The Self-Transform

MW01590841

The Self-Transforming School combines an insightful meta-analysis of factors contributing to the success of schools with an examination of powerful mega-trends shaping developments in education, to offer the first mega-analysis in education policy and practice. The book spans 50 years, beginning with Caldwell and Spinks's ground-breaking work *The Self-Managing School*, which advocated innovative approaches that are now accepted as preferred practice, before offering a prognosis and plan for the future.

This book argues that all schools in all settings can secure success for all students in an era when both society and the economy are changing constantly and dramatically. Although schools find some support in local and global networks, externally designed restructuring, restaffing or command-and-control direction is not sufficient to achieve transformation. Instead of replicating particular approaches to achieve modest improvement, leadership of the highest quality needs to be deeply embedded in schools and their systems. Caldwell and Spinks propose three important points that need to be taken into consideration:

- schools are often at different stages of self-transformation;
- self-transformation requires a high level of professionalism and must include teacher education and ongoing professional development;
- funding is critically important and efforts to build a capacity for self-transformation are constrained by what is available.

The book gives particular attention to developments in Australia, Brazil, Canada, England, Finland, Hong Kong, India, New Zealand, Shanghai, Singapore and the United States. It will be of key relevance to school leaders and policymakers, to academics and postgraduate students engaged in research on equity, to student performance in highly disadvantaged settings and to education policy.

Brian J. Caldwell is Managing Director and Principal Consultant at Educational Transformations, Australia, and Professorial Fellow and former Dean of Education at the University of Melbourne, Australia.

Jim M. Spinks is Director of All Across the Line and a former school principal who consults widely on student-focused planning and resource allocation, both in Australia and internationally.

The Self-Transforming School

Brian J. Caldwell and
Jim M. Spinks

Routledge
Taylor & Francis Group

LONDON AND NEW YORK

First published 2013
by Routledge
2 Park Square, Milton Park, Abingdon, Oxon OX14 4RN

Simultaneously published in the USA and Canada
by Routledge
711 Third Avenue, New York, NY 10017

Routledge is an imprint of the Taylor & Francis Group, an informa business

British Library Cataloguing in Publication Data
A catalogue record for this book is available from the British Library

Library of Congress Cataloging in Publication Data
Caldwell, Brian, author.
The self-transforming school / Brian J. Caldwell, Jim M. Spinks.
pages cm
1. School management and organization—Cross-cultural studies.
2. Educational leadership—Cross-cultural studies. 3. School
improvement programs—Cross-cultural studies. I. Spinks, Jim M.,
author. II. Title.
LB2805.C236 2014
371.2–dc23
2013002730

ISBN: 978-0-415-66058-7 (hbk)
ISBN: 978-0-415-66059-4 (pbk)
ISBN: 978-0-203-38798-6 (ebk)

Typeset in Galliard by Prepress Projects Ltd, Perth, UK

MIX
Paper from
responsible sources
FSC
www.fsc.org   FSC® C013056

Printed and bound in Great Britain by
TJ International Ltd, Padstow, Cornwall

Contents

Foreword

Last year, the world's population was said to have exceeded 7 billion, of whom over 2 billion were children. The future of the planet will be in their hands so how and what they are taught now, and the life skills they develop, could not be more important. It seems to me that almost every aspect of life is going through radical change. Nowhere are these changes more keenly felt than amongst school leaders and governors. However, schools and the ways in which children are taught are slow to change. In the West, some would say, schools have not fundamentally changed in over 100 years. That is why I found this book so inspiring and challenging. The authors acknowledge the crisis in education in many countries and offer an unparalleled global perspective and review of policy and practice over the past 25 years. Significantly using research evidence, they set the scene for what will happen in the coming decades, consider what kind of leadership will be required and, importantly, illuminate the way for schools to move from being self-managing to self-transforming.

It has been 25 years since the authors inspired me with their book *The Self-Managing School*. That book, and its sequels, provided me with the research evidence that supported what I felt to be true: that, in order to bring about systemic transformation, we need to develop the capacity to lead that change at a local level rather than to introduce more and more measures and bureaucracy. In the West, a command-and-control culture has cascaded down through the system over decades so that many people now do not know what it means to take up their own authority. A dependency culture creates not only inefficiencies but, all too often, low morale. The recent financial crisis may actually be what reverses this trend. Autonomy is partially a result of the current austerity and this has resulted in schools in many countries becoming largely responsible for their own destinies. With less central backing, schools are beginning to develop their own support networks. Collaboration is the watchword and an essential aspect of the educational landscape.

What is being suggested by the fascinating research in this book is that a different approach is needed, a change of mindset. As we all know, it is often very hard and painful for people to discard ways of working that they have developed over many years and that have served them well in the past. I know from personal experience that the way in which leaders lead or resist change, and how they engage with their staff, sets the climate of a school that either promotes trust and innovation or reinforces rigidity and resistance to change. This sounds like common sense, but is often deeply counter-cultural.

I co-founded Creating Tomorrow five years ago with the sole aim of developing a process that would help schools everywhere bring about transformational change for themselves. I had been struck by the fact that senior leaders usually have a sound knowledge of the theory of change, are able to visualise where they want to take their school, but find it very hard to distribute leadership whilst retaining accountability. There is a huge untapped wealth of talent and enthusiasm in schools for doing things differently. It is the role of the principal to unleash this and free him- or herself to embrace a more strategic role. I refer to this as 'leading change, changing leadership'.

Having spent the last decade working with schools and educational systems around the world, I agree wholeheartedly with the book when it says that schools need to build the capacity to reinvent themselves, to create an education with a better fit for today and tomorrow. The authors are clear that this transformation will require a creative use of resources and a higher level of professionalism of teachers, leaders and those that support them. Like them, I believe it should be the aim of every jurisdiction to build each school's capacity to be self-transforming as only this will make education available in radical new ways in order to ensure future success for all children.

The impact of the work of Caldwell and Spinks on policymakers and practitioners over the past 25 years has been enormous and this new book takes their thinking to a new and exciting frontier, one that will inspire the next generation of teachers wherever they are in the world.

Dame Pat Collarbone, Creating Tomorrow Ltd

Preface

This book is the fifth in a series that commenced with *The Self-Managing School* in 1988. It thus marks the twenty-fifth anniversary of our initial collaboration in print, the outcomes of which included extended work in England during the implementation phase of the 1988 Education Reform Act. However, the decision to write a fifth book was not just to mark these anniversaries, important though they may be in a personal sense. It is now evident that the tipping point for school self-management has been passed in several countries and is approaching in many more. What is now coming into sharper focus is a vision for what schools with a deep capacity for self-management can accomplish, that is that they may become self-transforming.

We are in no doubt that the concept of the self-transforming school will be challenged, as was the initial concept of the self-managing school. The latter referred to a school in a system of public education that has been granted a degree of authority and responsibility to make important decisions within a centrally determined framework. The success of the first book was derived from its description and illustration of the inter-related processes of goal setting, policymaking, planning, budgeting, implementing and evaluating in teaching and learning, and the support of teaching and learning. Looking back, it was a common-sense approach that proved useful to thousands of practitioners in many countries, not just Australia and England, who had been empowered to lead and manage in an era when the balance of centralisation and decentralisation shifted, at least in part, to the latter. The authors never intended it to be, nor did it ever become, a process that undermined the notion of public education, let alone become the means for privatising public schools.

It has become increasingly apparent that a powerful capacity for decision making at the local level is absolutely essential if there is to be improvement in outcomes across a system of public education in which each community is unique and each school contains a unique mix of needs, interests, aptitudes, ambitions and passions of students. Moreover, there is unprecedented breadth and depth in knowledge regarding what works and why in learning and teaching under different conditions. A capacity to draw on this knowledge is necessary if there is to be success for all students in all settings.

Whereas the first book described and illustrated the basic processes of self-management, its successors focused on leadership (*Leading the Self-Managing School* in 1992), the link between self-management and learning (*Beyond the Self-Managing School* in 1998) and aligning resources, broadly defined but especially financial resources (*Raising the Stakes* in 2008). Each of the first four books drew on knowledge gleaned from the best policies and practices in self-management. It is now time to draw from the best again in describing how self-managing schools have become self-transforming schools and to illustrate how others that are building their capacities for self-management can do the same.

We have maintained the definition of transformation in these and related publications, that is transformation is significant, systematic and sustained change that secures success for all students in all settings. A self-transforming school is a school that has the capacity to make decisions that lead to such an outcome. Again, anticipating an initial reaction as with the first book, this does not mean the privatising of public education or breaking up a system of schools. It does mean, however, that the self-transforming school is in a position to 'call the shots' on how it will achieve transformation. It may draw its support from any source, including 'the system', and may network with any number of schools or other learning organisations in any country at any time without weakening its commitment to the values that bind the schools that form a system of education.

We offer several important qualifications or preconditions in describing the self-transforming school. First, we are mindful of recent studies that make it clear that systems are on different stages of a journey towards transformation. Self-transformation may be many years away for those that struggle to get students, or even teachers, to attend school. We acknowledge this in several chapters. Second, and related, self-transformation requires a higher level of professionalism than ever before on the part of teachers and their leaders and those who support them. A precondition for self-transformation is likely to be the transformation of initial teacher education and ongoing professional development, as has been achieved in several countries reported in the book. Third, resources in the form of funding are critically important and efforts to build a capacity for self-transformation will be constrained by what is available, especially in hard times. This is why we continue to focus on the design of models for needs-based funding of schools.

As is made clear in several chapters, we believe that many schools with a capacity for self-management are needlessly constrained and contend that they should be 'unchained'. It should be the aim of every jurisdiction to build the capacity of all of its schools to be self-transforming. Self-transforming schools are a precondition for self-transforming systems. Command-and-control or carrot-and-stick approaches may work for a time under particular circumstances, but they have no place in a self-transforming system. It is 10 years since Sir Michael Barber wrote in a publication for the Organisation for Economic Co-operation and Development (OECD) that 'the era of the large, slow moving, steady, respected, bureaucratic public services, however good by earlier standards, is over'. We are not there yet, but we know how to get there. It is for this reason that *The Self-Transforming School* is for policymakers as much as it is for practitioners.

Although this book marks 25 years since the publication of our first book on self-managing schools, we devote relatively little space to reflecting on the past. Our primary purpose is to map the way forward for schools and school systems that seek to be self-transforming and our horizon is in fact the next 25 years, even though we cannot specify particular innovations or their timing and sequencing, such is the pace of change. However, consistent with the approach we first took in 1992, we describe the mega-trends which, taking the book as a whole, span a total of 50 years.

Illustrations are drawn from many countries and from the private as well as the public sectors. It is intended that *The Self-Transforming School* be relevant to all jurisdictions and to all sectors, regardless of their starting points and progress. It is also intended that the concept of self-transformation apply to the individual as well as to the institution; indeed, this should be the starting point for all who commence the journey.

Brian Caldwell, Melbourne, Victoria
and Jim Spinks, Paradise, Tasmania
May 2013

1 Narratives in self-management

There is a crisis in education in many nations around the world. Nations that have been proud of their systems of education for more than a century are now struggling to keep pace with others that are performing at the highest levels in international tests of student achievement and whose economies, in some instances, are almost certain to dominate in the twenty-first century. The former include Australia, England, New Zealand and the United States and the chief concern, apart from the overall quality of schooling, is the disparity in achievement between low- and high-performing students. Moreover, the performance of the best students is declining while the gap is growing wider. The latter include Canada, Hong Kong, Finland, Shanghai, Singapore and South Korea, where the gap between low- and high-performing students is relatively narrow and the best students in several instances are a year or more ahead of their counterparts in the former.

Some governments appear to be at their wits' end over how to improve. A major theme of this book is that they must go beyond improvement; they will never catch up by persisting with current strategies. They must plan for the transformation of their schools. They will not achieve this outcome by trying harder to do the same things that have been done for years during the period of decline. Unrelenting pressure on schools to do better is not resulting in improvement, let alone transformation.

The seriousness of the situation in England was conveyed in an Organisation for Economic Co-operation and Development (OECD) Economics Department Working Paper entitled *Reforming Education in England* (Braconier, 2012). Henrik Braconier is Senior Economist on the United Kingdom/Finland desk in the Economics Department of the OECD. He concluded from a deep analysis of school performance in England that 'despite significant increases in spending on child care and education during the last decade, PISA [Programme for International Student Assessment] scores suggest that educational performance remains static, uneven, and strongly related to parents' income and background' (ibid.: 2).

Media comment on the OECD study was illustrated in a graphic newspaper headline. Referring to indicators of decline in England's performance as reported by Braconier, the *Mail Online* (Harris, 2012) declared: 'Failed,

failed, failed: Blair said his priorities were education, education, education. But Labour billions did nothing to raise standards, says report'. Yet there is a more positive view of what occurred in England and what might lie ahead (Adonis, 2012).

Australia was embarrassed when results for 2011 in the Trends in International Mathematics and Science Study (TIMSS) and the Progress in International Reading Literacy Study (PIRLS) were released in December 2012. No one was prepared for results that revealed Australia was ranked twenty-seventh out of 48 countries for Year 4 in PIRLS, or eighteenth out of 52 countries for Year 4 Mathematics in TIMSS (Thomson *et al.*, 2012). Australia finished behind England, Canada, Chinese Taipei, Finland, Hong Kong, Japan, Singapore and the United States in all rankings. One headline read 'Australia's Disaster in Education' (Topsfield, 2012: 1).

This is an astonishing state of affairs given that knowledge about improvement and transformation is richer and more dependable than ever. There have been tens of thousands of impressive studies around the world. What stands out is the quality of the different meta-analyses, that is the increasing number of reports that bring together the findings of these studies to provide general patterns to guide the efforts of policymakers and practitioners. These include many studies under the auspices of the OECD, based on outcomes in PISA; the several robust international comparative reports of McKinsey & Company (especially Barber and Mourshed, 2007; Mourshed *et al.*, 2010); the extraordinary work of John Hattie (2009), who drew on the findings of more than 800 separate meta-analyses; the narrative of 'the fourth way' provided by Andy Hargreaves and Dennis Shirley (A. Hargeaves and Shirley, 2011); the *Oceans of Innovation* report (Barber *et al.*, 2012); and the comprehensive study by the Grattan Institute in Australia (Jensen *et al.*, 2012) that has gone a long way to explaining why students are doing so well in Asia.

There are paradoxes in these studies. One is the intriguing finding (Zhao, 2012: Chapter 4) that there appears to be a negative relationship between a nation's score in PISA, which focuses on literacy and numeracy, and entre-preneurship, at a time when the latter is considered an important indicator of a nation's social and economic success in the twenty-first century. Especially noteworthy is the willingness of the best-performing nations to dramatically change their approaches, as illustrated in statements by Singapore's Prime Minister, Lee Hsien Loong (*The Economist*, 2012a: 31), who decried the excessive coaching of three- and four-year-olds in favour of more play-based learning. Excessive coaching is a stereotype, if not the reality, of approaches to learning in his country. Underpinning his concern is the need for citizens to be more innovative and inventive.

Another paradox is that, despite the broad national decline summarised above, there are exceptions in the performance of different schools. Some of the most impressive examples of leadership and governance, accompanied by ground-breaking developments in curriculum and pedagogy, may be found in schools in Australia, England, New Zealand and the United States. Although these schools work within a centrally determined framework, they are characterised by high-quality teaching and a capacity to tailor their programmes to local priorities for the needs, interests, aptitudes, ambitions and passions of their students. That is, these schools are self-managing and, because they have achieved significant, systematic and sustained change that secures success for their students regardless of their settings, they have used their capacities for self-management to also become self-transforming, even though they have drawn in varying degrees on support from within and beyond the school and school system. Noteworthy among these examples are the academies (England) and charter schools (United States) described in more detail in Chapter 4.

Although the 2012 edition of OECD's *Education at a Glance* found a decline in the proportion of decisions made at the school level since its previous survey in 2007, there has been a general trend over several decades to provide schools with higher levels of autonomy – or, to use a preferable term, a higher level of self-management – and a purpose of this book is to review the outcomes and to outline possible directions for further change as schools use their capacities for self-management to achieve transformation. It is not possible or appropriate to predict the particular practices that may emerge in schools over the next 25 years but it is possible to offer a 'mega-analysis' of developments now under way.

There is solid evidence that a capacity for self-management, or a relatively high level of autonomy, is associated with higher levels of student achievement, provided it is accompanied by accountability, and that self-managing schools use their capacities to transform learning. However, it is apparent that self-management in countries such as Australia, England, New Zealand and the United States has been overwhelmed by more centralised arrangements in what may be described as a powerful and excessive command-and-control approach. Sahlberg (2011) referred to these and some other countries as being 'infected' by the GERM (Global Education Reform Movement) in contrast to the 'Finnish Way'.

This is the fifth book by the authors, and the publication of *The Self-Transforming School* marks the twenty-fifth anniversary of the first, entitled *The Self-Managing School* (Caldwell and Spinks, 1988). It is also the twenty-fifth anniversary of the 1988 Education Reform Act in England, in which a capacity for self-management, or local management as it was called at the time, was one of several major changes in education. *The Self-Managing School* was an important resource for schools in England, as it was in Hong Kong, New Zealand and Victoria, Australia, shortly thereafter. It is timely to review developments in the intervening years and to document some of the examples of outstanding transforming practices in schools in these and other countries at the same time that command-and-control approaches have tended to characterise the effort to improve all schools in contrast with what has occurred in high-performing nations.

After providing some important definitions, Chapter 1 is organised into five parts. The first briefly summarises the work of the authors over the aforementioned 25 years. The second provides more information from a sample of the meta-analyses that have been conducted in recent years. The third refers to a first effort at mega-analysis in 1992, when the concept of the 'mega-trend' was adopted to describe powerful forces and associated developments that were emerging towards the end of the twentieth century. Subsequent developments are summarised. The fourth describes the pitfalls of forecasting what may occur in the next 25 years but summarises in broad terms some of the expected mega-trends in the years ahead. The chapter concludes with an overview of the book, in which most chapters are devoted to describing and illustrating capacities for self-transformation. Implications for policymakers and practitioners are highlighted in a final statement that concludes the chapter.

Definitions and related concepts

A *self-managing school* is one to which there has been decentralised a significant amount of authority and responsibility to make decisions on the allocation of resources within a centrally determined framework of goals, policies, curriculum, standards and accountabilities. Resources are defined broadly to include staff, services and infrastructure, each of which will typically entail the allocation of funds to reflect local priorities. A self-managing school has a high level of autonomy, though not complete autonomy given the centrally determined framework.

Whereas a capacity for self-management is chiefly concerned with process, self-transformation is intended to shift the focus to outcomes. A *self-transforming school* achieves, or is well on its way to achieving, significant, systematic and sustained change that secures success for all of its students regardless of the setting.

The self-transforming school includes but goes beyond the concept of the *self-improving school*. David Hargreaves has written a series of 'think pieces' for the National College for School Leadership in England organised around the idea of a self-improving school system (SISS). He described how school improvement has 'come to be defined in terms of the processes of intervention in schools that are deemed, by whatever measure, to be underperforming' (D. Hargreaves, 2010: 4). He captured an argument in the current book that an SISS, once established,

> reduces the need for extensive, top-down systems of monitoring to check on school quality, the imposition of improvement strategies that are relatively insensitive to local context, with out-of-school courses not tailored to individual professional needs, and external, last-ditch interventions to remedy schools in difficulties, all of which are very costly and often only partially successful.
>
> (ibid.: 23)

Hargreaves considers a capacity for self-management to be a prerequisite for self-improvement. However, limiting the approach to improvement does not address the need for transformation when one considers what is occurring in many nations. Improvement occurs within current approaches to schooling; transformation seeks success for all in what are certain to be dramatically different approaches to schooling in the years ahead.

In the statement cited above, Hargreaves captured some important features of what may be defined as *command-and-control* ('extensive, top-down systems of monitoring to check on school quality, the imposition of improvement strategies that are relatively insensitive to local context'). A related practice is when schools are provided with inducements for accepting funds to implement programmes determined at a system level in what is basically a *carrot-and-stick* approach. Carrot-and-stick is also an apt descriptor of practice when a higher level of government, with more resources, provides funds to a lower level of government, with fewer resources, and requires acceptance by the latter of strict terms and conditions that are not necessarily those that would have been accepted if there was no such dependence.

Those involved in Catholic education often refer to the principle of *subsidiarity* in describing the distribution of authority and responsibility. Pope Pius XI is often cited:

> Still, that most weighty principle, which cannot be set aside or changed, remains fixed and unshaken in social philosophy: Just as it is gravely wrong to take from individuals what they can accomplish by their own initiative and industry and give it to the community, so also it is an injustice and at the same time a grave evil and disturbance of right order to assign to a greater and higher association what lesser and subordinate organizations can do. For every social activity ought of its very nature to furnish help to the members of the body social, and never destroy and absorb them.
>
> (Pope Pius XI, 1931: paragraph 79)

Such a view in no way detracts from a commitment to a system of schools that share the same values and mission or that develop mechanisms for mutual support. In addition to education departments in systems of public education, or the Catholic Education Office in a diocese or archdiocese, even independent schools establish such mechanisms. For example, the Association of Independent Schools (AIS) in New South Wales employs a staff of 82 people, most of whom provide support to member schools.

Dennis Higgins, former Director of Education in the Catholic Education Office, Sandhurst (Australia), shifted the focus from self-management to *self-leadership* in a powerful reflection on his career in Catholic education:

> No system should talk of 'self-managed' schools. The notion is to have 'self-led' schools, and the system can do its schools its greatest favours by encouraging and enabling local schools/settings to take responsibility for

all of the big decisions, and to help out by providing the resources and support for that to happen.

(Higgins, 2011: 32)

Higgins went on to observe that 'schools become dependent on the system, and this is a weakness. Schools can become independent of the system and this is also a weakness'. His reflections and observations are consistent with the principle of subsidiarity and a major theme in this book.

An author narrative

The Self-Transforming School has been published 25 years after *The Self-Managing School*. In the intervening period, the authors have been continuously engaged in research and consultancy in dozens of countries and this has provided them with an opportunity to shape policy and practice in several instances but, especially, to learn about what has been achieved. The following is a brief summary of their work.

The foundation for Caldwell's work was laid in his doctoral dissertation at the University of Alberta, Canada, in the mid-1970s, which examined the objectives, adoption, operation and perceived outcomes of decentralised school budgeting in seven school systems in Alberta, including the pilot project in the Edmonton Public School District (Caldwell, 1977). What was accomplished in Edmonton became a landmark reform that continues to this day; indeed, it has been institutionalised to the extent that it is now accepted as the way things are done in that system.

In 1983, he was chief investigator in a Project of National Significance (PNS) in Australia, known as the Effective Resource Allocation in Schools Project, which was conducted in South Australia and Tasmania with a focus on resource allocation at the school level under the limited decentralisation in place at the time. A model was developed from practice at Rosebery District High School in Tasmania, where Spinks was principal, which had received the most nominations from knowledgeable people for effectiveness, both in a general sense and in the manner in which resources were allocated. This model shaped the design and delivery of a professional development programme for school councils, principals, teachers and students in Victoria, where the Cain Labor government had adopted a policy of school-based policymaking, planning and budgeting. Fifty-two workshops were conducted from 1984 to 1986 for approximately 5,000 people from 1,200 schools. The workshop materials were incorporated into a book, initially published for a limited market in Australia, but updated as *The Self-Managing School* (Caldwell and Spinks, 1988) and released to an international audience at about the time of the 1988 Education Reform Act in England, and shortly before the Tomorrow's Schools initiative in New Zealand and the School Management Initiative (SMI) in Hong Kong. These were historic initiatives. Caldwell and Spinks conducted many workshops for school and school system leaders in these countries. Spinks alone conducted more than 100 in England.

It is important to note that Caldwell and Spinks referred to self-managing schools, not self-governing schools or autonomous schools, because they were working within and were committed to maintaining, indeed strengthening, systems of public education. Autonomy implies a degree of independence that was not intended at the time and is not intended now.

Caldwell and Spinks monitored implementation, especially with respect to the changing role of principals and other school leaders, and *Leading the Self-Managing School* (Caldwell and Spinks, 1992) was published shortly before the landmark Schools of the Future initiative of the Kennett Liberal–National government in Victoria. Caldwell worked in partnership with Max Sawatzki in 1996 to present workshops for more than 1,000 principals in this state.

Extensive research on the links between self-management and learning led to *Beyond the Self-Managing School* (Caldwell and Spinks, 1998). This research included a longitudinal study of Victoria's self-managing schools that mapped these links through the Cooperative Research Project. The project was a partnership of the Victorian Primary Principals Association (VPPA), the Victorian Association of State Secondary Principals (VASSP), the Education Department of the Victorian Government and the University of Melbourne. The initiative was taken by leaders in the VPPA. The research team was assisted in this effort by three eminent scholars at the University of Melbourne: Professor Peter Hill, more recently CEO of the Australian Curriculum, Assessment and Reporting Authority (ACARA); Dr Ken Rowe, an international expert in structural equation modelling; and Professor Hedley Beare, who was the founding CEO of the Australian Capital Territory (ACT) Schools Authority, which led the nation in self-management in the early 1970s.

It became apparent in the early years of the twenty-first century that a new conceptualisation of leadership in the self-managing school was emerging and this was described by Caldwell (2006) in *Re-imagining School Leadership*. Following retirement as a principal in Tasmania, Spinks engaged in an extended consultancy in Victoria on student-focused planning and resource allocation. A broader view of resources and a deeper focus on the student resulted in *Raising the Stakes* (Caldwell and Spinks, 2008). This book drew on further developments in Victoria under the Bracks Labor government that extended what had been introduced under the Kennett Liberal–National government, which, in turn, built on what had been achieved under Labor governments in the 1980s.

This continuing and connected narrative is important and developments in Victoria paralleled the alternating bipartisan initiatives in England under Conservative and Labour governments and in New Zealand under Labour and National governments. Twenty-five years on, a tipping point has been reached, to the extent that the terms 'self-management' and 'autonomy' are rarely used in places such as England, New Zealand and Victoria, or in systems such as that of Edmonton in Canada. It is simply 'school management'.

An England narrative

It is appropriate to refer to a narrative for developments in England, given that this book was published in 2013, marking the twenty-fifth anniversary of the 1988 Education Reform Act. Much of the author narrative in the preceding section was set in the context of this legislation and the work undertaken by the authors in building the capacity of schools to implement that part of the Act that was concerned with the local management of schools.

A powerful narrative was provided by Andrew Adonis in *Education, Education, Education: Reforming England's Schools* (Adonis, 2012). At first sight, his book was about the academies movement in England, about which he supplied an insider account of his work as an education advisor to the Labour Prime Minister, Tony Blair, and then a minister whose role included the design and delivery of this new model of schools. It did indeed provide such an account but it did much more. First, it provided a broader historical account of the shortcomings of state education in England over more than half a century. Second, it acknowledged the contributions of his predecessors and successors in Conservative governments: notably, Kenneth Baker, Secretary of State for Education in the Thatcher government ('a highly dynamic reformer'), who played an important role in an early form of the academies (City Technology Colleges) as well as in the implementation of the local management of schools; and Michael Gove, Secretary of State for Education in the Cameron government ('a brilliant blaze of rhetorical fireworks on Michael Gove's part'), who drove the dramatic expansion of the academies. Adonis believed that the local management of schools was 'an unalloyed and almost immediate success' (Adonis, 2012: 27–28). Third, Adonis provided a vision if not a broad plan for the future of academies, but going further to provide the same for a more comprehensive transformation of state education in the years ahead. The academies movement continues to be contentious and there are competing narratives, notably in *The State and Education Policy: The Academies Programme* (Gunter, 2011).

Meta-analyses

Four examples of meta-analyses are briefly summarised here, two by McKinsey & Company, one by Hattie and one by the Grattan Institute. Strictly speaking, only Hattie's is a meta-analysis; the others may be better described as evidence-based international comparative studies. The meta-analyses/international comparative studies of the OECD are summarised in Chapter 2 in the context of international evidence of the impact of self-management. Features of 'the fourth way' in the narrative provided by Andy Hargreaves and Dennis Shirley (A. Hargreaves and Shirley, 2011) and the *Oceans of Innovation* report (Barber *et al.*, 2012) are included in other chapters.

In 2007, a report by McKinsey & Company entitled *How the World's Best-Performing Systems Come out on Top* (Barber and Mourshed, 2007) described practice in several countries and school systems. The report drew extensively on approaches in Finland that attracted headlines for their consistently high performance in PISA, but also on other high performers including Alberta (Canada), Australia, Belgium, Finland, Hong Kong (China), Japan, the Netherlands, New Zealand, Ontario (Canada), Singapore and South Korea. The main finding was concerned with the quality of teaching, with the key themes being getting the right people to be teachers, developing effective instructors and ensuring every student performs well.

The findings in another report of McKinsey & Company (Mourshed *et al.*, 2010), entitled *How the World's Most Improved School Systems Keep Getting Better*, highlighted the need for a nuanced approach, depending on the setting. The study was concerned with school systems that were already high performing and getting better, and others that were starting from a low base and were showing noteworthy improvement. Examples of the former included Singapore, Hong Kong and South Korea. The latter included Western Cape in South Africa, Minas Gerais in Brazil and Madhya Pradesh in India. There were three main findings:

1 'it's a system thing, not a single thing': there is a common pattern in the interventions that improving systems use to move from one stage to the next, irrespective of geography, time, or culture;
2 'prescribe adequacy, unleash greatness': there is a strong, correlation between the stage of a school system's improvement journey and the tightness of central control over an individual school's activities and performance;
3 'common but different': the findings indicated that six interventions occur with equal frequency across all the improvement journeys, though manifesting differently in each one.

One of the most comprehensive studies was conducted by Hattie (2009), formerly at the University of Auckland and now at the University of Melbourne, who synthesised more than 800 meta-analyses to specify the effects of various interventions on student achievement. He was able to rank order the effects of 138 interventions. For example, he drew conclusions from the literature on leadership to identify practices with positive effects, the most successful being goal setting and team building and the least successful being 'techno-structural' interventions, such as job redesign and job enrichment. Overall, the effects of school leadership were indirect rather than direct, that is they involved the creation of conditions under which these 138 interventions could be established and made effective.

The Grattan Institute in Melbourne took a similar approach to McKinsey & Company but focused on high-performing systems in East Asia: Hong Kong, Shanghai, Singapore and South Korea. The authors (Jensen *et al.*, 2012) found that stereotypes of East Asian education did not stand up to critical scrutiny in wholly explaining the success of these countries; for example,

Confucian culture and the influence of 'tiger mums'. Although many may challenge this contention and refer also to differences in terms of the longer school day and special tutoring and coaching, the central theme is difficult to challenge, namely the quality of teaching. The focus in these countries is on building the capacity of teachers through the preparation and selection of outstanding applicants and devoting substantial amounts of time to school-based professional development and research. These findings are described in more detail in Chapter 5.

Mega-trends

In 1992, Caldwell and Spinks (1992: 7–8) used the concept of the 'mega-trend', coined by John Naisbitt and Patricia Aburdene (Naisbitt, 1982; Naisbitt and Aburdene, 1990) in the 1980s, to describe the broad trends in school education that were emerging in many countries in the 1990s. It is helpful to first list these predictions, followed by a summary of what has transpired in the intervening years:

1   There will be a powerful but sharply focused role for central authorities, especially in respect to formulating goals, setting priorities and building frameworks for accountability.
2   National and global considerations will become increasingly important, especially in respect to curriculum and an education system that is responsive to national needs within a global economy.
3   Within centrally determined frameworks, government [public] schools will become largely self-managing, and distinctions between government and non-government [private] schools will narrow.
4   There will be unparalleled concern for the provision of a quality education for each individual.
5   There will be a dispersion of the educative function, with telecommunications and computer technology ensuring that much learning that currently occurs in schools or in institutions of higher education will occur at home and in the workplace.
6   The basics of education will be expanded to include problem-solving, creativity and a capacity for life-long learning and re-learning.
7   There will be an expanded role for the arts and spirituality, defined broadly in each instance; there will be a high level of 'connectedness' in the curriculum.
8   Women will claim their place among the ranks of leaders in education, including those at the most senior levels.
9   The parent and community role in education will be claimed or reclaimed.
10   There will be unparalleled concern for service by those who are required or have the opportunity to support the work of schools.
(Caldwell and Spinks, 1992: 7–8)

'A powerful but sharply focused role for central authorities' (1) gathered momentum in the 1990s, continuing in the early years of the twenty-first century. This took the form of more tightly prescribed curricula and the emergence of the standards movement, accompanied by national testing programmes. 'National and global considerations' (2) have characterised school reform, as evidenced by international testing programmes, such as PISA, and awareness in most nations that their future depends on their integration into a global economy. The trend to self-management or higher levels of school authority and responsibility in systems of public education (3) has continued, but fallen back in some places, as reported by the OECD (2012), and distinctions between public and private schools have narrowed in some respects, although most of the former are still funded, built, owned and operated by the government or another public authority. The 'unparalleled concern for the provision of a quality education for each individual' (4) is evident in national and international concern for equity, or at least in the adoption of strategies to narrow the gap between low- and high-performing students.

Although the terminology may be different, there is no doubt that developments in information and communications technology (5) are powerfully shaping learning and teaching. Expanding the 'basics' to include 'problem-solving, creativity and a capacity for life-long learning and re-learning' (6) is central to the effort in developing the so-called 'twenty-first-century skills'. Working out ways to assess these skills is the focus of a major international project based at the University of Melbourne. Whether the role of the arts and spirituality has expanded (7) is debatable, especially in the light of evidence that these have been sidelined to some extent with the focus on literacy and numeracy and high-stakes testing. There seems to have been a steady increase in the number of women occupying senior leadership positions in education (8). About a decade ago in Australia every minister for education was female, and in many countries now most principals in primary schools and an increasing number of those in secondary schools are women.

There is stronger interest in engaging parents and the wider community (9) than there was in the early 1990s, extending over a range of functions. In some instances, this is a return to earlier times. It is difficult to assess the extent to which there has been 'unparalleled concern for service by those who are required or have the opportunity to support the work of schools' (10). This refers to those who work in education departments and their various agencies. The mega-trend was described at a time when there was pressure to reduce the size of bureaucracy. It is fair to say that bureaucracy has expanded in many countries and it is understandable that those who do not work in schools would claim that they are serving schools, even if their roles are primarily regulatory or concerned with accountability.

Further work in different countries in the course of the 1990s led Caldwell and Spinks (1998) to hone their view of mega-trends and to describe three 'tracks for change'. The image of a track seemed appropriate because the three movements were occurring at the same time in most places but schools, school systems and nations varied in the distance they had travelled down each track: (1) building systems of self-managing schools; (2) unrelenting focus on learning outcomes; (3) creating schools for the knowledge society. Rather than describe or propose a particular set of strategies to be implemented with fidelity in all schools, they provided a list of 'strategic intentions' that would help shape strategies as schools and systems navigated in a time of complexity and change. A total of 100 strategic intentions were proposed.

The three tracks for change and these strategic intentions are as relevant now as they were 15 years ago and they are useful for describing work in the self-transforming school. However, much more is known now about learning and teaching and the terminology has changed.

A futures perspective and innovation in education

What lies in store for the next 25 years? The mega-trends are still evident. Schools and school systems are moving down the 'tracks for change'. It is another major purpose of this book to look forward as far as possible, and in as much detail as possible, to what may occur in the future. However, it is important to declare at the outset that it is not possible to predict the future as far as particular developments, events or sequences of events are concerned. After all, who could have predicted with any certainty in 2009 that the workplace for students and staff would be transformed by the tablet computer within three years? It was possible to declare that this workplace would be changed in profound ways by further developments in technology, as described in the mega-trends, but the particularities would have defied prediction. Further change of the same order can be expected and the ways in which schooling is being transformed by technology are illustrated in many of the chapters.

There is arguably more thoughtful, if not exciting, work under way than ever before in describing alternative or preferred futures in education. In most instances, there is a powerful connection between a 'futures perspective' and innovation. Examples include the Global Education Leaders' Program (GELP), the Innovation Unit (IU) (England), the Centre for Strategic Education (CSE) (Australia) and the World Innovation Summit in Education (WISE). The Innovation Unit was formerly part of the government but is now an independent company. Some of its most stimulating thought pieces about the future of schooling are in the public domain. GELP is a loose consortium of leaders from different countries, energised in the first instance by Cisco but now with several partners including the Bill and Melinda Gates Foundation, which has met twice each year since 2009; for example, leaders from one or more jurisdictions in nine countries met in Helsinki and Rio de Janeiro in 2012 (Australia, Brazil, Canada, China, Finland, India, New Zealand, South Korea and the United States). CSE publishes powerful thought pieces on a regular basis and contributes to and facilitates programmes of these and other projects. WISE meets annually and, at its 2012 meeting in Doha, six projects received awards under the theme of Transforming Education (Bangladesh, Cambodia, Chile, Denmark, India and the United States).

There is a common source of energy among these enterprises, with the secretariat for GELP located in the IU, and the CSE contributing to and drawing from these entities. The CSE's Executive Director, Anthony (Tony) Mackay, also serves as Deputy Chair of the Australian Curriculum, Assessment and Reporting Authority (ACARA) and Chair of the Australian Institute for Teaching and School Leadership (AITSL). Valerie Hannon, Director of the IU, provides common thought leadership. Her contributions, and those of others in these interlocking organisations, are cited in subsequent chapters.

Urgency

There are several accounts in this book of schools that are self-transforming within current models of schooling. However, it is urgent that, in countries where there is much hand-wringing about the contribution of schools to social and economic well-being, all schools have the capacity to be self-transforming. Working harder to make incremental change will not suffice.

Houle and Cobb (2011) have labelled 2010–2020 'the transformation decade' for many institutions, including schools. For example, they contend that 'it will be the single most transformative decade in the history of energy' and that 'the accelerating, almost exponential increase in technological innovation will present realities that stagger the mind'. More specifically, for education 'it is essential that we completely transform all our educational institutions, constructs, methods, and vision to keep pace. It is now time to fully embrace the potential of this new century and seek new ways to prepare our young for what lies ahead' (ibid.: 49–50).

Chapter outlines

Chapter 1 ('Narratives in self-management') has highlighted what is at stake in many countries where performance in public education is declining. A crisis will not be averted with incremental improvements. The capacity of schools to be self-managing must be built to the point at which they become self-transforming. The key terms have been defined and a narrative that brings coherence to what has occurred in recent decades has been presented. The key themes in four meta-analyses, or evidence-based international comparative studies, have been highlighted. A futures perspective and serious innovation must be harnessed if self-managing schools are to become self-transforming schools and several promising initiatives to help develop such a perspective have been identified. Capacity for self-transformation is urgent.

Chapter 2 ('Expectations and impact of self-management') makes clear that, although the expectations for the self-managing school have often been overstated by proponents or puffed up for easy demolition by sceptics, there is a robust body of evidence that, when combined with accountability and provided that schools have the required capacities, there is a link to learning. However, a simple reading of broad national or even sub-national trends can be misleading. Although impact across a system is the aim, the most helpful lessons are probably learned from studies of successful self-transformation at the school level. *Education at a Glance* (OECD, 2012) drew attention to a recentralising trend as systems in some countries tightened their centrally determined frameworks of accountability and extended their testing regimes. Chapter 3 ('Unchaining the self-managing school') takes up this theme and proposes a model that highlights the dangers of an excessive command-and-control approach. It is argued that a better approach is to 'unchain' the self-managing school, which can then become self-transforming if the required capacities have been built.

Chapters 4 to 6 provide an opportunity to test the robustness of this model. Within a broader framework of education policy, particular attention is given to the extent to which schools have authority and responsibility. Chapter 4 ('A study of contrasts in the West') compares policy frameworks and governance arrangements in Australia, England, New Zealand and the United States – each of which is declining in performance on international tests of student achievement – with what occurs in Finland, which has maintained its position near the top, and in Canada, which also occupies the high ground. The evidence supports the argument of Sahlberg (2011) that the first four nations have been 'infected' by the excesses of what he described as 'the Global Education Reform Movement (GERM)'. Serious questions are raised about processes and outcomes when several levels of government try to direct the effort, especially in countries that are federations of states. Chapter 5 ('Can the West catch up?') provides the counterpoint by summarising what has been accomplished in Hong Kong, Shanghai and Singapore. Both sides of the question posed in the chapter title are canvassed. Chapter 6 ('Possibilities for the powerhouses') provides an overview of developments in Brazil and India. The state is being tested in these nations and it may be that many of the approaches that characterise the West should be bypassed. Reference is made to developments in South Africa.

Chapter 7 ('Contours of change') returns to the big picture and describes five major inter-related issues, the resolution of which will give shape to the contours of the terrain that lies ahead for schools on the journey to self-transformation. These issues are: (1) what assumptions underlie efforts to bring about change in schools and school systems; (2) what assumptions have been made about the role of innovation; (3) what is measured – what counts as performance; (4) how it is measured – the economics of transformation; and (5) how fast – the speed and scale of transformation.

Chapters 8 to 13 include illustrations of how the self-managing school may become the self-transforming school. Examples are drawn from each of the countries considered in Chapters 4 to 7. Chapter 8 ('Innovation everywhere') provides a description of the scope and scale of innovation that is required to achieve transformation, with illustrations at a national level. Particular attention is given to Finland, which, despite its sustained success, recognises the need for new approaches. Three key questions are then addressed: How can capacity for innovation be embedded in a system? What capacities are required of system leaders? What capacities are required at the school level?

It is argued in Chapter 9 ('The transformation of learning') that policymakers may be powerless in the face of the revolution in technology, with the student holding the whip hand in determining what to learn, how to learn it and when to learn it. Private providers are proving more nimble than slow-moving bureaucratically organised systems of public education.

Chapters 10 to 13 organise the illustrations of self-transforming practice according to the resources that are needed, using a classification of forms of capital developed by Caldwell and Spinks (2008) and Caldwell and Harris (2008): financial, social, spiritual and intellectual. Co-author Jim Spinks makes special contributions in Chapter 10 ('Financial capital and transformation') and Chapter 11 ('Funding models and their fitness for purpose'). In each of our books, we have given particular attention in several chapters to what has occurred in Victoria, Australia, and we do so again in Chapters 10 and 11 to report approaches to needs-based student funding in Victoria's highly autonomous public schools. These approaches have evolved over two decades and may well constitute best practice. Criteria for assessing funding models are provided.

Promising practices in Australia and Hong Kong are reported in Chapter 12 ('Rediscovering social and spiritual capital'). An array of illustrations is provided in Chapter 13 ('The knowledge'), which deals with the knowledge and skills of those who work in or for schools and how they acquire them.

There is a formidable agenda for policymakers and system leaders, as well as school leaders, and its elements are proposed in Chapter 14 ('Governance ethos leadership policy'). In the case of some, mainly Western, nations, this may mean a significant change in direction in some matters. However, for all nations, it is possible to see the policymaker and the system leader as more of an enabler than a regulator or controller, although they will continue to have an important role for the latter. School leaders will be empowered or 'unchained', to use the imagery introduced in Chapter 3.

The point is consistently made throughout the book that it is neither possible nor desirable to predict the future. On the other hand, it is possible to describe the broader trends – mega-trends – within which particular policy and practice in certain settings will emerge. It is also possible to describe in general terms possible and preferred scenarios and several are presented in Chapter 15 ('Narratives in self-transformation').

It is intended that the practitioner be the primary reader and, consistent with the title of the book, strategies for the self-transforming school are described and illustrated throughout. Several have already emerged in this first chapter, as highlighted below.

Important messages for policymakers and practitioners

Each chapter concludes with three important messages for policymakers and practitioners. The following are those that have emerged from Chapter 1:

1   Leaders of government, ministers, system leaders and school leaders should be able to articulate a narrative for what has occurred over the last 25 years as authority and responsibility have been decentralised to schools. A connection to learning and teaching should lie at the heart of this narrative.
2   A capacity for self-management is important in a self-improving school or self-improving system. Such a capacity is a prerequisite but it is not sufficient if there is to be a transformation of schools.
3   It is not possible to predict what may be in place in 25 years but there are powerful and clearly discernible mega-trends that are likely to determine the particular features of the self-transforming school. A futures perspective and a capacity for innovation at all levels are prerequisites.

2 Expectations and impact of self-management

What has been the impact of self-management? Of central concern should be the impact on learning. In addition, given that it involves a higher level of authority, responsibility and accountability at the school level, there should also be concern about workload and complexity. Chapter 2 contains a summary of evidence on these matters.

Expectations for the self-managing school

A key issue and useful starting point are the expectations for the self-managing school. These are addressed in two ways. First, given that this book was published on the twenty-fifth anniversary of the 1988 Education Reform Act in England, it is reasonable to look back at what was expected at the time, that is on the discourse surrounding the legislation. Second, it is worth critically examining the extent to which self-management was proposed as a dominant reform that might, of its own accord, make a powerful impact on learning. Was it held out as a 'silver bullet'?

The 1988 Education Reform Act in England included provision for more authority and responsibility to be assumed by schools through the extension across the country of a form of local management that had already been in place for several years in a small number of local authorities. The Act implemented what was promised in the manifesto of the Conservative Party for the 1987 election (Conservative Party, 1987), which had been shaped by concerns about aspects of state education.

Two interest groups were influential in shaping public debate. The Hillgate Group manifesto (Hillgate Group, 1986) recommended greater centralisation on the one hand – 'we believe that a national curriculum is essential' (Hillgate Group, 1986: 7) – but also greater decentralisation – 'schools should be self-governing' (ibid.: 10). The group believed that 'the first and most important step in any comprehensive reform of the state educational system is to give more power to the parents' (ibid.: 10). In a paper for the Institute of Economic Affairs (the second interest group), Stuart Sexton, one-time advisor to the former Secretary of State Sir Keith Joseph, based his case (Sexton, 1987) for the self-management of schools on popular perceptions about poor academic standards, poor standards of discipline and behaviour, inadequate response to technology and employment needs, low teacher morale, under-funding and inefficient management. He believed that

> the only choice left is to devolve the system to the schools themselves, and to create a direct relationship between the suppliers of education, the schools and the teachers, and the consumers, the parents and their children. It is to create, as near as practicable, a 'free market' in education. To use a popular word, it is in some sense to 'privatise' the State education system.
>
> (ibid.: 10)

Much of the criticism of the reform was that its intention was to privatise public education. The critics stood on firm ground because that was indeed the language employed by its proponents, as illustrated by Sexton, who went further by advocating a voucher system, with self-management and a devolved budget being an intermediate step. He acknowledged that there would be difficulties in determining the budget allocation to a school and establishing an appropriate mechanism for accountability, but the intention was clear: 'It can be cogently argued that this single step of financial devolution could do more, now, both to raise standards and to produce a more effective and efficient use of money, than any other measure' (ibid.: 24).

Despite Sexton's view that the proposals, if enacted, would in some sense 'privatise' state education, and that self-management would be an intermediate step to a voucher system, nothing of the kind was embodied in the 1988 Education Reform Act (ERA) or in what unfolded in the succeeding 25 years, either in England or in the increasing number of countries where there has been a significant increase in authority, responsibility and accountability at the school level. State schools are still owned, staffed and substantially funded by a public authority. The fact that state schools also draw support from a range of private sources and that parents have a choice among schools does not mean that the state education system has been 'privatised'.

It is therefore apparent that the introduction of self-managing schools under the ERA did not lead to the privatisation of public education. It is also clear that the claims of its proponents for what it would achieve were extravagant. As noted above, Sexton based his case for self-management on popular perceptions about poor academic standards, poor standards of discipline and behaviour, inadequate response to technology and employment needs, low teacher morale, under-funding and inefficient management. There is considerable evidence to support a view that these matters have not been resolved to any great extent through any combination of policies in the ensuing years.

The early absence of evidence of impact on learning led some observers to discount the idea of the self-managing school as an important strategy for school improvement. In one sense, this was setting up a kind of 'straw man' expectation, since it was never claimed in the series of books on self-managing schools that the strategy, in and of itself, would have a direct cause-and-effect relationship with outcomes for students. *The Self-Managing School* (Caldwell and Spinks, 1988) was a straightforward exposition of a more-or-less cyclical process of goal setting, policymaking, planning, budgeting, implementing and evaluating that should be applied to decisions about curriculum, learning, teaching, services and infrastructure. It described a capacity that is needed in any approach to the management of schools but should be well developed if schools were to assume a higher level of authority and responsibility within a centrally determined framework. There should be alignment in decision making on a range of functions if self-management was to make a contribution to school improvement.

The importance of aligning different strategies was made clear in *Beyond the Self-Managing School* (Caldwell and Spinks, 1998) in several of the 'strategic intentions' that should shape the work of the self-managing school. The following is a sample that illustrates this alignment:

- The primary purpose of self-management is to make a contribution to learning, so schools that aspire to success in this domain will make an unrelenting effort to utilise all of the capacities that accrue with self-management to achieve that end.
- There will be clear, explicit and planned links, either direct or indirect, between each of the capacities that come with self-management and activities in the school that relate to learning and teaching and the support of learning and teaching.
- There is a strong association between the mix and capacities of staff, and success in addressing needs and priorities in learning, so schools will develop a capacity to optimally select staff, taking account of these needs and priorities.
- There is a strong association between the knowledge and skills of staff and learning outcomes for students, so schools will employ their capacity for self-management to design, select, implement or utilise professional development programs to help ensure these outcomes.

(ibid.: 217)

Impact on learning

There has been a consistent demand for evidence that self-management leads in cause-and-effect fashion to improved student outcomes, and this is understandable despite the unrealistic or inappropriate expectations that have been held for the process. It was sobering to note the consistent finding in early research that there appeared to be few, if any, direct links. Such an impact was unlikely to be achieved in the absence of purposeful connections between capacities associated with self-management and what occurs in the classroom in learning and teaching and in the support of learning and teaching.

A review of research suggests that there have been three generations of studies and it is only in the third that evidence of the impact of decentral-isation on outcomes has emerged, and then only when certain conditions were fulfilled. The first generation in the 1970s was when impact on learning was not a primary or even secondary purpose. The second generation was in the 1980s, when such purposes may have been brought to the fore but the database was weak. The third, emerging in the late 1990s and gathering momentum in the early 2000s, coincided with a pre-eminent concern for learning outcomes and the development of a strong database. The most strik-ing findings have come from analyses in PISA.

These findings confirm that the most successful systems of schools secure an optimal balance of autonomy, accountability and choice. Particularly note-worthy are two studies conducted for the OECD by staff at the Ifo Institute for Economic Research at the University of Munich (Department of Human Capital and Innovation). One focused on the level of student achievement and the other on equity of student achievement. As far as the level of student achievement is concerned, 'on average, students perform better if schools have autonomy to decide on staffing and to hire their own teachers' and 'stu-dents perform substantially better in systems where private school operation creates choice and competition' (Wößmann *et al.*, 2007: 59). As far as equity is concerned:

> rather than harming disadvantaged students, accountability, autonomy, and choice are tides that lift all the boats. There is not a single case where a policy designed to introduce accountability, autonomy, or choice into schooling benefits high-SES students to the detriment of low-SES students.
>
> (Schütz *et al.*, 2007: 35)

Andreas Schleicher leads the OECD effort in PISA. He provided a helpful synthesis of the findings on school and system characteristics in high-per-forming systems (Schleicher, 2011). He made it clear that self-management is but one element in a constellation of approaches that must be aligned if the desired outcomes are to be achieved. He referred to high-performing systems 'in which teachers and school principals act as partners and have the authority to act, the necessary information to do so, and access to effective support systems to assist them in implementing change' (ibid.: 63).

Schleicher acknowledged the importance of lateral (internal) accountability as well as external accountability. Consistent with the 'Finnish Way' reported by Sahlberg (2011), Schleicher noted that a distinguishing characteristic of Finland was the 'networks of schools that stimulate and spread innovation as well as collaborate to provide curriculum diversity, extend services, and professional support' (Schleicher, 2011: 63).

Although a balance of centralisation and decentralisation is evident in the above, it is important to note that, even now, there may be no impact on learning unless purposeful links are made at the school and classroom levels. Fullan, Hill and Crévola (2006) demonstrated the limits to improvement by describing how gains in literacy had plateaued in England and how the decentralisation of decision making in Chicago, Milwaukee and Seattle had not led to large-scale improvement: 'They contain glimpses of what will be required, but they fail to touch deeply day-to-day classroom instruction, and to touch it in a way that will get results for all' (Fullan *et al.*, 2006: 6).

The most comprehensive Australian study that explored the links between self-management and learning was conducted in Victoria over five years from 1994 to 1998 following the further empowerment of approximately 1,700 schools under the rubric of Schools of the Future. The research was conducted by a consortium of the Education Department, Victorian Primary Principals Association, Victorian Association of State Secondary Principals and the University of Melbourne, as summarised by Caldwell and Spinks (1998). The touchstone for the project was the objectives of the initiative, which were to:

- encourage the continuing improvement in the quality of educational programs and practices in Victorian schools to enhance student learning outcomes;
- actively foster the attributes of good schools in terms of leadership, school ethos, goals, planning and accountability process;
- build on a state-wide framework of quality curriculum, programs and practices;
- encourage parents to participate directly in decisions that affect their child's education;
- recognise teachers as true professionals, able to determine their own careers and with the freedom to exercise their professional skills and judgements in the classroom;
- allow principals to become true leaders in their school with the ability to build and lead their teaching teams;
- enable communities, through the school charter, to determine the destiny of the school, its character and ethos;
- within guidelines, enable schools to develop their own programs to meet the individual needs of students;
- be accountable to the community for the progress of the school and the achievement of its students.

(ibid.: 48–49)

Surveys of all principals were conducted each year for five years as the programme was expanded from early volunteers to the point where all but a handful of schools were included in the scheme. Substantial reports were prepared and widely disseminated. After the first base-line survey, the questions in succeeding years included the same items, enabling the researchers to track the views of principals over the period of the project.

The objectives were generally perceived to be achieved at a high level. A noteworthy feature was the identification in the base-line survey of 25 expected benefits, with progress monitored in the surveys that followed. These were grouped in four domains: curriculum and learning, planning and resource allocation, personnel and professional, and school and community. Structural equation modelling of responses resulted in an explanatory model of direct and indirect effects among factors influencing principals' perceptions of curriculum and learning benefits.

The limitations of the research were acknowledged at the time. It was a second-generation study in the three generations described earlier; it drew on the perceptions of principals since there were no consistent data sets on student achievement at the time.

Impact on workload

An enduring issue is the impact of self-management on the role of the principal and other school leaders. A study was conducted in Victoria (Department of Education and Training [DET], Victoria, 2003) on the workload in public (state) schools and its impact on the health and well-being of the principal and assistant principals. On workload, the number of hours worked per week by principals in Victoria was similar to that worked by principals in England, as reported in a survey at about the same time, being about 60 hours. This was well above the average of leaders in other professional fields in several European nations (about 45 hours per week). The report contained evidence of a negative impact on the emotional and physical well-being of principals.

A study in Sweden reported by Lindberg (2012) was concerned with levels of stress experienced by principals when a management by objectives approach was implemented in association with school-based management (SBM). School-based management has been a feature of trends in school reform in Sweden over the last two decades. Implementation was in the hands of municipalities, which have authority and responsibility for the administration of schools while operating in a broad framework of national policy on education. The study compared the impact of school-based management at the senior secondary level in two municipalities, one which retained a largely traditional role for schools and their principals and the other which implemented a relatively high level of decentralisation. The former provided no choice on which schools students could attend and decentralised only decisions on the allocation of funds for materials, supplies and professional development. Students were free to choose their schools in the latter, with principals able to make decisions on the number of employees, salaries, materials, supplies, investments, professional development and actions concerning income.

Surveys and interviews of principals in the Swedish study focused on aspects of stress, including role conflict, role ambiguity and role overload. There were important and significant differences in the responses of the two groups:

Principals with more traditional roles experience less role ambiguity, but greater role conflict and role overload [whereas] principals with SBM-influenced roles experience less role conflict and role overload, but much more role ambiguity . . . They have space to manoeuvre.

(Lindberg, 2012: 168)

Assessing the impact

Self-management is one manifestation of a general trend to decentralisation in public education in many countries since the late 1960s, with bipartisan political support and more widespread practice in the early years of the twenty-first century. The phenomenon is not a 'fad', as stated in a report to the Review of Funding for Schooling in Australia in which the Nous Group stated that '"Autonomy" has arguably been one of the more faddish concepts that has informed education reforms internationally in the past decade' (Nous Group, 2011: 63).

The practice was introduced for a range of reasons but much of the heat from often contentious debates about its efficacy has dissipated as most governments and system authorities settled on the enhancement of learning as its primary purpose. The logic of the argument was relatively straightforward: each school contains a unique mix of student needs, interests, aptitudes, aspirations and passions, and those who work at the school level are best placed to determine the particular mix of all of the resources available to the school to achieve optimal outcomes. Early research was generally unable to confirm the logic, either because the design of the reform did not include a connection to learning or because the database on student achievement was poorly constructed, thus thwarting any effort to determine the connection. Research at macro and micro levels tends to confirm the association but it requires purposeful efforts by a skilled profession to make it effective.

Early efforts placed an inappropriate emphasis on management, with particular attention being given to planning and resource allocation, rather than the more integrated view of self-management along the lines of the strategic intentions cited earlier, which stressed the links to learning. However, with heightened expectations for schools, especially in terms of success for all students in all settings, the focus continues to shift to leadership and the building of professional capacity to achieve an alignment of all kinds of resources, including curriculum and pedagogy, with the mix of learning requirements at the school level. Table 2.1 provides a summary of evidence on nine assertions often made about the self-managing school.

Aligning the effort

Although the focus in this book is on the self-managing school and how it may become the self-transforming school, it is important to place the evidence on impact into a larger framework and to stress again the importance of aligning the effort. One approach is to follow the lead of Barber, Donnelly

Table 2.1 An evidence-based assessment of nine assertions about the self-managing
school

Assertion	Summary of evidence
Self-management is an attempt to privatise public schools	Self-managing schools have remained in the public system. Contributions from the not-for-profit, philanthropic and corporate sectors have not changed the relationship between government and public schools
Self-management is a fad	There has been a consistent trend to self-management for more than four decades
Self-management is about capacity to hire and fire	'Hire' and 'fire' imply an authority to employ or dismiss that is not evident in public schools except for short-term appointments. The loose use of these terms has often given rise to heated debate when the correct terms for the processes are 'select' and 'transfer', since the contract of employment remains with a central authority
Self-management harms efforts to achieve equity	Evidence from OECD studies suggests the opposite, provided there is a balance of autonomy, accountability and choice. The trend to self-management has been invariably accompanied by efforts to develop a student needs-based approach to the allocation of funds to schools and these normally contain an equity component. The issue is the overall quantum of resources available to schools regardless of the degree of centralisation and decentralisation
Self-management is associated with efforts to reduce public expenditure on government schools	Self-management has been introduced in good times and bad as far as the resourcing of schools is concerned
Self-management should not be implemented because it fails to address the needs of struggling schools, small schools or schools in remote settings	A one-size-fits-all approach is not supported by the evidence on successful policy and practice and there are no advocates for such an approach. There are circumstances where a more centralised approach is necessary, including for schools described in the statement
Self-management has no impact on learning	Although evidence was mixed at best in the first decades of self-management, this was because there was no purposeful link to learning and there was an absence of data on student achievement that would enable a judgement to be made. The weight of evidence since the turn of the century supports the case for a positive impact, provided that decision making at the local level is focused on learning and teaching and on the support of learning and teaching and that staff have the capacities to design and implement a student-centred approach

Assertion	Summary of evidence
Self-management is a distraction for principals and others who should focus instead on educational leadership	This statement captures a legitimate concern and there is evidence in some settings that this has been the case. Management support has not always been available to principals of public schools when authority, responsibility and accountability have been decentralised
Self-management reflects a lack of commitment to the needs of the system	Networking professional knowledge and resources is arguably more evident now than ever before, as is the connection between autonomy and accountability

and Rizvi (2012) in their report for the Institute for Public Policy Research in London, entitled *Oceans of Innovation*, which drew from developments around the Atlantic and Pacific. Some of its findings are taken up in more detail in Chapter 8 ('Innovation everywhere').

Barber and his colleagues proposed nine building blocks of 'world-class education systems', including standards and accountability (globally bench-marked standards, transparent data and accountability, concern for every child); human capital (identify and prepare great people, continuous improvement in knowledge and skills, outstanding leadership); and structure and organisa-tion (enabling or empowering central organisations and agencies, capacity to manage change at every level, operational authority and responsibility at the school level) (Barber *et al.*, 2012: 59). They believed that the system should be reorganised so that it 'becomes a dynamic driver of change rather than a static bureaucracy – a driver of quality rather than an enforcer of compliance' (ibid.: 59). Failure to give effect to this belief is identified in Chapter 3 as a barrier to moving from self-management to self-transformation.

Oceans of Innovation also drew attention to the danger of false dichoto-mies, proposing that AND should replace OR to provide the following set of seven: universal standards AND (not OR) personalisation; whole systems AND autonomous schools; best practice AND innovations; teaching AND technology; disciplinary AND interdisciplinary; public AND private; strategy AND implementation (ibid.: 62).

Pitfalls in national and international generalisations

A small trend away from self-management was reported in the 2012 edition of the OECD's *Education at a Glance*. For example, the proportion of deci-sions made at the school level, at the lower secondary level, has declined since 2007 in 10 of the 21 countries that provided a report, with an increase in only four, including Australia (OECD, 2012: 500–501). Care should be taken in interpreting this trend, and trends reported in earlier editions of *Education at a Glance*, because the balance of centralisation and decentralisation varies among systems within particular countries. For example, Australia ranks twelfth among the 21 responding nations but there is wide variability among its eight systems of public education. New South Wales, the most populous state, has the most centralised approach and it is only since 2010 that a small-scale trial of self-management has been implemented. In contrast, Victoria, the neighbouring and second most populous state, has the most far-reaching and long-standing approach to self-management in Australia. Only one other state, Western Australia, has a comparable level of self-management at the time of writing, but this does not yet extend to all schools. This is the 'independent public schools' initiative.

There are similar variations in Canada and the United States. However, the Canadian province of Alberta, for example, has a relatively high level of self-management, especially in the Edmonton Public School District, which has more than 30 years' experience of landmark reform in this respect. There are significant developments in districts across the United States but these represent a small minority.

These variations within countries highlight the importance of a smaller frame of reference, not only particular systems within a country, but also particular schools that have built capacity and have become self-transforming. This finer-grained analysis is undertaken in succeeding chapters.

Broad descriptions of policy and practice in different countries should be treated with caution. Consider, for example, the international comparative study conducted by the World Bank (Barrera-Osorio *et al.*, 2009). It had a sharp focus on school-based management. Although it drew from Western literature in explaining the concept, it dealt mainly with policy and practice in developing countries in Latin America and the Caribbean, Africa, Asia, the Middle East and North Africa. It offered sweeping generalisations in several instances; for example, it stated erroneously that in the 1970s Australia 'increased efficiency through near total autonomy' and noted that 'unfortunately there are no rigorous evaluations of the Australian, New Zealand, or UK programs so there is no convincing evidence of the effects of these reforms on student achievement' (ibid.: 11). In apparent contradiction, the report observed that 'SBM reforms of the strongest type appear to have been introduced and been successful in achieving their goals' in developed countries, including Australia and New Zealand (ibid.: 103). The study did not refer to the OECD studies and other research cited earlier in this chapter.

It is important, nevertheless, to appreciate why there has been the recent slight trend towards centralisation in some countries. The OECD report suggests that 'some of the shift toward more centralised decision-making can be explained by the heightened interest in measures of accountability that involve national assessments and national examinations that are based on centrally established curricula or frameworks' (OECD, 2012: 500–501). A key issue is the extent to which this is counter-productive, and this is a major theme in Chapter 3.

Important messages for policymakers and practitioners

1 Initial expectations for self-management were often unrealistic, especially when they embodied a claim that the practice in and of itself leads to improvement in learning.
2 The processes of self-management and associated capacities must be powerfully and purposely linked to the implementation of strategies that evidence shows are likely have an impact on learning.
3 Generalisations about the extent of school autonomy in particular countries should be critically scrutinised, for there is a range of policies and practices in particular systems within a country, and sometimes between particular schools within a system.

3 Unchaining the self-managing school

The evidence in Chapter 2 affirmed the contribution that a higher level of autonomy can make to improved outcomes for students, but the relationship is heavily qualified or moderated by a range of factors. The OECD studies, based on findings in several iterations of PISA, highlighted the importance of getting 'the right balance' of autonomy and accountability. Other research referred to the need for purposeful links with strategies that are known to have a positive impact on learning.

In general, there is logic in the links. Each school contains a unique mix of student needs, interests, aptitudes, ambitions and passions, and each is located in a community that differs from others in important ways. A capacity to determine local priorities and the mix of resources required to address them calls for a high level of authority and responsibility at the school level. However, confounding the logic and findings in these national and international studies is the fact that several countries that provide a relatively high level of autonomy are declining in their performance on international tests such as PISA. Why is this so?

The consequences of dysfunctional command-and-control

It is argued in this chapter that the logic and the evidence in Chapter 2 are often confounded by the constraints placed on schools through the application of inappropriate strategies of command-and-control. England is a case in point. There has been steady incremental growth in autonomy, with significant advances on occasions such as the passing of the 1988 Education Reform Act; schools have been supported by a dramatic increase in funding; some of the most impressive approaches to the development and support of school leaders have been adopted, for example, at the National College for School Leadership. There have been severe cutbacks in recent years but government took the view that additional funding had not made a difference; indeed, the country had gone backwards, as described in the OECD report (Braconier, 2012) cited in Chapter 1.

Seddon's general critique of public sector reform in England is instructive:

The public-sector reform that is most needed is the one that is never talked about – that of the regime itself, the vast pyramid, hundreds of thousands strong, of people engaged in regulating, specifying, inspecting, instructing and coercing others doing the work to comply with their edicts.

(Seddon, 2010a)

Seddon provided evidence to refute the claim that standardisation of services is the most efficient way to proceed. He believed that managers will be dismayed when confronted by this apparently counter-intuitive finding and will be challenged when confronted with the evidence:

The reality that standardisation drives costs up will be resisted, rationalised and angrily denied. But studying the work obliges managers to confront the evidence of their own eyes: while specialisation and standardisation of work lower transaction costs, overall costs of service go up because the factory design creates more handovers, fragmentation, duplication and errors and hence re-work, and generates massive failure demand. Studying the work, they understand a paradox: managing costs creates costs.

(Seddon, 2010b)

Seddon (2010b) argued that there are greater efficiencies, as well as better outcomes, if the focus is on local services: 'Local services are human, receptive, engaging and productive. Counter intuitively, they are also high quality and low cost. So if the idea of local services goes against the grain – as it does – it is the grain we have to change'. He suggests that 'economy comes from flow, not scale'.

Seddon takes aim at people such as Sir Michael Barber, who headed the Prime Minister's Delivery Unit (PMDU) at 10 Downing Street from 2001 to 2007 after leading the School Effectiveness Unit. Barber, described by Adonis (2012: 27) as 'brilliantly can-do and insightful', now at Pearson after a senior appointment at McKinsey, has written in detail of his experience in *Instruction to Deliver* (Barber, 2007) and in a guide for system leaders under the title of *Deliverology 101: A Field Guide for Educational Leaders* (Barber *et al.*, 2011). He was a strong supporter of higher levels of autonomy for schools in England, but Seddon would argue that this and related strategies have been overwhelmed by the approach to 'deliverology'. In *Oceans of Innovation*, cited in Chapter 2 and referred to elsewhere, especially in Chapter 8 ('Innovation everywhere'), Barber and colleagues (Barber *et al.*, 2012) include standardisation and accountability in the three-dimensional description of the building blocks of a world-class school system. They proposed 'deliverology' as a strategy for achieving this end.

Finland's Pasi Sahlberg explains the shortcomings of the approach in England and comparable countries in his account of the Global Education

Reform Movement (GERM), which has the following characteristics (the 'Finnish Way' is summarised in parentheses): standardised teaching and learning (customised teaching and learning), focus on literacy and numeracy (focus on creative learning), teaching prescribed curriculum (encouraging risk-taking), borrowing market-orientated reform ideas (learning from the past and owning innovations) and test-based accountability and control (shared responsibility and trust) (Sahlberg, 2011: 103). He argued that GERM was an outcome of concern for literacy and numeracy in the face of the constructivist approaches to learning in the 1980s, a demand from the public for guaranteed outcomes, and the competition and accountability movement in the reform of public services (ibid.: 99–100). Whatever the reasons or the forces that underpinned it, GERM has a poor track record in comparison with the 'Finnish Way'.

Despite the critique, some of the outstanding examples of the self-transforming school may be found in England and several other countries allegedly 'infected' by the GERM, and some are described in subsequent chapters.

An explanatory model

A model that explains the critique and maps in broad terms the journey from the self-managing school to the self-transforming school may be illustrated by the series of tables and explanations in the pages that follow.

The starting point is the identification of three dimensions, each of which provides a continuum on which systems may differ. One is the extent of school *autonomy*. Although there are sound reasons for not using the concept of autonomy, it is employed here because of its wide use. It refers to the extent to which a school has the authority and responsibility to make decisions within a centrally determined framework of goals, policies, standards and accountabilities. The relationships and distinctions between self-management and autonomy were described in Chapter 1. Schools may have relatively low or relatively high levels of autonomy.

The second dimension is the extent of system *control* over schools, which may be relatively tight or relatively loose. Although there is a relationship between autonomy and control, it is possible for a system to exercise relatively tight control over schools on important matters whereas they may have a high level of autonomy on others. The third dimension is the *outlook* of the system, which may be relatively closed or relatively open, referring to the extent to which it is open to outside ideas and influences.

There are eight ways of classifying systems on these dimensions, as illustrated in Table 3.1, and these are designated as 'types'. Before explaining these, it is important to note that they are broad classifications and there may be different ways of classifying a system for different functions. Expressed another way, systems may have the characteristics of more than one type.

Table 3.1 Systems classified by type according to autonomy, control and outlook

Dimension	Type							
	1	*2*	*3*	*4*	*5*	*6*	*7*	*8*
Autonomy	L	L	L	L	H	H	H	H
Control	H	H	L	L	H	H	L	L
Outlook	C	O	C	O	C	O	C	O

Note: L=Low; H=High; C=Closed; O=Open.

Type 1: Low autonomy, high control, closed outlook

In Type 1, schools have minimal authority and responsibility to make decisions over important matters and the system exerts tight control over their operations. The system is generally impervious to developments in its external environment. Type 1 may be a preferred approach if a sense of coherence and order is required to raise standards across the system, especially if its leaders have high levels of expertise. This is a classic command-and-control approach but ultimately unsustainable in a time of complexity and change.

Type 2: Low autonomy, high control, open outlook

For Type 2, schools have minimal authority and responsibility to make decisions over important matters and the system exerts strong control over their operations. The system is open to new ideas from its external environment. Type 2 is a preferred approach if a sense of order and coherence is required to raise standards across the system and its leaders have a capacity to draw ideas from within and outside in times of complexity and change. Although still command-and-control, Type 2 is likely to be more sustainable than Type 1.

Type 3: Low autonomy, low control, closed outlook

Type 3 is likely to be a fragmented system, making slow progress in building a sense of order and coherence. It does not seek ideas from outside the system. Things do not augur well for such a system.

Type 4: Low autonomy, low control, open outlook

Prospects for the system are likely to be better under Type 4 than under Type 3 because its leaders are open to new ideas but they continue to exert minimal control over schools that have limited capacity to make decisions that may improve their lot.

Type 5: High autonomy, high control, closed outlook

Type 5 involves a higher level of autonomy than Type 4 and a relatively high level of control may be appropriate where there is a need for a stronger sense of coherence and order. There is an opportunity for schools to make decisions that reflect their particular mix of needs and priorities. However, a closed outlook suggests that leaders in the system are shielding themselves from learning about a better way to do things.

Type 6: High autonomy, high control, open outlook

Type 6 may be more effective and sustainable than Type 5 if leaders are open to ideas from outside the system. The danger is maintaining elements of command-and-control for longer than necessary.

Type 7: High autonomy, low control, closed outlook

Type 7 provides an opportunity to move from self-management to self-transformation as the chains of an excessive command-and-control approach are cast aside and schools have the capacity to take charge of their operations. The approach will be constrained to the extent that the system and its schools are shielded from ideas from outside.

Type 8: High autonomy, low control, open outlook

Type 8 maximises the opportunity for self-transformation if schools have the capacity to take charge. The system and its schools are open to developments from outside.

It is important to stress that these classifications are silent as far as capacities and outcomes are concerned. Whether schools in each type of system are effective depends on their capacities and the kinds of support they receive. Many of the chapters in this book include examples of such schools and strategies for achieving success, with a particular focus on self-transforming schools.

A major source of concern is the extent to which a command-and-control approach is unnecessarily constraining the efforts of self-managing schools, or has been maintained if not strengthened beyond what is necessary to achieve coherence in a system that is focusing its efforts on improvement. An inappropriate 'chaining' of self-managing schools is illustrated in Table 3.2.

The appropriate response under these circumstances is to break the chain, as illustrated in Table 3.3. It is important to stress that the chain does not entirely disappear, for it is necessary to ensure transparency and accountability where public funds are concerned. However, in some places the chains may fall away to a large extent, or may not have existed to any great degree, as in Finland and in other systems of self-managing schools.

Table 3.2 Chaining the self-managing school

Dimension	Type							
	1	*2*	*3*	*4*	*5*	*6*	*7*	*8*
Autonomy	L	L	L	L	H	H	H	H
Control	H	H	L	L	H	H	L	L
Outlook	C	O	C	O	C	O	C	O

Note: L=Low; H=High; C=Closed; O=Open.

Table 3.3 Unchaining the self-managing school

Dimension	Type							
	1	*2*	*3*	*4*	*5*	*6*	*7*	*8*
Autonomy	L	L	L	L	H	H	H	H
Control	H	H	L	L	H	H	L	L
Outlook	C	O	C	O	C	O	C	O

Note: L=Low; H=High; C=Closed; O=Open.

Table 3.4 From self-management to self-transformation

Dimension	Type							
	1	*2*	*3*	*4*	*5*	*6*	*7*	*8*
Autonomy	L	L	L	L	H	H	H	H
Control	H	H	L	L	H	H	L	L
Outlook	C	O	C	O	C	O	C	O

Note: L=Low; H=High; C=Closed; O=Open.

This 'unchaining' provides a window of opportunity, as it were, for many schools to move from self-management to self-transformation, as illustrated in Table 3.4.

A simplified version of the model is illustrated in Figure 3.1. It includes two dimensions only – autonomy and control – with four quadrants labelled fragmented, command-and-control, self-managing and self-transforming. The outlook may be relatively open or relatively closed for schools and systems in each quadrant. As noted earlier, schools and systems may be in more than one quadrant depending on the function under consideration.

Whether self-transformation is in fact achieved depends on schools having the capacity and obtaining the support they need to make 'significant, systematic and sustained change that secures success for all students in all settings' (Caldwell and Harris, 2008: 3).

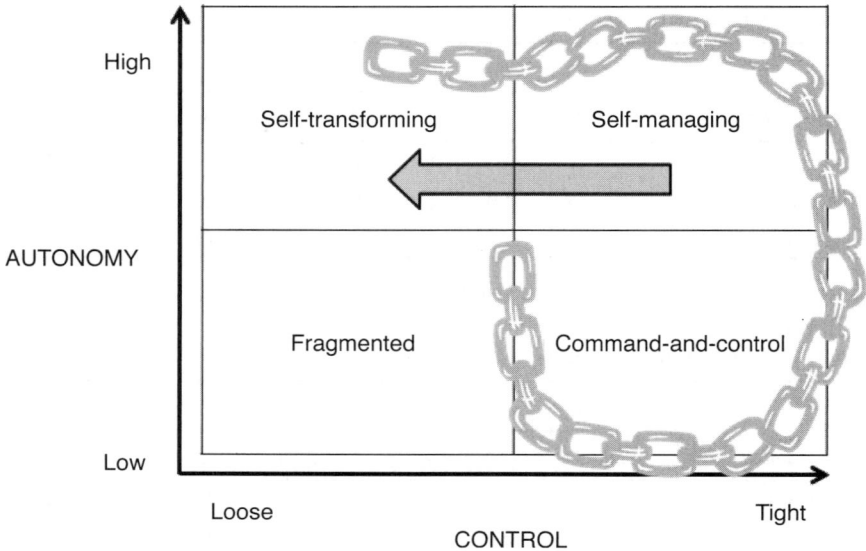

Figure 3.1 The simplified model.

Houle and Cobb were cited in Chapter 1 in respect of their declaration that 2010–2020 should be the decade of transformation. In describing the realities of exponential developments in technology and how these may apply to schools, they used imagery that is consistent with Figure 3.1 in stating that 'we need to break out of the box entirely' (Houle and Cobb, 2011: 71).

A small-scale field test

Caldwell conducted a small-scale field test of the model, as brought together in Table 3.4 and simplified in Figure 3.1, by illustrating the 'unchaining' metaphor. The occasion was the 2012 Trans-Tasman Conference of the Australian Primary Principals' Association (APPA) and the New Zealand Principals' Federation (NZPF) conducted on the theme 'Our Primary Purpose: Leading Learning'. He provided a list of five characteristics of a self-transforming school, that is a school that operates as Type 8, and explained that these were illustrations of many possibilities.

1   The self-transforming school calls for higher levels of autonomy to the extent that the school is unchained from the constraints of a command-and-control and carrot-and-stick approach.
2   The self-transforming school is unchained to choose the support it needs from sources of its choice even though system support may be on offer. The culture of 'the system' should shift to service.
3   The self-transforming school is unchained from the constraints of

local networks, which in many cases are simply administrative units in a command-and-control, hierarchical approach to line management, although it may include such networks in the many constantly changing networking arrangements in which it engages to share knowledge, address problems of common concern and pool resources.

4   The self-transforming school is unchained from the need to wait for and adopt so-called best practice innovations that are scaled up for implementation in all schools. What is scaled up is a capacity for innovation and freedom to choose the innovations that best suit local circumstances.

5   The self-transforming school is unchained from the myriad of often unsustainable short-term conditional grants, each of which calls for lengthy submissions and centrally managed accountability with its seemingly endless paperwork, to an approach canvassed in the Gonski Report (Recommendation 24) in which needs-based recurrent funding is rolled into allocations to schools.

The Gonski Report (Australian Government, 2011) is the report of the Review of Funding for Schooling conducted in Australia from 2010 to 2011, named after the chairman of the review committee, David Gonski. Recommendation 24 raised the possibility of rolling multiple short-term grants into a single needs-based funding mechanism for schools.

Those attending were principals of primary schools in Australia and New Zealand. Most of the former were from the host state of Victoria, where there is a relatively high level of self-management. Others from Australia came from other states and territories where autonomy lies in the mid-range, but is considerably less than in Victoria. Primary schools from New Zealand have about two decades of experience of a comparatively high level of autonomy (see Chapter 4). Some were from relatively autonomous Catholic and independent (private) schools but the majority were from public schools.

All had just attended keynote presentations by Pasi Sahlberg, Director General of CIMO (Centre for International Mobility and Cooperation) in Helsinki, Finland, and Yong Zhao, Presidential Chair and Associate Dean for Global Education, College of Education at the University of Oregon, United States, with the former describing the stand-out achievements of students from Finland on international tests and the latter focusing on innovation and entrepreneurship.

Participants in two workshops were invited to rate the desirability and feasibility of each of the above five characteristics on a scale from 0 (low) to 5 (high). Table 3.5 contains a summary of ratings.

Each of the five characteristics was considered highly desirable, with mean ratings ranging from 4.15 to 4.88. The lowest rating was given to Characteristic 3, concerned with networking. Comments suggested a higher value was placed on local system networks than implied in the statement. The

Table 3.5 Participant ratings of desirability and feasibility of five characteristics of the 'unchained' self-transforming school (conducted at the Trans-Tasman Conference of Primary Principals in Australia and New Zealand, September 2012) (45 participants)

Characteristic no.	Description	Mean desirability*	Mean feasibility*	Sample comments
1	The self-transforming school calls for higher levels of autonomy to the extent that the school is unchained from the constraints of a command-and-control and carrot-and-stick approach	4.77	3.08	High desirability (4) if there is needs-based funding. Feasibility low (3) while funds are allocated as they are
2	The self-transforming school is unchained to choose the support it needs from sources of its choice even though system support may be on offer. The culture of 'the system' should shift to service	4.75	4.00	Low feasibility (2) while resources are stretched so thinly across schools
3	The self-transforming school is unchained from the constraints of local networks, which in many cases are simply administrative units in a command-and-control, hierarchical approach to line management, although it may include such networks in the many constantly changing networking arrangements in which it engages to share knowledge, address problems of common concern and pool resources	4.15	4.15	Schools value the benefits of their local networks. Schools can already join other networks. 'Regional networks still dictate and insist on too much data and bureaucracy that just causes work not creates change'
4	The self-transforming school is unchained from the need to wait for and adopt so-called best practice innovations that are scaled up for implementation in all schools. What is scaled up is a capacity for innovation and freedom to choose the innovations that best suit local circumstances	4.73	3.80	There is an issue with use of scarce public funds for innovation. Distribution may be inequitable. Prefer 'next practice' to 'innovation'
5	The self-transforming school is unchained from the myriad of often unsustainable short-term conditional grants, each of which calls for lengthy submissions and centrally managed accountability with its seemingly endless paperwork, to an approach canvassed in the Gonski Report (Recommendation 24) in which needs-based recurrent funding is rolled into allocations to schools	4.88	4.88	Low feasibility (2): 'after-hours is always about chasing the paper trail'. High feasibility (4) but 'does not lead to real change'

* Participants provided ratings on a scale from 0 (low) to 5 (high).

highest rating was given to Characteristic 5, which called for schools to be 'unchained from the myriad of often unsustainable short-term conditional grants'.

Feasibility was considered to be moderate to high, with mean ratings in the range 3.08 to 4.88, with the lowest mean rating for unchaining schools 'from the constraints of a command-and-control and carrot-and-stick approach'. Concern about this issue was raised by a New Zealand principal who observed that 'New Zealand schools are becoming more and more externally controlled and sadly less likely to be given the opportunity to be self-transforming'. Another principal stated that self-transformation will be possible only if schools 'have a clear vision of the direction we need to create the best education possible for all and the resourcing to enable this to occur'. One principal rated feasibility as 5 for each characteristic if the approach in Finland were adopted but this will require 'a change of attitude/practice by our Ministry of Education'. A Catholic principal felt that transformation was more feasible in a smaller system.

Participants were invited to make additional observations and these included the following:

- The self-transforming school has time to develop/evolve what it sees as the best pathway and is allowed to pursue it for long enough to develop mastery/excellence, unchained from constant meaningless, ideologically driven change.
- The self-transforming school can recruit, reward and retain the best education professionals.
- The self-transforming school can unchain the existing limitations/controls on school enrolments and rid schools of 'local area only' enrolment requirements.
- How can we 'regain' or 'unchain' the trust between our political leaders and us as professionals? We need a dramatic cultural shift in our political context – one based on trust and support to schools, not based on command and control.
- Small remote schools do not fit this. There is a need to build in support but also accountability as often teachers/principals are inexperienced and they do not have another school 'just down the road' to visit. Given the right person in the District Director position, we can create a vibrant learning community between these schools but there is a price in terms of full autonomy.
- We need to learn from successful and effective international experience, for example Finland, Singapore and Ontario.
- The self-transforming school is able to set its own value/belief statement that underpins the ethos and move forward with this as a strong focus of strategy and goals underpinned by the school's values.
- We need to design a personalised curriculum that is a living document and can change to suit the changing needs of the students/community.

Other responses referred to the challenges of working with students whose first or even second language is not English. One recalled the harmful competitive effects of the self-managing Schools of the Future programme in Victoria in the 1990s (Chapters 2 and 4 include a description of Schools of the Future and themes from research on its design and implementation).

'Unleashing greatness'

The model should not be understood as the 'one best way' to proceed. There is a time and place for a command-and-control approach, especially when a system is fragmented and student achievement is generally low. Particularly helpful in explaining this in the international arena is the McKinsey & Company report *How the World's Most Improved School Systems Keep Getting Better* (Mourshed *et al.*, 2010). There were 18 countries in the study (a total of 20 systems, including three from the United States). These were classified on a robust evidence base in four 'journeys': poor to fair ('achieving the basics of literacy and numeracy'), fair to good ('getting the foundations in place'), good to great ('shaping the profession') and great to excellent ('improving through peers and innovation'). There were three main findings, the first of which highlights the importance of strategic coherence across a system of schools. The second provides direct support for the model in Figure 3.1:

> There is a strong, correlation between a school system's improvement journey stage and the tightness of central control over the individual schools' activities and performance. Systems on the poor to fair journey, in general characterised by lower skill educators, exercise tight, central control over teaching and learning processes in order to minimise the degree of variation between individual classes and across schools. In contrast, systems moving from good to great, characterised by higher skill educators, provide only loose, central guidelines for teaching and learning processes, in order to encourage peer led creativity and innovation inside schools, the core driver for raising performance at this stage.
>
> (ibid.: 33–34)

The third highlights the commonalities across the four journeys, including curriculum, standards, remuneration, high-quality teachers and leaders, and the use of data. There is an important qualification as far as commonalities are concerned, namely that all schools in a system do not move together in their journeys: some may be moving from poor to fair and others from good to great. Approaches that chain all schools to the same command-and-control strategies, even when the majority of schools in the system are poor, are not appropriate when there is even one that should be unchained because it has the capacity to move to greatness.

Authors of the report label the second finding as 'prescribe adequacy, unleash greatness', and this is critical for moving from self-management to self-transformation. Chaining self-managing schools to excessive command-and-control structures is a barrier to greatness.

Framing the work of the self-transforming school

The school that succeeds at self-transformation must have powerful capacity if it is to achieve the goal of success for all of its students no matter what the setting. Much of this book is concerned with how these capacities are acquired and applied. Illustrations in Chapters 10 to 13 are framed by a classification developed by Caldwell and Harris (2008), based on studies of self-transforming schools and the systems that support them. They adopted the same definition of transformation as used in the current book: significant, systematic and sustained change that secures success for all students in all settings.

The groundwork was laid from 2004 to 2007 in 73 seminars and workshops involving about 4,000 school and school system leaders from 11 countries. These events combined input from Caldwell, Harris and Spinks, but the main features in most instances were scores of short case studies from school leaders about how their schools had achieved, or were making progress in achieving, transformation as defined above. The purpose of the workshops was to share and test ideas. It was an iterative programme, with findings from one event being reported at those that followed. Hypotheses were created to explain how transformation was achieved and these were tested in more focused studies in Australia, China, England, Finland, the United States and Wales. Schools that had been transformed or had made good progress to transformation were adept at strengthening and aligning four forms of capital – intellectual, social, spiritual and financial – achieving this strength and alignment through outstanding governance.

Caldwell and Harris (2008: 10) described each kind of capital as follows: intellectual capital refers to the level of knowledge and skill of those who work in or for the school; social capital refers to the strength of formal and informal partnerships and networks involving the school and all individuals, agencies, organisations and institutions that have the potential to support and be supported by the school; spiritual capital refers to the strength of moral purpose and the degree of coherence among values, beliefs and attitudes about life and learning (for some schools, spiritual capital has a foundation in religion; in other schools, spiritual capital may refer to ethics and values shared by members of the school and its community); financial capital refers to the money available to support the school. The alignment of these four forms of capital and their focus on the student are illustrated in Figure 3.2.

Ten indicators of each form of capital were identified in these international studies. Arguably the most potent are those concerned with intellectual capital and these indicators include (1) staff allocated to or selected by the school are at the forefront of knowledge and skill in required disciplines and pedagogies and (2) the school has built a substantial, systematic and sustained capacity

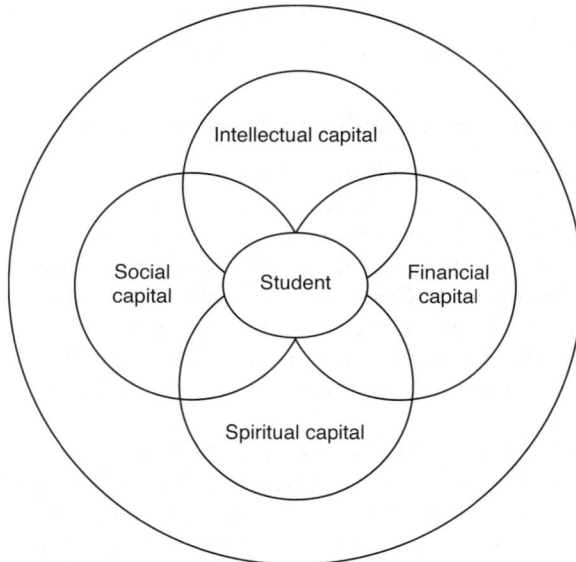

Figure 3.2   A model to frame the transformation of schools (adapted from Caldwell and Harris, 2008; Caldwell and Spinks, 2008).

for acquiring and sharing professional knowledge. Schools in Finland and some Asian jurisdictions generally have these capacities. Indicators of social capital include a high level of alignment between the expectations of parents and other key stakeholders and the mission, vision, policies, plans and programmes of the school.

Conclusion

Highly focused research on the efficacy of various system-wide strategies often highlights the negative impact of aspects of command-and-control and the positive impact of more flexible and supportive arrangements at the system level. For example, Lee, Seashore Louis and Anderson (2012) reported the impact of an emphasis on learning targets and the use of data on subsequent learning in a set of school districts in the United States and compared these with the impact of new arrangements for networking. They found that the former had a negative impact and the latter a positive impact. However, they did not conclude that target setting and the use of data are inappropriate: 'In the end we conclude that pressure for data use without support will not yield the desired results' (Lee *et al.*, 2012: 149).

A telling observation is made by Hannon in one of her powerful thought pieces for the Innovation Unit in England and prepared for discussion and reflection in the Global Education Leaders' Program (GELP) in Helsinki in 2012:

Governments lack the skills and impulses to be good facilitators and brokers: they cannot resist the temptation of becoming controllers and regulators, because they are, ultimately, responsible and their electorates will hold them to account.

(Hannon, 2012: 10)

Herein lie the dilemmas and challenges in unchaining self-managing schools.

Important messages for policymakers and practitioners

1 School systems vary according to how much autonomy they provide their schools, how much control they exercise over the decision-making process in schools and the extent to which they are open to new ideas from outside the system. High autonomy, low control and high openness are the optimum conditions for self-managing schools to become self-transforming schools, provided they have the necessary capacities to accomplish this.
2 Some systems maintain a command-and-control approach far longer than is necessary, as they attempt to achieve coherence across the system, and, under these circumstances, there should be an 'unchaining' of self-managing schools when they have the capacity to become self-transforming.
3 Schools in systems where there is a high degree of school self-management considered sample characteristics of the self-transforming school to be highly desirable and moderately feasible. These characteristics and strategies for their implementation are described and illustrated in subsequent chapters.

4 A study of contrasts in the West

Chapter 4 looks at policy and practice in Australia, England, New Zealand and the United States, each of which has declined in international tests of student achievement this century, and contrasts them with policy in Finland, which has maintained its position near the top, although slipping a little in recent times, and in Canada, which also occupies the high ground. The evidence supports the argument of Sahlberg (2011) that three of the first four nations have been 'infected' by the excesses of what he described as the GERM, with New Zealand thus far largely avoiding the 'infection' but being at the crossroads.

The chapter is not intended to provide an overview of education in these countries. The focus is on the framework for governance and the extent to which their schools are self-managing. Evidence of an inappropriate commitment to command-and-control is presented in several instances. The chapter concludes with a reflection on the complexities and dysfunctions of multiple levels of government, giving particular attention to the role of a federal government when constitutional powers to make laws in relation to education lie with the states.

Performance in PISA

OECD provides helpful frameworks for analysing the performance of nations in PISA and these form the basis for contrasting Canada and Finland, on the one hand, and Australia, England, New Zealand and the United States on the other. Countries are classified as low or high in terms of quality (mean score on PISA) and equity (variance or spread of scores on PISA). For 2009 (as reported by Sahlberg, 2011: 38), the three countries with the highest scores for quality and equity (high quality–high equity) were Canada, Finland and South Korea. Australia is also high quality–high equity, but is close to the OECD mean on equity. New Zealand and the United States are both high quality–low equity, with the latter much closer to the OECD mean than the former in respect of quality. The United Kingdom is marginally below the OECD mean for quality and marginally above the mean for equity.

The trends among these nations are especially noteworthy. As reported by Sahlberg (ibid.: 66), in PISA results for 15-year-olds in mathematics from 2000 to 2006, scores steadily declined in Australia, Canada, New Zealand, the United Kingdom and the United States but steadily increased for Finland, although there has been a decline for Finland in more recent tests.

Australia

Australia was established as a federation of six states in 1901. There is a federal government, often referred to as the 'commonwealth government'. Two territories created more recently have similar powers to the states, but are subject to federal control on some matters. Constitutional powers in respect of education lie with the states and territories, but the federal government has a powerful influence because it can distribute grants from general revenue and is the sole level of government that has the power to levy an income tax (this summary will refer to states only).

The federal government can set conditions on how grants to the states can be used and, in recent years, these conditions have been set out in a series of 'national partnership agreements' that reflected a desire in 2007 for 'cooperative federalism' when all governments were of the same persuasion (Labor). States are dependent on the federal government for a large portion of their total revenue, especially smaller states without a strong revenue base (in the case of Tasmania, the federal share exceeds 60 per cent). There are signs that consensus among the states is breaking up as governments of different persuasion (Liberal–National coalition) are elected, for example, in the three most populous states of New South Wales, Queensland and Victoria.

About 65 per cent of students attend public schools in Australia, with more than 50 per cent in private schools at the senior secondary level in the largest cities. Private schools are normally classified as either Catholic or independent. State and federal grants are distributed to authorities representing the interests of these schools. There are Catholic education commissions in each state and territory, which distribute the money to schools in their jurisdiction. Grants are distributed directly to independent schools, although an association representing the interests of such schools may be involved in certain instances; for example, funds to support building projects or professional development. These funding mechanisms are always the subject of debate, with federal funding renegotiated every four years. New arrangements will be implemented from 2014 if the different levels of government reach agreement on how recommendations of the Review of Funding for Schooling (Australian Government, 2011) are to be addressed.

For most of its history, there has been very limited autonomy for schools in the public sector in Australia and a negligible role for the federal government. This changed in the late 1960s, accelerating in the 1970s, when a review (Interim Committee of the Australian Schools Commission, 1973) recommended an expanded role for the federal government in terms of level of funding and programmes to be supported. A high level of self-management through 'devolution' was recommended, but states varied in the extent to which they empowered their public schools as a result. Victoria has had more than three decades of experience with self-management, with about 90 per cent of the state's recurrent budget for schools devolved for local decision making since the early 1990s. Western Australia now provides more authority and responsibility for some of its schools through what are known as 'independent public schools'. Queensland is following the same path as Western Australia. The federal government is implementing through national partnership agreements a scheme for empowering local schools, but states are, for the most part, using associated grants to build capacity through existing approaches rather than creating new levels of autonomy, as are Catholic and independent schools, which are virtually self-managing by definition although, as explained below, they are increasingly constrained by funding arrangements and accountability requirements.

Grants from state and federal governments tend to be of short duration, often only for one year and never for more than three, and there are heavy demands for paperwork to obtain the funds and be accountable for their deployment. Billions of dollars are tied up in national partnership agreements. An army of bureaucrats at every level of government is involved in the administration of grants. Most staff in the offices of associations supporting independent schools are employed in this kind of work. Some agreements are endeavouring to implement schemes that have minimal support in the profession, for example, a performance-based reward/bonus scheme for teachers.

The federal government established the Australian Curriculum, Assessment and Reporting Authority (ACARA) in 2009 to design and implement the nation's first national curriculum. ACARA also administers the National Assessment Program – Literacy and Numeracy (NAPLAN) for students in Grades 3, 5, 7 and 9, with school performance published on the My School website. Comparisons with 'like schools' are made possible using the Index of Community Socio-Educational Advantage (ICSEA). Sources of income and fields of expenditure are reported on My School for every public and private school in the country. There are national partnership agreements that commit states to participation in NAPLAN and My School, both of which are highly contentious in the profession.

The federal government also set up the Australian Institute of Teaching and School Leadership (AITSL), which established National Professional Standards for Teachers (NPST) and a National Professional Standard for Principals (NPSP). All ministers for education at both levels of government signed off on these standards and the way they will be used to shape policy and practice. There is a national accreditation scheme for programmes in initial teacher education offered by universities that is based on NPST. There is general support for the work of AITSL.

Although several of these initiatives are overdue, such as a national curriculum and national professional standards, most of the national partnership agreements, as with their predecessors, have been embraced by the states because they need the funds – the federal government neither owns nor operates a single school. The complexity of the funding arrangements is illustrated in the case of Victoria, which has designed an impressive needs-based funding mechanism to support its self-managing schools (described in Chapters 10 and 11), on to which has been grafted a large number of conditional grants from state and federal sources, each to be applied and accounted for. A review of funding arrangements to be implemented from 2014 recommended a similar needs-based approach for all schools in the country, into which should be added the large numbers of conditional grants. This is contained in Recommendation 24 of the report of the Review of Funding for Schooling (Australian Government, 2011).

Despite the additional funds and the entry of the federal government, there has been no overall improvement in outcomes for students after four decades of relentless change and after a nearly 300 per cent increase in funding (as reported in Barber and Mourshed, 2007). Australia's performance in PISA has declined relative to other countries and outcomes in NAPLAN have generally flatlined since the tests were introduced in the mid-2000s. Greater transparency of school performance in NAPLAN has not led in any measurable way to the exercising of greater parent choice. Despite these general patterns, there have been outstanding examples of particular schools that have been transformed and these are described in later chapters.

Overall, Australia has the characteristics of the GERM described by Sahlberg (2011) and, despite the good intentions of each level of government over many years, serious questions may be raised about priorities for funding and an excessive command-and-control or carrot-and-stick approach.

England

England is of special interest in the context of this book, the publication of which, in 2013, has occurred 25 years after the publication of *The Self-Managing School* (Caldwell and Spinks, 1988) and the passing of the 1988 Education Reform Act (ERA). The latter triggered the introduction of the self-managing school across England, after successful experience in a small number of local authorities, as well as the design and implementation of a national curriculum and a national testing programme.

England differs from other countries considered in Chapter 4 in several ways. First, there is a unitary system of government in the United Kingdom, with significant devolution of powers to governments in Northern Ireland, Scotland and Wales. There are different systems of public education in the four countries and what follows applies to England only, where a high level of autonomy was provided in the self-managing reforms of the ERA. Setting aside these differences, the mantra since 1944 has been about a national system, locally administered. Local in this context referred to the role of the local education authority. There was no local management in the sense of the self-managing school. Schools had boards of governors but their powers were limited, if not largely ceremonial. Second, schools that are usually described as 'private' in some other countries are fully funded by the state in England. Most faith-based schools are also maintained in this way. There are relatively few truly private schools in England which receive no funds from the public purse. Third, and significantly in the context of this book, there have been dramatic changes in the governance and funding of schools since 1988.

On the one hand, schools have become self-managing; on the other, there has been unprecedented activity on the part of government in setting standards and building frameworks of accountability. For much of the last two decades, it has been a tightly controlled form of self-management. Following the defeat of the Labour government in elections in 2010, the Conservative–Liberal coalition government moved to reduce the amount of regulation and encouraged greater diversity in the governance of schools. In respect to the latter, the government is extending the already far-reaching changes initiated by the Thatcher government and continued under Labour governments led by Tony Blair and Gordon Brown. To use a derogatory term, 'the bog-stand-ard comprehensive school' has apparently passed into history.

The transformation of governance commenced with the creation of City Technology Colleges (CTCs), the introduction of grant-maintained schools and the encouragement of specialisation, all at the secondary level. The CTC was a new kind of school with a focus on technology, established in disad-vantaged communities, with a significant injection of funds from the private sector, usually with sponsorship or naming rights. The grant-maintained school was a class of school that elected to withdraw from the control of a local education authority and to receive additional funds to enable it to employ its own staff and select its own support services. Initially derived from the CTC, specialist secondary schools grew rapidly in number during the Blair and Brown years to the point that virtually all secondary schools became specialist secondary schools, offering one or more specialisations for which they received additional public funding that effectively doubled the extra cash or in-kind support they received in partnership with public or private entities. The specialist programme was abandoned with the change of government in 2010, drawing this response from Andrew Adonis, former education advisor to Tony Blair and subsequently a minister: 'It was a serious mistake of the Cameron government to abolish the specialist schools programme under which, for the previous twenty years, comprehensive schools and academies had been encouraged to develop centres of curriculum excellence' (Adonis, 2012: 255).

Arguably the most significant of recent changes in governance has been the creation of the academies. These were an initiative of the Blair government to replace low-performing secondary schools in areas of severe disadvantage in cities around the country. Private sector contributions in cash and the membership of governing bodies were required. They were free of control by local education authorities. There was slow but steady growth in the number of 'city academies' throughout the Blair and Brown years, but accelerating dramatically since the election of the Cameron government.

Andrew Adonis declared that 'without Tony Blair there would be no academies' (ibid.: 64), but the academies have survived Tony Blair. 'During the Blair–Brown transition, both Gordon Brown and David Cameron had pledged their support, sealing a political consensus which even a few months ago I would have thought improbable' (ibid.: 120).

Academies now include primary schools and they may be located in any kind of community. By mid-2012, more than half of England's 3,261 secondary schools were already academies or had applied for academy status. About 5 per cent of primary schools had applied to become academies. Academies remain contentious for a range of reasons (the arguments for and against are canvassed in Gunter, 2011). A key issue in the context of this book is the extent to which these self-managing schools (now self-governing schools) are also self-transforming, or have the potential to become self-transforming. Illustrations are included in several chapters.

Another contentious initiative of the Cameron government is the establishment of 'free schools' based on a Swedish model. The take-up has been small, with only 55 opening at the start of the 2012–2013 school year. They are also free of local education authority control and tend to be very small.

Taking all things into account, given the trends in PISA reported at the start of the chapter, and general concerns about the contribution of schools to social and economic well-being, it is no wonder that the government is willing to try so many new arrangements as far as the governance of schools is concerned.

New Zealand

New Zealand has a small population supporting about 2,600 schools but it is one of the most interesting countries as far as school reform and self-managing schools are concerned. Its mean scores on PISA are relatively high but equity is lower than the OECD average. The country has a substantial population of Māori and South Pacific Islanders, and others (Pakeha). There are pockets of serious disadvantage, and closing the gap between low- and high-performing students is a matter of enduring concern. Some of the world's leading scholars have been based at the University of Auckland, including Viviane Robinson and John Hattie (now at the University of Melbourne).

New Zealand is not a federation and has a national unitary government. A feature of governance was the passing in 1975 of the Conditional Private Schools Integration Act, in which most Catholic and independent private schools became part of the fully publicly funded system but could charge no fees (ownership arrangements were not affected).

New Zealand has been a leader in self-managing schools since the late 1980s. Its relatively centralised system of schools was the subject of review and dramatic change followed the adoption by the Lange Labour government of the Tomorrow's Schools policy, which saw significant decentralisation of authority and responsibility to schools and the establishment of powerful school boards which appointed principals and had oversight of finances and human resources. Regional support arrangements were abandoned so it essentially became a national system of self-managing schools. An Education Review Office (ERO) was established as part of the new accountability arrangements.

These developments brought together two streams of thought about governance and management. The more powerful role for the community struck a chord with Prime Minister David Lange, who had been an influential community lawyer in the 1970s. The review that led to Tomorrow's Schools took on board much of the philosophy that has become known as 'new public management'. The outcome was sweeping change that was opposed by much of the academic community in education and the teachers' unions. However, the reform proceeded with the extensive professional development of principals and members of school boards, with workshops conducted by Caldwell and Spinks over three years starting in 1989, using *The Self-Managing School* (Caldwell and Spinks, 1988) and associated materials.

As in Victoria, Australia, and England, self-managing schools continued under successive governments of different persuasions, with several issues attracting attention from time to time, including the mechanism for allocating funds to schools, employment arrangements for teachers, the nature and extent of support for schools, the development of a national curriculum, the review of schools, assessment and testing, and accountability. A contentious development in 2013 is a trial of a small number of charter schools, designated 'partnership schools' in New Zealand.

New Zealand appears to be resisting many of the characteristics of the GERM (Sahlberg, 2011) and may well position itself as an international exemplar in building the capacity of its self-managing schools so that they make the transformation to self-transforming schools. Evidence of this possibility is drawn from two sources. First, there are statements in a Ministry of Education discussion paper on assessment (Ministry of Education [New Zealand] 2010), which called for a balance of the qualitative and quantitative and explicitly warns against the misuse of data. John Hattie was a contributor to the paper. Second, a report of the Education Review Office (2012) included details of strategies required to close the gap in achievement and each called for building the capacity of New Zealand's self-managing schools.

The Ministry's discussion paper could not have been clearer about the misuse of data:

> The Ministry maintains that the publishing of raw, highly aggregated assessment data without qualitative context information will both undermine this collegial environment and subvert the reliability of the assessment data collected. The Ministry of Education considers that it is not appropriate to compare schools on a simplistic and misleading basis.
>
> (Ministry of Education [New Zealand], 2010: 50)

The discussion paper highlighted the importance of 'overall teacher judgements' that are based on both 'tacit information' and 'explicit information' that are drawn from multiple sources (ibid.: 16).

The Education Review Office (ERO) is a department of the New Zealand government that evaluates and reports on education in schools and early childhood services. It employs approximately 150 review officers in four regions. In 2010–2011, it conducted 1,265 reviews of early childhood services, 807 reviews of schools and other education services, and self-review workshops for more than 3,000 participants. It prepares reports for policymakers on national issues in education. The Ministry, or Minister, may intervene in schools on the basis of adverse reports from the ERO. Reviews of schools are differentiated according to the track record of the school, leading to decisions on the next review being in either the short term or the long term. The ERO provides advice on interventions and support that may be needed in particular circumstances.

Of particular interest is a report of the ERO in 2012 that provided a synthesis from 15 national evaluations and reports of good practice published in the preceding four years, highlighting three key issues facing the system. The ERO believed that 'these issues, in particular, are hindering efforts to raise the achievement of New Zealand's lowest performing school students, our priority learners' (Chief Review Officer Graham Stoop, Education Review Office, 2012: 2). 'Priority learners' are those who do not experience success; these include many Māori and South Pacific Islander students and those in low socio-economic settings or with special education needs.

The first issue is to shift the focus to student-centred learning: 'in the most successful schools, the trustees, leaders and teachers have an uncompromising focus on fostering students' interests and strengths, and on addressing their learning needs' (Education Review Office, 2012: 7). The second is knowledgeably implementing a responsive and rich curriculum: 'ERO's national evaluation reports identified that, generally, schools are not developing and managing their curricula in ways that are responsive to learners' (ibid.: 12). The third is using assessment information to know about and plan for students' learning: 'Issues and challenges for the 50 percent of schools still developing their systems included helping leaders to better understand the standards so that they were in a stronger position to help teachers make judgements about students' achievement, progress and next learning steps' (ibid.: 17).

The report included comprehensive links to findings in earlier reports and to a range of practices that should be part of a school's repertoire. It is crystal clear that the various strategies are within the power of schools to design and implement so it is a matter of utilising existing levels of authority and responsibility to transform the learning of their students. It concludes on an optimistic note and highlights the importance of innovation and creativity in the responses of schools, a theme that is taken up in Chapter 8.

United States

The constitution of Australia of 1901 is modelled in significant ways on that of the United States, which took effect in 1789. At the federal level, in each country there is a Senate and a House of Representatives, with each state electing the same number of senators regardless of its population. Constitutional power to make laws in relation to education lies with the states. In the United States, as in Australia, the federal government exerts a powerful influence on the states and their schools because it makes conditional grants to the states. At the federal level, there is a Secretary for Education and a Department of Education. There are notable differences related to the funding of private schools. As noted earlier, both federal and state governments in Australia make substantial grants to private schools. In the United States, this is not possible for private schools connected to churches because of the constitutional requirement for the separation of church and state.

Schools in each state of the United States are administered by school districts, of which there are more than 14,000, with policy in each instance set by an elected school board that appoints a superintendent to supervise the operations of schools. There has been steady growth in the number of charter schools over the last two decades, these being publicly funded schools that operate independently of their school district. In 2012, there were more than 5,600 charter schools enrolling more than 2 million students. Most states have legislation that enables the formation of charters, which are similar to academies in England. They are very popular among parents in disadvantaged settings in large cities, with ballots often being required at some schools when demand exceeds supply. There is mixed evidence on the impact of charter schools on student achievement.

Although the United States is considered to have a decentralised system of education, this generally goes only as far as school districts, most of which are highly centralised in terms of the authority and responsibility that have been devolved to individual schools. Only a small minority of districts have self-management as extensive as that found in parts of Australia (especially Victoria), Canada (especially Alberta), England, Finland and New Zealand. Early developments in self-management, or school-based management as it is more generally known in the United States, predated the landmark initiative in the Edmonton Public School District in Alberta (described below), but several of its large city systems, notably Seattle, subsequently drew on the Edmonton experience, especially with respect to its transparent student needs-based funding mechanism. The United States, therefore, has a highly constrained form of self-management with a long hierarchical chain of influence from Washington to the state capital to the school district to the school. The rules and regulations at each level above the school are vast in number and powerfully prescriptive. The 'education code' in California, for example, extends to thousands of pages.

It seems that presidents have for several decades vied to be 'the Education President', determined to lift the performance of schools across the country.

The most notable initiatives this century have been the 'No Child Left Behind' (NCLB) bipartisan legislation passed under George W. Bush and the 'Race to the Top' initiative of Barack Obama. In each instance, states have been required to sign up to a demanding set of requirements if they are to receive federal funds. The intentions are impeccable, given the performance of America's students in PISA cited at the start of this chapter and, especially, the wide gap in achievement between low- and high-performing students that is cast along racial and socio-economic lines. Although some school districts and many schools do outstandingly well under often difficult circumstances, the fact remains that performance across the nation has been declining for decades, despite the billions of dollars that have been allocated to solve the problem.

There are many paradoxes in education in the United States. In addition to the pockets of excellence referred to above, some of the world's leading scholars in curriculum, leadership and pedagogy may be found in its universities, many of whom continue to be influential in developments around the world. Some of the most striking innovations may also be found in the United States.

In the context of this book, it is fair to conclude that the general approach is command-and-control, consistent with being 'infected' by the GERM, as described by Sahlberg (2011). Yong Zhao, Presidential Chair and Associate Dean for Global and Online Education at the University of Oregon, offered a devastating critique in *Catching Up or Leading the Way: American Education in the Age of Globalization* (2009):

> As we enter a new world rapidly changed by globalization and technology, we [United States] need to change course. Instead of instilling fear in the public about the rise of other countries, bureaucratizing education with bean-counting policies, demoralizing educators through dubious accountability measures, homogenizing school curriculum, and turning children into test takers, we should inform the public about the possibilities brought about by globalization, encourage educational innovations, inspire educators with genuine support, diversify and decentralise curriculum, and educate children as confident, unique, and well-rounded human beings.
>
> (Zhao, 2009: 198)

Zhao noted that 'while the United States is moving toward more standardization and centralization, the Asian countries are working hard to allow more flexibility and autonomy at the local level' (ibid.: 63). These developments in Asian countries are considered in more detail in Chapter 5.

Canada

Although Finland often captures the headlines, it is important that Canada also moves to centre stage for several reasons. First, it is a high performer in PISA, coming second to Finland among nations in the West. Second, it is a much larger nation than Finland, with a more diverse population; indeed, cities such as Toronto, Montreal and Vancouver are as multi-cultural as any in the West, with suburbs that have significant socio-economic disadvantage. This addresses a common argument that Finland is not a good comparator when the search is on for strategies that might be adopted or adapted elsewhere. Third, unlike its neighbour, the United States, or Australia, its federal government has virtually no role in school education.

Although national performance is important for Canada, as for any other country, one must look more closely at performance in particular provinces, or in particular systems within provinces, to seek the explanation. Under Canada's constitution (originally the British North America Act passed by the Parliament of the United Kingdom and the Parliament of Canada in 1867, now 'patriated' within the Constitution Act of 1982), the federal government has no role in education apart from the delivery of schooling for First Nation (indigenous) children, children of those who serve in the armed services, and those incarcerated in federal institutions. There is no federal minister for education and no federal department of education. With the aforementioned exceptions, there is no federal funding for schools. Across Canada, more than 90 per cent of students are in either public or separate school districts, the latter being for the children of residents who declare their support for either a Catholic or a non-Catholic system – the public system is always the larger of the two. Both kinds of systems are publicly funded on the same basis. There are relatively few students in private schools, some of which may receive limited state aid. Cooperation and coordination among the 10 provinces and three territories is achieved through the Council of Ministers of Education, Canada (CMEC).

The performance of Alberta and Ontario, in particular, warrants attention because the former came second to Finland in PISA in early iterations of the tests, now equalled or exceeded by Ontario. The policies and programmes that characterise these provinces are noteworthy, but different in some respects. When combined, they provide potent lessons for other systems of public education.

There is a relatively high level of autonomy for schools in Alberta's school districts, with many taking the lead from the Edmonton Public School District, which was a pioneer of school-based management from the late 1970s. Edmonton's student needs-based funding mechanism has influenced practice in other nations (more information about this approach is included in Chapter 11). However, there are other noteworthy features. There is, for example, the Alberta School Improvement Initiative (AISI) administered by the Department of Education of the Government of Alberta, which pays funds to school districts on a per student basis to support the improvement of student learning by encouraging teachers, parents and the community to work collaboratively on innovative projects that reflect local needs and circumstances. More than 2,000 projects were funded in the first 10 years of the scheme, which was formally evaluated by Andy Hargreaves and an international team that included Pasi Sahlberg from Finland. Sahlberg considers AISI to be closely related in nature and purpose to the Aquarium Project in Finland, which involved more than 1,000 projects in 700 schools in 163 municipalities (Sahlberg, 2011: 36). The authors concluded that: 'AISI is a unique, world-leading strategy for developing innovation, and improving professional quality and engagement in teaching' (A. Hargreaves *et al.*, 2009: 107). They considered developments in the province to be consistent with the need in the twenty-first century to achieve 'outcomes beyond conventionally tested basics in order to create flexible cultures of creativity and innovation in schools and society' (ibid.: 108).

The review team considered Alberta to be an exemplar of 'the fourth way' (A. Hargreaves and Shirley, 2011), which calls for continuing or discontinuing themes in previous 'ways'. Inspiration, innovation and autonomy should be retained from the first way (dating from the end of the Second World War to the mid-1970s); common standards with local interpretation from the 'interregnum' (from the mid-1970s to the late 1980s); urgency, consistency and all-inclusive equity from the second way (from the late 1980s to the mid-1990s); and balance and inclusiveness, public involvement, financial reinvestment, better evidence and professional networks from the third way (from the late 1990s to the present). Cut-throat competition, excessive standardisation, persistent autocracy, imposed targets and obsession with data should be abandoned from the second and third ways (ibid.: 48).

Developments and achievements in Ontario have also been well documented, notably by the international expert on change in education Michael Fullan, who serves as Special Advisor to the Premier and Minister for Education in Ontario, and Ben Levin, who served as Deputy Minister for Education (chief civil servant) in Ontario, and previously in a similar position in Manitoba. He is Canada Research Chair in Education Leadership and Policy at the Ontario Institute for Studies in Education (OISE) at the University of Toronto.

Achievement in Ontario is indicated by an increase in the number of high-school graduates from 68 per cent in 2004 to 82 per cent in 2011. Teacher attrition has dropped significantly (Levin, 2012: 10). Levin drew from experience in Ontario to describe system-wide strategies for success. He provided illustrations in each instance:

1 Small number of publicly stated and achievable goals
2 Positive outlook for improving all schools and achieving success for all students
3 Emphasis on capacity building and focus on results
4 Multi-level engagement through strong leadership
5 Innovation and effective use of data
6 Focus on key strategies
7 Effective use of resources
8 Strong implementation effort

(ibid.: 11)

Levin identified pitfalls, such as allowing measures to displace goals; coaching to the test; narrowing the curriculum to limit attention to art, music and physical activity; and connecting results to sanctions or incentives (ibid.: 12–13). He stressed the importance of building trust and forging partnerships with key stakeholders. Looking ahead, he declared that:

> The next phase of large-scale education improvement will have greater emphasis on strategies that affect all classrooms and on elements that foster ongoing quality and equity or are essential to societal reform. Reforms primarily focused on structure and governance should be less dominant.
>
> (ibid.: 31)

Levin demonstrated that a strong system-wide strategy does not mean a command-and-control or carrot-and stick approach.

Finland

No account of strategies to transform schools is complete without reference to Finland, which has been at or near the top in international tests of student achievement such as PISA for more than a decade. After early profiling of this success, international interest tended to drop off a little when some observers pointed to the special characteristics of the country, including its relatively homogeneous population compared with, say, Australia, Canada, England, New Zealand and the United States. Inaccurate reference was made to the high levels of expenditure on schools when, in reality, it was about the OECD average. An associated comment was the country's commitment to equity and high levels of taxation, conditions that could not be readily implemented in these other places. It was pointed out that the language was relatively easy to learn and this accounted for the high levels of literacy.

There has been renewed and strong interest as observers realised that many of the particular factors that explained Finland's success, including the relatively narrow gap between low- and high-performing students, could be replicated in other places; for example, the very demanding requirements for admission to initial teacher education, the priority in appointments to school staff of a cadre of teachers who could assist students who, for whatever reason, fell behind (over the course of schooling, about one-third of students require special support of this kind). Large numbers of teachers and school leaders now visit Finland whereas, in the early days, visitors were mainly academics and senior system leaders. A powerful influence has been the contributions of well-informed and articulate people who were centrally involved in policy and practice in Finland, with Pasi Sahlberg perhaps the best known and most influential. Sahlberg is Director General of the Centre for International Mobility and Cooperation (CIMO) at the Finnish Ministry of Education and

Culture. His book *Finnish Lessons* (Sahlberg, 2011) is an international best-seller. His comments about the GERM are cited in several chapters.

Finland is a nation of about 5 million, which makes it about the same size in population terms as Victoria, Australia. Although there is a national ministry, it is relatively small compared with the very large bureaucracies that shape what occurs in Victoria: at the national level, through the Department of Education, Employment and Workplace Relations (DEEWR) of the Australian government and, at the state level, the Department of Education and Early Childhood Development (DEECD) of the Victorian government. The framework for policy and practice in Finland is determined by the National Board of Education, whose functions include the design of a relatively broad curriculum framework that lends itself to local adaptation. Although schools may draw on tests that are set by the National Board of Education, this is at a school's discretion; there is no system of national testing at different levels of primary and secondary education.

Schools are administered by municipalities in Finland, of which there were 336 in 2011 (this relatively large number is contentious and there is pressure for amalgamations). Several municipalities may work together to provide secondary education. These municipalities have the right to levy an income tax. Larger municipalities have the status of cities. School starting age is seven. Most parents avail themselves of pre-school programmes but these are not compulsory.

According to the Ministry of Education, Finland's success in PISA is largely explained by the education system itself with its equitable provision across all age groups, its highly competent teachers, and the autonomy given to schools. A capacity for self-management is one element of the 'Finnish Way' described by Sahlberg, which involves, among other things, 'setting a clear but flexible national framework for school-based curriculum planning' and 'encouraging local and individual solutions to national goals' (Sahlberg, 2011: 103).

Finland, therefore, has a national system of self-managing schools that have the capacity for self-transformation because of the competence of its teachers, but there is a further critical requirement if this capacity is to be realised, namely that there is an open outlook as far as innovation is concerned with a priority on adaptability to meet the social and economic needs of the nation. This is a challenge for Finland, which seems determined not to rest on its laurels, especially given its recent performance in PISA revealing a slight decline. The place of innovation in Finland is explored further in Chapter 8 ('Innovation everywhere').

Role of federal or national governments

There are some important differences among the nations represented in this chapter as far as governance is concerned. Australia, Canada and the

United States have federal governments but only two have powerful roles in education, namely Australia and the United States. Although their respective constitutions leave policy to the states, these federal governments exert influence through power to make grants to the states to which conditions are attached. They have powerful ministers (Australia) or secretaries (United States). Their roles expanded and became more complex as the decades passed, with approaches of the command-and-control variety, because states must adhere to an extraordinary array of terms and conditions in order to receive grants. Federal bureaucracies are vast in each instance. In contrast, the federal government in Canada has no minister and no department, with cooperation and coordination across the 10 provinces and three territories achieved through a council of ministers. Although there are many factors at work, the question must be raised whether in Australia and the United States there is not one level of authority in the mix too many. It is striking that student performance has declined in both countries and the gap between low- and high-performing students is as wide as ever. In contrast, Canada is consistently a top performer.

Finland is also interesting, although its size limits the comparison. It is not a federation. Policies are steered through the National Board of Education. Schools are administered by municipal governments and they have a substantial capacity for self-management.

There is a national unitary government with oversight of education in England but its role could not be more different from Finland. There is a team of ministers, a secretary of state for education and a very large department. Until recently, most public schools were administered through local education authorities. Schools have been weighed down by an increasing burden of rules and regulations that constrained the efforts of self-managing schools. There is a concerted effort to reduce the number of constraints and free schools from central control.

New Zealand is also not a federation and has what is effectively a national system of self-managing schools. It is challenged by relatively high levels of inequity. However, the ERO has identified a range of strategies that schools can adopt to reduce inequity and they point to the need to build capacity of a kind that will help self-managing schools become self-transforming.

A counter-argument to the view that federal governments may get in the way of the efforts of state/province-based schools was mounted by Chad Lykins and Stephen Heyneman at Vanderbilt University in research commissioned by the Centre on Education Policy in Washington, DC, for its project on Rethinking the Federal Role in Education (Lykins and Heyneman, 2008). They compared the roles of federal governments in Australia, Canada and Germany with the role of the federal government in the United States (Germany is like Canada and has no national department or ministry); they observed that 'Canadian provinces more closely resemble independent countries rather than dependent provinces' (ibid.: 7). They argued for a strong role for federal governments, in particular in the United States: 'the federal government, in addition to fostering a culture of accountability, must help create an environment that enables success' and 'success depends on a second wave of reform that will increase the federal government's role not just in setting standards, but in helping states achieve them' (ibid.: 15–16). Such a counter-argument does not stand up to critical scrutiny in the face of evidence and the arguments presented by Sahlberg (2011) and Zhao (2012).

On the other hand, they contend, there is no one best way to structure the governance of education in a federal system, or any system with several layers of government, each of which seeks a role in education: 'Policies that are best implemented at the national level in one country may be better implemented at the state or local level in another' (Lykins and Heyneman, 2008: 2). The central issue is whether the field is so crowded, with every leader wanting to be 'the education [president, prime minister, premier]', that schools are unnecessarily constrained from doing the very best for their students.

Finally, there is the interesting perspective from an Australian study that presented a case that a federal system with powers divided between two levels of government inhibits innovation in education, especially in governance, but flowing through to schools. The study was conducted by Bronwyn Hinz and reported in a paper presented at the Annual Conference of the Canadian Political Science Association in 2010 (Hinz, 2010). The setting is pertinent to this chapter, given the accounts of the roles of different levels of government in Australia and Canada.

Hinz conducted an independent study of the design and implementation of the Schools of the Future initiative in Victoria in the 1990s, in which a high level of self-management was delivered to schools. In financial terms, more than 90 per cent of the state's recurrent (annual) budget for public schools was decentralised to schools for local decision making. Hinz triangulated her sources of data, one of which was an extended interview with several of the key policy actors. She concluded that Victoria was able to design and implement Schools of the Future without reference to the federal government (the respective governments were of different political persuasion at the time). None of the actors could recall a single piece of correspondence or a single phone call on the matter between the two levels of government. There was no difficulty meeting the terms and conditions of grants from federal to state level since none were connected to the distribution of authority and responsibility within the system.

Hinz referred to views of supporters and detractors alike that this was 'the most radical Australian education reform in the last century' (ibid.: 1). She suggested that an innovation on this scale might not have been possible if agreement between the two levels of government or broad agreement among the states on the particular matter of school autonomy were required. She suggested that the successful initiative 'undermines the belief, prominent especially among education academics, media commentators and federal politicians, that a greater federal role and policy uniformity is necessary to improve outcomes and accountability in school education', and went on to note that 'Canada has one of the world's top-performing education systems and possesses close convergence among provincial school system organization and per-pupil expenditure, despite the absence of national government programs, directives, or tied grants for schooling' (ibid.: 14).

Hinz also described how various forms of self-management have permeated the state system in Australia over the years and that this occurred without tight federal–state agreements. Although there is general bipartisan agreement at the federal level that a higher level of autonomy for public schools is desirable, reaching agreement on an across-the-board approach is difficult. It is interesting to note that the governing Australian Labor Party went to the federal election in 2010 with a policy for further autonomy (Empowering Local Schools) but it was softened (some would say, watered down) to some extent by the time the policy was rolled out in 2012. Although higher levels of authority and responsibility were still possible, the emphasis was on building the capacity of public and private schools to operate more effectively within existing levels of authority and responsibility. This is, of course, desirable anyway, as made clear in subsequent chapters, but the Australian government had to accommodate a range of views among the states and organisations representing the interests of Catholic and independent schools, as well as key stakeholders, such as the Australian Education Union, before progress could be made. In Victoria, the highly innovative if not radical Schools of the Future project proceeded because the state government of the day was in a position to implement it without federal involvement or approval. The same has occurred in the second decade of the century with 'independent public schools' initiatives in Western Australia and Queensland and the Local Schools, Local Decisions project in New South Wales.

Important messages for policymakers and practitioners

1   There is a strong case for changing governance arrangements in countries with a federal system and where powers to make education lie with states or provinces. Powerful roles for federal governments that involve a complex system of conditional grants to state governments that are constitutionally responsible for schools have not been associated with improvement in educational performance and may, instead, be a manifestation of a command-and-control approach that constrains self-managing schools rather than empowers them to be self-transforming.

2   Competition between states may result in more innovative and effective approaches to improvement in outcomes than a uniform one-best-way approach that is implemented by a federal government. Innovation will be disseminated as a matter of course if states are open to ideas, policies and practices in other jurisdictions. There is no evidence that different states will not pursue the national interest under these circumstances.

3   Nations and their systems of education should now take stock of the successes and failures of approaches that have epitomised efforts to improve their schools in recent decades, retaining the best and discarding those that have had no effect or have proved to be dysfunctional.

5 Can the West catch up?

In recent times, attention around the world has shifted to education systems in Asia for two reasons. First is that several jurisdictions in the region now perform at the top in PISA. Three are described in Chapter 5: Hong Kong (China), Shanghai (China) and Singapore. Two of the three are part of a single nation, China, hence the reference in places to 'systems' or 'jurisdictions' rather than countries and nations. Second, there is a consensus emerging that the twenty-first century will be the 'Asian Century', following Britain (nineteenth century) and the United States (twentieth century). It is a good idea, say the commentators, to look closely at why these systems are performing so well. Reference is frequently made to the apparently stronger connection that is made between the quality of schooling and social and economic well-being. If these systems are already strong and making plans to become even stronger, it is fair to pose the question 'Can the West catch up?'. With PISA rankings in mind, Australia's Prime Minister, Julia Gillard, announced in mid-2012 that Australia should be in the top five globally by 2025. Is this possible?

The chapter is organised into four parts, looking at (1) how these jurisdictions in Asia perform in PISA compared with their counterparts in the West; (2) factors explaining their superior performance; (3) the drive for innovation in Asia, raising the possibility that the West may find it hard, if not impossible, to catch up; and (4) how schools in Asia have deep capacities for self-management in things that matter that give them a start in the journey to self-transformation.

Terms such as 'East' and 'Asia' are used in several places in the pages that follow. This is a convenient generalising shorthand but the focus throughout is on the three jurisdictions of Hong Kong, Shanghai and Singapore. Similarly, the West is used in a general sense but the focus is on countries considered in Chapter 4, especially Australia, the United Kingdom and the United States. There are particular features of education in Finland that are also selected for special mention.

Where these jurisdictions stand in PISA

Hong Kong, Shanghai and Singapore have all attracted international attention because of their high standing in PISA, which was first reported for tests in 2009. The overall performances of each are shown in Table 5.1. Shanghai achieved top ranking for reading, mathematics and science, with Hong Kong ranked fourth and Singapore fifth. This chapter therefore reports on education in three of the top five jurisdictions in PISA 2009. Four others in the top 10 were described in Chapter 4 (Finland – third, Canada – sixth, New Zealand – seventh, and Australia – ninth). Noteworthy are the rankings of the United States (seventeenth) and the United Kingdom (not included in the top 20).

Reservations are expressed from time to time about the significance of PISA. Doubts about the merit of the OECD itself are reported in Chapter 7. PISA and many national and sub-national tests are often criticised for their narrow focus. The quality of education, it is argued, is indicated by much broader outcomes. Nevertheless, PISA is conducted by the OECD on behalf of participating jurisdictions, which take very seriously where they finish in the rankings. This has led to several powerful studies of why some systems finish at the top. Particular attention is given in this chapter to the report of

Table 5.1 Top 20 rankings in PISA 2009 (OECD, 2010)

Rank	Country	Reading	Mathematics	Science
1	Shanghai (China)	556	600	575
2	Korea	539	546	538
3	Finland	536	541	554
4	Hong Kong (China)	533	555	549
5	Singapore	526	562	542
6	Canada	524	527	529
7	New Zealand	521	519	532
8	Japan	520	529	539
9	Australia	515	514	527
10	Netherlands	508	526	522
11	Belgium	506	515	507
12	Norway	503	498	500
13	Estonia	501	512	528
14	Switzerland	501	534	517
15	Poland	500	495	508
16	Iceland	500	507	496
17	United States	500	487	502
18	Liechtenstein	499	536	520
19	Sweden	497	494	495
20	Germany	497	513	520

a Melbourne-based think tank, the Grattan Institute, entitled *Catching up: Learning from the Best School Systems in East Asia* (Jensen *et al.*, 2012).

Especially noteworthy is the gap in the performance of students between those in Hong Kong, Shanghai and Singapore, and their counterparts in Australia, the United Kingdom and the United States. The OECD (2010) provided estimates of how many months students in the second set were behind those in the first set in reading, mathematics and science among 15-year-olds. These differences are presented in Table 5.2. For example, students in the United States are 17, 33 and 23 months respectively behind their counterparts in Shanghai. For mathematics this is equivalent to being nearly three years behind.

Critics of these comparisons, and the apparently superior performance of students in these three jurisdictions in Asia, usually refer to longer hours of study, after-hours coaching, Confucian culture and the influence of the 'tiger mums'. However, these do not stand up to critical scrutiny, since the performance of students in each of the Asian jurisdictions improved dramatically in recent years during which time these factors remained unchanged.

The criticism of comparisons with Asian countries is similar to that levelled at comparisons with Finland when its superior performance in PISA was revealed in earlier iterations of the tests. It was claimed that there were reasons to explain the difference: it has a relatively homogeneous population, the language is easier to learn, a higher value is placed on education, there is a stronger commitment to equity, and even the long and cold winters were conducive to long hours of indoor study. Apart from the fact that it spends less per student on schooling than Australia, the United Kingdom and the United States, and that students start school later at seven years of age and do less homework, there was a lack of awareness among the critics or a discounting of factors that explained its superior performance. As with similar factors at work in the three jurisdictions in Asia, these can be replicated or adapted in other places. The frequent reference to rote learning in Asia should also be discounted in the light of what is measured in PISA, whose tests are designed to assess how well students can apply academic skills to real-life situations. Students are also asked to compose long form answers in addition to responding to multiple-choice questions. PISA plans to test students' skills in collaborative problem solving in 2015 and it will be interesting to see the performances of all of the jurisdictions considered in this book, from both the East and the West.

Factors accounting for superior performance

The Grattan Institute, led by its School Education Program Director, Ben Jensen, published a widely read report on 'the best school systems in East Asia'. A round table in Melbourne of leaders in the region was followed by visits of the research team to four systems, with South Korea added to the three described in this chapter. It met with government officials, principals,

Table 5.2 The number of months that students in Australia, the United Kingdom and the United States are behind their 15-year-old counterparts in Hong Kong, Shanghai and Singapore in reading, mathematics and science (adapted from OECD, 2011)

	Australia			United Kingdom			United States		
	Reading	Mathematics	Science	Reading	Mathematics	Science	Reading	Mathematics	Science
Hong Kong	6	12	7	14	18	8	10	20	15
Shanghai	13	25	15	19	32	19	17	33	23
Singapore	3	14	5	12	20	11	8	22	13

teachers and educational researchers and concluded that 'these four systems focus on the things that are known to matter in the classroom, including a relentless, practical focus on learning and the creation of a strong culture of teacher education, research, collaboration, mentoring, feedback and sustained professional development' (Jensen *et al.*, 2012: 2). Findings included the following:

- Teachers in Shanghai spend just 10–12 hours per week in face-to-face teaching, allowing the rest of a 38-hour working week to be devoted to classroom observation, team teaching, school-based research and modelling good practice.
- Hong Kong designed a whole-of-system transformation over 20 months that included intensive community, as well as professional, consultations. High-stakes public examinations were abandoned.
- Initial teacher education in Singapore is characterised by a close relationship between the sole provider (National Institute of Education) and the Ministry of Education. There is a strong focus on practical skills, with philosophy and history of education removed from the undergraduate curriculum. Academics are promoted on the basis of their contribution to improved learning in schools, as well as on research and publications.
- There are strong programmes of preparation and professional development for principals. In Singapore, for example, the six-month full-time programme includes a fully funded two-week visit to an international educational institution.

They are not standing still!

There is another sweeping generalisation that needs to be challenged as far as education in Asia is concerned, and that is the view that jurisdictions under consideration in this chapter and others, such as South Korea, are standing still, as it were, able to maintain their high performance simply because of cultural factors and the educational practices summarised earlier, including longer school hours, coaching, Confucian culture and the influence of the 'tiger mums'. Closer examination reveals that these jurisdictions are well aware of the need to change; some would say they recognise the need to move closer to the West on some matters related to curriculum and pedagogy (Zhao, 2009). As shown in the pages that follow, significant innovation has been under way for several years and, along with factors that account for superior performance on PISA, as summarised above, most are either transferable to or worthy of adaptation in the West.

Hong Kong

There are approximately 1,200 schools in Hong Kong, with about 10 per cent of students attending approximately 300 government schools. Most schools are owned and operated by foundations, trusts and churches, each of which is funded by the government. There are very few truly private schools. Hong Kong thus has a system of self-managing schools, with a major thrust happening in the early 1990s through the School Management Initiative (SMI). It is evident from performance in PISA and TIMSS, as well as strategies for innovation summarised below, that many if not most are also self-transforming schools. This is a remarkable achievement given the degree of difficulty, as it were, with dramatic increases in population since Hong Kong was returned to China in 1997.

A major development in Hong Kong, aspects of which involved a high level of innovation, was the change in curriculum, which in turn was an important driver of new approaches in pedagogy. The Grattan Report described the connection in these terms: 'Curriculum reform helped shift teachers' thinking from "what" students should learn to "how" they learn. It focused teachers on providing "learning experiences" for students rather than simply transmitting knowledge' (Jensen *et al.*, 2012: 18).

In general, innovation flourishes in schools in Hong Kong, energised to a large degree by the remarkable Quality Education Fund (QEF) established in 1998 with a capital of HK$5 billion. By its tenth anniversary, it had supported over 7,000 applications and grants totalling about HK$3.5 billion. It is important to note that projects are funded from income on the capital investment, thus ensuring the long-term sustainability of the programme. There appears to be no counterpart in any other system around the world.

Twenty projects received Outstanding Project Awards at the QEF Projects Exposition to mark its tenth anniversary in 2008. For example, the Accelerated Schools for Quality Education Project (ASQEP), based in the Faculty of Education at the Chinese University of Hong Kong, received a grant of more than HK$60 million (the largest single grant at the time) to enhance university–school partnerships in three areas: school administration, curriculum and teaching, and parents and community. The three-year project involved 50 schools, with findings shared through a network of conferences and workshops involving more than 60,000 teachers, students and parents. Although there were literally thousands of relatively small projects, it is probable that the larger projects had the greatest impact in the shortest time across the system of schools in Hong Kong.

Apart from many seminars, workshops and conferences for dissemination, the QEF Cyber Resource Centre (CRC) was established in 1999 to support the transfer of knowledge. After a decade, the CRC included 5,600 project proposals, 4,800 project reports and 13,000 project deliverables.

Two observations are offered. First, innovation pervades the system. Although small numbers of grants were given to universities, these had to be implemented through partnerships with schools. In simple gross terms, there was an average of nearly six grants per school over the first 10 years. Second, significant amounts of money were involved, ranging up to more than HK$60 million in the case of the ASQEP.

Shanghai

In addition to factors summarised in the previous section, the rapid pace of successful reform in Shanghai has been the result of a commitment to cultural change and innovation. This is remarkable not only for the end result but also for the speed of turnaround.

Shanghai is the largest city in China, with a population of over 22 million people, and is one of four Chinese municipalities with the status of a province. Shanghai is considered to be the business capital of China and has a large population of immigrants from rural areas. Shanghai, as with all of China and many other Asian cultures, has strong traditions that value education very highly. These traditions have assisted innovation in education, as students are highly engaged and families and communities are supportive. It is also an area of concern in terms of student workload and examination pressure. An educational plan for 2020 included a call 'to reduce the academic burden on students' (Ministry of Education [People's Republic of China], 2010). Innovation in schools in Shanghai has occurred within a framework developed by the national Ministry of Education and the Shanghai Education Commission.

Important changes to the examination regime allowed schools to expand their curriculum. Shanghai removed examinations for entry into primary and junior secondary schools and implemented a neighbourhood attendance policy, which allowed teachers at these levels to broaden the curriculum. Shanghai also modified its higher-level examinations to 'serve the purpose of curriculum and pedagogy reform' (OECD, 2011: 92). Examinations are often integrated across subjects and test students' capacity to apply their knowledge to real-life or unfamiliar problems. Examinations are also developed more flexibly to enable them to reflect local contexts.

Shanghai leads China in reaching goals of universal education from preschool to senior secondary levels. It has a large number of very high-achieving students, as assessed in PISA, and relatively few students demonstrating low levels of proficiency (OECD, 2010). The Shanghai Education Commission and its schools have shown a commitment to shared responsibility for achievement across school boundaries. There are several examples of successful schools supporting less successful counterparts and of a culture among educators that is focused on sharing knowledge and good practice. Principals and other staff members work with partner schools to support change. In some cases, successful schools have been designated as 'experimental schools' or 'demonstration schools', networking with local schools to support reform.

Shanghai has made curriculum a high priority and it is given extra freedom by the national ministry to experiment with reforms. Curriculum reform follows national and municipal guidelines but there has been encouragement for schools to develop their own curricula to reflect their local contexts. Control of curriculum has also been broadened to allow participation from agencies outside the school system. Museums and other organisations are influencing a broader and more innovative curriculum.

China has rapidly increased the level of education and training that is required to become a teacher, and Shanghai has led the country in requirements for continuous professional development for teachers. Shanghai has encouraged reform in teaching practice that has paralleled reforms in curriculum. Major change in classroom practice has occurred across the system through the use of slogans designed to change perceptions of a good classroom and good teaching. For example, 'Return class time to students' has seen a decrease in lecturing and an increase in student-centred activities (OECD, 2011: 94).

There is a belief among educators that 'good practices and indeed creative practices are meant to be copied' (OECD, 2011: 94). The Shanghai Education Commission has facilitated this predisposition by developing a web-based platform for teachers to develop and share curriculum and approaches to learning and teaching.

Oriental Green Ark is a facility established by the Shanghai Education Commission that includes a broad range of resources for schools, including museums, 'challenge centres' and a 'global village' of homes and hotels. This is an example of institutions outside schools influencing curriculum and pedagogy (OECD, 2011: 93).

Innovation in Shanghai has been exceptional in recent decades. In contrast with Finland, Shanghai has a much more centralised approach to innovation. However, although these approaches were initiated by the Shanghai Education Commission, most are intended to encourage schools to innovate in curriculum and teaching to meet local contexts and the emerging modern learning needs of their students. As well as removing or reforming the structures that were constraining schools to narrow, outdated curriculum and pedagogy, the Shanghai Education Commission also provided resources and programmes to encourage schools and educators to network and share their innovative achievements for the benefit of the whole system and for all students. Adopting the imagery from Chapter 3, it is a remarkable example of schools being 'unchained' in their journey to self-transformation.

Singapore

Education in Singapore is characterised by an impressive array of innovative practices. Commitment to innovation has seen Singapore grow into one of the world's top-performing education systems, which is consistently at or near the top of most major international education ranking systems (OECD, 2011). This is a remarkable achievement considering that this small nation gained independence only in 1965, when there was no common school system and its population had a variety of different cultural, religious and language backgrounds. Singapore quickly united its people with a commitment to the pledge of 'One united people regardless of race, language or religion' (National Library Singapore, 2011). There was recognition that human resources were the most precious of assets. Education quickly became an essential and valued investment and Singapore successfully aligned the education system with the social and economic needs of the nation (Subramaniam and Lee, 2011).

The Ministry of Education (MOE) in Singapore has had a significant leadership role in the three major phases of the country's development. There was strong alignment with other government departments and economic agencies, as well as with research and teacher training. A key strength of the system has been its ability to innovate to meet the social and economic needs of the country through the education of its citizens (OECD, 2011). This has been evident in the most recent era, which started with the Asian financial crisis in 1997. At that time, Singapore recognised that success in the world's economic environment would require transition to a knowledge-based economy.

In 1997, the government embarked on an ambitious programme to change the nation's education system with the *Thinking Schools, Learning Nation* policy. This new vision for education, which has captured international attention, was launched by the then Prime Minister, Goh Chok Tong, whose belief was that 'A nation's wealth in the 21st Century will depend on the capacity of its people to learn' (OECD, 2011: 162). This vision is still the key strategic framework. *Thinking Schools, Learning Nation* included a wide range of policies for innovation that were generally implemented in a system-wide, top-down approach. These included changes to teacher education and career paths, and moving curricula and assessment towards creative thinking and project work. There was also a strong commitment to ICT (information and communications technology) provision across schools, which enabled a new type of learning that was more self-directed and collaborative. The MOE also moved away from a strongly centralised system towards greater school autonomy. It introduced a 'School Excellence Model' of annual review and 'Cluster Superintendents', who 'were appointed to mentor leaders in schools and to promote innovation' (OECD, 2011: 163). Singapore is, therefore, moving towards a system of self-managing schools that are on a journey to self-transformation.

In 2004, the MOE introduced the *Teach Less, Learn More* strategy, which aimed to move education in Singapore from 'quantity' to 'quality'. This strategy has guiding principles of 'teaching to truly engage the hearts and minds of students . . . [and] . . . to continue to provide more flexibility and choice to learners' (Hogan and Gopinathan, 2008: 372). In 2005, an initiative of 'White Space' was introduced. This aimed to open up the curriculum by reducing the content by 10–20 per cent, thus providing time and space for teachers to engage students more deeply in learning. This strategy has been supported by action-research orientated, school-based curriculum development in about 60 'prototype' schools. The MOE has facilitated the sharing of innovations by prototype schools through publications and seminars.

'Nurturing Innovation and Enterprise Spirit' is a key guideline provided by the MOE that highlights the value of developing such a 'spirit' in students. It recognises the benefits of a strong focus on innovation and enterprise in individual students and in the broader society. The guidelines for schools include five 'key tenets' that encourage a core set of life skills and attitudes: a spirit of inquiry and original thinking; a willingness to take risks; strength of character and resilience; ability to work collaboratively as part of a team; and a sense of community connection (Ministry of Education [Singapore], 2011).

Singapore is one of only six countries in the world that are committed to positioning themselves as an International Education Hub (Knight, 2011). The intention is to attract a broad range of cross-border educational activities that position the country as a centre for higher education and research, and therefore a leader in the global education market. The Global Schoolhouse initiative has attracted 16 foreign branch campuses of higher education institutions and 44 pre-tertiary schools offering international curricula (Singapore Economic Development Board, 2011). A key element of Global Schoolhouse is building the capacity of local educational institutions to undertake research and curriculum innovation (Knight, 2011). This illustrates Singapore's economic commitment to a global knowledge economy and enhancement of innovation across the education system through international perspectives and strong research capabilities.

There are strong relationships between policy developers, researchers and educators. As noted earlier, the National Institute of Education (NIE), the country's only teacher-training facility, has close links with the MOE. For example, as a part of the *Teach Less, Learn More* strategy, the MOE funded the development of the Centre for Research in Pedagogy and Practice at the NIE, which worked closely with schools and reported back to the MOE. These partnerships have allowed the Singapore education system to close the gap between policy and practice in classrooms and to implement change and innovation more effectively.

Taking these developments as a whole, it is clear that the MOE has nurtured a culture that seeks continual improvement. It has developed effective mechanisms for recognising and implementing worthwhile innovation. The centralised nature of the system is responsive to wider socio-economic forces and has the capacity to produce change quickly to meet needs. This connection to broader issues, combined with the successful policies described above, has enabled the development of a structure that encourages 'bottom-up initiatives' and provides 'top-down support' to enable long-term substantial and sustainable pedagogical innovation in Singapore's classrooms (Hogan and Gopinathan, 2008).

Singapore's successful education system is now strongly based on its culture of innovation. Since the birth of the nation in 1965, Singapore has developed an education system that is central to the country's social and economic success. Most recently, commitment to become a nation that is competitive in a twenty-first-century global knowledge economy has enabled the development of a system that embraces, encourages and supports educational innovation in all parts of the education system.

The challenge for East and West

Both East and West require a deeply embedded capacity for innovation at all levels if their systems of education are to meet social and economic needs in the twenty-first century. The East cannot rest on the laurels of its high performance in PISA and TIMSS, and the West faces the challenge of catching up and providing an education that is fit for purpose. In *Oceans of Innovation*, Barber, Donnelly and Rizvi expressed the challenge for the East in the following terms:

> Given their success and the deeply rooted nature of educational progress in the region, it would be tempting for leaders to conclude that they should leave the educational systems well alone. The region could rest on its laurels while the rest of the world scrambles to catch up . . . If the Pacific is to assume global leadership, it needs to lead the world in innovation and, if it is to do that, its education systems will need to adapt from their stunning success in what might be thought of as the 20th century paradigm and take the lead in developing a new 21st century paradigm.
>
> (Barber *et al.*, 2012: 98)

Yong Zhao is Presidential Chair and Associate Dean for Global and Online Education, College of Education at the University of Oregon. In *Catching Up or Leading the Way: American Education in the Age of Globalization* (Zhao, 2009), Zhao puts another perspective on the challenges facing both Asia and the United States:

> While the United States is moving toward more standardization and centralization, the Asian countries are working hard to allow more flexibility and autonomy at the local level. While the United States is investing resources to ensure all students take the same courses and pass the same tests, the Asian countries are advocating for more individualization and attending to emotions, creativity and other skills. While the United States is raising the stakes on testing, the Asian countries are exerting great efforts to reduce the power and pressure of testing.
>
> (ibid.: 63)

On the evidence presented in this chapter and elsewhere in the book, it is Asia that is responding to the challenge, and likely to maintain its supremacy, while the West struggles to achieve at current levels, let alone catch up.

Why self-managing schools in Asia are also self-transforming schools

There is a profoundly important lesson for the West in reviewing these accounts. Hong Kong, Shanghai and Singapore are characterised by outstanding programmes in initial teacher education and ongoing professional learning. Teachers and other professionals have the capacity to work within centrally determined frameworks to secure performance at the highest levels by international standards. They are outstanding in the way they work within these frameworks to ensure that the curriculum and approaches to learning and teaching suit students in the local setting. Especially striking is the substantial amount of time that teams of teachers invest in preparing how these approaches will be implemented in their classes and in sharing their experiences after delivery to make further adaptation. Innovation is now deeply embedded in the culture of the profession, contrary to a common stereotype. These are all characteristics of what a profession should do in the journey from good to great and from great to excellent, to use the descriptors of the journeys in education reported by McKinsey & Company (Mourshed *et al.*, 2010) (see summary in Chapter 1).

With these capacities spread fairly evenly across all schools, it should be no surprise that bureaucracies at the central level are relatively lean compared with those in the West. As in Finland, one can count on most schools being staffed by well-trained teachers, and mechanisms to support teachers that are evident in many jurisdictions in the West are not necessary or such large numbers are not required. Examples include the need for the 'professional coach' to support teachers in many schools in Australia, England and the United States. Combined with the now deeply embedded approaches to innovation, there can be a high degree of confidence that the self-managing schools in these jurisdictions in Asia now have the capacity also to be self-transforming schools.

The title of this chapter posed the question 'Can the West catch up?'. On the evidence presented, this is going to be a very difficult task. However, to maximise the probability of doing so, a good start can be made by adopting or adapting many of the practices that explain success in the three jurisdictions considered in this chapter. Deeply embedded cultural or professional practice that cannot, or should not, be transferred should not be used as an excuse for inaction. Embedding a capacity for innovation is also an important strategy for unchaining the self-managing school in the West. Strategies for innovation are addressed in more detail in Chapter 8.

Important messages for policymakers and practitioners

1 The West should stop using stereotypes of education in Asia as a reason why it should not pay attention to policies and practices that account for the success of the latter in international tests of achievement, just as stereotypes of Finland have been abandoned as realisation grows that policies and practices that account for success in that country can be adopted or adapted elsewhere.

2 There is as much, if not more, innovation in schools and school systems in Asia as there is in the West. However, all systems in all parts of the

world must continue to adapt; it is not sufficient to maintain or improve performance in a twentieth-century paradigm of schooling.

3 The generally high standard of teaching in all schools in Hong Kong, Shanghai and Singapore means that large numbers of staff are not required outside schools. Large bureaucratic superstructures are not needed but support is available to assist schools. Schools in these systems are largely self-managing, especially in curriculum and pedagogy, and therefore have a capacity to be self-transforming.

6 Possibilities for the powerhouses

Brazil and India are invariably included in lists of nations that will become powerhouses in the twenty-first century. They are not among the top performers on key indicators today and they will need to move up the ranks if their economies are to be as strong as expected. This chapter includes summaries of developments in school education and strategies that are in place to secure improvement. Promising innovations are identified. It is acknowledged at the outset that these countries are vast, in both population and geography, and it is difficult to generalise what has occurred or been planned. South Africa is included because of its potential and also because a transformation of its school system is a prerequisite if this potential is to be realised.

The McKinsey & Company project that resulted in the report entitled *How the World's Most Improved School Systems Keep Getting Better* (Mourshed *et al.*, 2010) included accounts of developments in three jurisdictions in these countries: Minas Gerais (Brazil), Madhya Pradesh (India) and Western Cape (South Africa). Each was on a journey from poor to fair in the different stages described in the report (poor to fair, fair to good, good to great, great to excellent). Excerpts from the report are included in this chapter to illustrate the kinds of strategies that have been adopted in these countries.

This chapter provides a further opportunity to test the model in Chapter 3 that proposed that self-managing schools should be 'unchained' from excessive command-and-control or carrot-and-stick approaches if they are to become self-transforming schools, that is if they are to develop the capacity to take charge of the agenda or 'call the shots' to achieve the significant, systematic and sustained change that secures success for all students regardless of the setting. The model acknowledged that there are circumstances in which high levels of central control with a low amount of autonomy are appropriate, especially when a sense of coherence in a fragmented system is needed. The key issues are whether these constraints are maintained for longer than necessary and whether some of the features of other systems should be bypassed if they have proved to be dysfunctional.

Brazil

In data reported in the OECD's statistical profile for 2011–2012, Brazil had a population of approximately 195 million with a growth rate of 0.9 per cent. Life expectancy at birth is 72.7 years. In 2010, annual growth in GDP was 7.5 per cent, inflation was 5.0 per cent, unemployment was 6.7 per cent and tertiary attainment for people aged 25 to 64 was 10.9 per cent.

Growth on key indicators as reported in *Education at a Glance* (OECD, 2012) is impressive. For example, Brazil increased public spending on education from 10.5 per cent of total public expenditure in 2000 to 14.5 per cent in 2005 and 16.8 per cent in 2009. Brazil ranked fourth out of 32 countries that provided data on this indicator (the OECD average in 2009 was 13.0 per cent). Student population fell by 5 per cent between 2005 and 2009. Per student expenditure over this period increased by 149 per cent, the largest increase among the nations reporting. Overall, Brazil invests 5.55 per cent of GDP in education, which is below the OECD average of 6.23 per cent (all education).

A finer-grained analysis of enrolment trends reveals that participation in early education for three-year-olds rose from 21 per cent in 2005 to 32 per cent in 2010, well below the OECD average of 66 per cent. Enrolment rates among five-year-olds increased from 63 to 78 per cent over the same period, bringing Brazil closer to the OECD average for this age group of 88 per cent. Information provided to participants in the GELP held in Rio de Janeiro in November 2012 noted that 34 per cent of students reaching fifth grade cannot read.

Despite these generally positive indicators, UNESCO reported that 'Brazil is ranked among the 53 countries that have not achieved – and are not about to achieve – the Education for All Goals by 2015' (UNESCO, 2012).

Brazil's performance in PISA indicates the size of the challenge overall and in relation to other countries in Latin America. For example, in PISA 2009, its overall mean score was 401 compared with an OECD mean of 496. Brazil ranked fifty-fourth out of 65 countries that participated. Among eight Latin American countries, Brazil ranked fourth behind Chile, Uruguay and Mexico, but ahead of Columbia, Argentina, Panama and Peru. Brazil's performance in PISA is improving, as is the number of students participating. The mean score for reading in 2000 was 396 (4,893 students), rising very slowly to 412 in 2009 (20,127 students).

Brazil has 26 states grouped into five regions. Rio de Janeiro and Minas Gerais, described in more detail below, are in the south-east region. There are more than 5,500 municipalities. The constitution requires that states and municipalities take responsibility for school education. The municipalities are responsible for early childhood education (0–6). Municipalities and states share responsibility for compulsory primary education from first to eighth grade. States are responsible for secondary education. The constitution requires that 25 per cent of state and municipal taxes, and 18 per cent of federal taxes, be reserved for education.

The federal Ministry of Education has a broad strategic role. In 2007, it prepared and made available to states and municipalities the Education Development Plan, which covered educational management; professional formation (teachers, service and support personnel); pedagogical practices and evaluation; and physical infrastructure and pedagogical resources.

Minas Gerais

Minas Gerais, the third largest state in Brazil, is of particular interest because it is one of the jurisdictions reported in McKinsey & Company's *How the World's Most Improved School Systems Keep Getting Getter* (Mourshed *et al.*, 2010), in which 20 systems from 18 countries were mapped on journeys from poor to fair, fair to good, good to great and great to excellent (details of the study are contained in Chapter 3). The authors concluded that certain sets of strategies seemed well suited to each stage of the journey.

Minas Gerais demonstrated well the strategies for the journey from poor to fair. What transpired is a good match with the low autonomy, high control, open outlook connection, which is Type 2 in the model illustrated in Chapter 3. Type 2 was described in these terms: 'Type 2 is a preferred approach if a sense of order and coherence is required to raise standards across the system and its leaders have a capacity to draw ideas from within and outside in times of complexity and change'. As illustrated in Figure 3.1, the system moved from 'fragmented' (low autonomy, low control) to 'command-and-control' (low autonomy, high control). Here is how McKinsey & Company described what was accomplished in Minas Gerais:

> In 2006, a state-wide assessment showed that only 49 percent of its eight-year-olds were able to read at the recommended level of proficiency. The governor set the aspiration that by 2010, 90 percent of eight-year-olds would read at the recommended level. This involved 2,500 primary schools, 15,000 teachers and 500,000 students. The state's department of education translated this overarching goal into specific regional and school-level improvement targets. A 'results book', including baseline student achievement data, was created for each school so that teachers and principals could see their starting point and evaluate their progress. The Department of Education then developed prescriptive teaching materials for each lesson, to guide teachers in their classroom activities, and provided new workbooks for the students. The guides proved so effective that several private and municipal schools also voluntarily adopted the materials. It also strengthened its capacity across the 2,450 primary schools in the state, creating a central team of 46 members divided across the four regions. Each core team spent two weeks per month visiting

regional departments of education assigned with three tasks: to train the trainers, to disseminate and assess the implementation of the support materials developed by the Department of Education, and to act as a barometer and gather feedback from schools regarding their needs, challenges, and progress in implementing the literacy program.

(Mourshed *et al.*, 2010: 37–40)

These strategies proved to be highly effective, with the state moving from fifth to first between 2006 and 2009 on Brazil's National Education Index of student outcomes, thus justifying its inclusion in the McKinsey & Company project. The percentage of eight-year-olds reaching recommended levels in reading increased from 49 to 86 per cent, whereas the number who performed poorly fell from 31 to 6 per cent. Accountability requirements were tightly administered, but schools that did well were allowed greater autonomy. Teachers in schools that met their targets received up to one month's additional salary (ibid.: 40).

The key issue is whether a larger number of schools will in time become self-managing, consistent with the journey from good to great in the journeys described by McKinsey & Company, and then be 'unchained' to become self-transforming.

Rio de Janeiro

Rio de Janeiro was the site of the GELP in November 2012 (a description of GELP is contained in Chapter 1). The information in this section was compiled from notes prepared for participants.

The City of Rio de Janeiro has the largest municipal school system in Latin America, serving approximately 700,000 students in about 1,530 schools and employing an estimated 38,000 teachers. Students in the system improved their performance from 2009 to 2011 on the Basic Education Development Index with gains ranging from 6 per cent in the early years of primary to 22 per cent in the upper secondary years. Performance in the city was about the same as that in Rio de Janeiro state. There is, of course, wide variety among schools, ranging from those in communities with high socio-economic advantage to those in the favelas, where the challenge is to have large numbers of students attend school in the first place.

There has been a systematic effort to develop good systems for knowledge management under the title of Escola 3.0. The aim is to improve the collective intelligence of the system. One (Rioeduca) provides a portal and email system for staff and students. Another (Sistema de Gestão Acadêmica – SGA) supports centralised management of enrolments, classes, transfers, attendance, grades and lesson planning. A third (Educopédia) is an online platform to support digital learning where students and staff can gain access and practise, any place, any time.

Responding to a broad concern that schools are impersonal and standardised, fostering student compliance rather than autonomy, Rio de Janeiro has developed GENTE (Ginásio Experimental de Novas Tecnologias Educacionais) as a prototype for schools where there will be no years, classes or classrooms. Tablets and smart phones will replace notebooks and textbooks. The online digital platform (Educopédia) will be used. The intention is for students to become 'autonomous citizens, caring and competent and develop essential skills for a changing world, such as search, analyse and evaluate information and sources; solve problems and make decisions, and use creative productivity tools effectively' (GELP, 2012). This ambitious programme came into effect in 2013, but for just 210 students from Grade 7 to Grade 9 at one school (Municipal School André Urani in Rocinha).

The contrast between Minas Gerais and Rio de Janeiro is an interesting one, with the former on a tightly controlled journey from poor to fair and with the latter, although also on a journey of improvement, introducing digital technology that is transforming learning for students, but starting on a very small scale in 2013. As noted earlier, the issue for Minas Gerais is whether the tight control will be maintained for longer than necessary so that schools do not become self-managing, let alone self-transforming, when these are the capacities that should be developed and implemented as they continue the journey from good to great. The issue for Rio de Janeiro is whether schools that are transforming learning also become self-transforming schools.

A private role in public education

A development in the north-eastern state of Pernambuco is of interest because of the involvement of the Institute for Co-Responsibility in Education (ICE), a private educational foundation. The State Governor, Eduardo Campos, engaged ICE in an initiative to reform middle schools which are administered by the state:

> More than 200 of these now operate an eight-hour day, rather than the four-hour shifts common in Brazil. In return, the government has raised teachers' salaries and added bonuses tied to results. It is also trying to chivvy mayors into improving primary schools through extra funds and other initiatives. That is vital: on average, pupils arrive in middle schools aged 15 with a three-year learning deficit, says Marcos Magalhães, ICE's founder. Pernambuco is rising up the rankings of state educational performance.
>
> (*The Economist*, 2012b: 39)

This appears to be an effective use of the command-and-control and carrot-and-stick approaches. The issue is the extent to which these are sustained or even strengthened if the reported improvement stalls.

India

India has a population of more than 1.2 billion with an age distribution that presents an immediate challenge as far as education is concerned: 75 per cent are under 35; 50 per cent are under 25; and 32 per cent are under 15. Literacy rates for young people in the 15–24 age range are 87 per cent for males and 77 per cent for females. There are 35 cities with more than 1 million people; the national capital, Delhi, has more than 16 million. GDP growth is 6.8 per cent per year and inflation is 6.8 per cent (2011 in both instances).

Responsibility for education is shared between national, state and municipal governments (there are 29 states and seven territories). The national Department of Education within the Ministry of Human Resource Development has a coordinating role, prepares five-year plans and provides about 10 per cent of the funding. Ministries at the state level coordinate the work of municipalities, with the administration of public schools shared between these two levels of government. Most of the funding comes from state governments. Overall, funding for education is relatively low by international standards. For example, in 2001, India ranked 104th out of 143 countries in respect to the share of GNP devoted to education. This share rose slowly from 1.2 per cent in the early 1950s to about 4 per cent in 2001. Student enrolment has grown about 5 per cent per year in recent decades.

The Right of Children to Free and Compulsory Education (RTE) Act of 2009 secures the right of children to free and compulsory education until the end of primary school at a school in their neighbourhood. The Act specifies norms and standards for student–teacher ratios, buildings and infrastructure (see below in relation to a breach of this provision), working days and teacher working hours.

Private schools and social entrepreneurs

Private education is flourishing in India, with about 500,000 of India's 1.4 million schools enrolling about 300 million students. A special report on India in *The Economist* had this to say:

> By one estimate, 40 percent of Indian students now make some use of private education – either private schools or topping-up by tutors. A survey in 2011 by Credit Suisse suggested Indians typically spend 7.5 percent of their incomes on education, more than Chinese, Russians or Brazilians. Education is seen as a quick route to prosperity.
> (*The Economist*, 2012c: 13)

The Economist gave an example of students living in a poor part of Delhi where, in one small private school (Ebyon), 200 students learnt in the morning in large classes in poor facilities and moved to a public school in the afternoon, where they received a free lunch and had access to books and additional support.

In general, it seems that public schooling is struggling and that private schooling is preferred by parents where it is available. The energy for transformation lies in the private or third sector, with social entrepreneurs leading the way. Leadbeater and Wong (2010) provided interesting accounts of these developments in India and other developing countries. They developed a model for transformation based on their findings and this is described in Chapter 8. The following illustrates what they found in India:

> A 2006 survey by Pratham, the leading educational NGO, found that 47 percent of children in grade 5 could not read a story designed for grade 2. About 55 percent of those in grade 5 could not divide a three-digit number by a single digit, and this percentage rose to 75 percent in poorer states. The main problem is the poor quality, attendance, motivation, and management of the highly unionised Indian teaching workforce. One study, based on random visits to Indian schools, found that 25 percent of teachers were absent at any one time. In only half the schools was teaching actually in progress. About 90 percent of the Indian education budget goes to teacher salaries.
>
> (ibid.: 8)

In addition to these conditions, basic facilities are lacking, as illustrated in the absence of toilet facilities, especially for girls. The Right to Education Forum, a not-for-profit network of about 10,000 non-government organisations, reported that 95 per cent of schools across the country failed to comply with standards. India's Supreme Court determined in 2012 that the dreadful state of school toilets was a violation of the right to free and compulsory education guaranteed in the Indian constitution (BBC, 2012).

According to Leadbeater and Wong, Pratham (referred to above) is one of several companies of social entrepreneurs that are stepping in to lift the quality of schooling. Pratham has helped create thousands of low-cost pre-schools, employing and then training school-educated young women who provide basic education to about 21 million children. Satya Bharti has created a network of 158 pre-schools serving about 18,000 students. They drew the following conclusions from experiences in India and the other developing countries where they conducted their research:

> For all these reasons, innovation to supplement schools is unlikely to come from incumbents. It may prove unwise to ask schools to get too deeply involved in this work for which they are ill-equipped and which may distract from their core task of teaching and learning. The social innovation that is needed is much more likely to come from outside – from social entrepreneurs – as well as from integrating learning with other public services, such as healthcare.
>
> (Leadbeater and Wong, 2010: 18)

An example of how the not-for-profit sector contributes to public education is Project Nanhi Kali, which was initiated in 1996 by the K.C. Mahindra Trust, now in partnership with 21 other non-government organisations. It focuses exclusively on the support of under-privileged girls. According to its website (www.nanhikali.org) at the time of writing (2012), the project supports the education of over 75,000 girls from poor urban, remote rural, tribal and conflict-afflicted communities in nine states (Maharashtra, Andhra Pradesh, Rajasthan, Chhattisgarh, Madhya Pradesh, Karnataka, New Delhi, Haryana and Tamil Nadu). The participants, described as Nanhi Kalis, receive support through a 1- to 2- hour class conducted before or after school, where concepts in mathematics, science and language are taught to help bridge gaps in learning. Nanhi Kali claims a reduction of 10 per cent in dropout rate and a 20 per cent increase in learning outcomes.

There are many other accounts of developments in India that highlight the contributions of the private sector. One that complements the work of Leadbeater and Wong is the research of James Tooley carried out in India and other developing countries (Tooley, 2009). He reported that private schooling was preferred to public schooling in many slum communities, even if it meant that the poorest of people had to scrape small amounts together to ensure their children could attend. Moreover, he found that the private schools, more often than not, out-performed public schools when comparisons were possible. He summarised the themes of his research in the following terms:

> Private schools serving the poor are burgeoning across the developing world. In many urban areas they are serving the majority of poor school children. Their quality is higher than that of government schools provided for the poor – perhaps not surprisingly given that they are predominantly businesses dependent on fees to survive and, hence, are directly accountable to parental needs.
>
> (ibid.: 263)

These studies of Leadbeater and Wong as well as Tooley raise interesting issues about transformation. The energy for transformation came from outside the schools in the findings of Leadbeater and Wong, from the social entrepreneurs. The energy came from outside public schools altogether in the study by Tooley. The entrepreneurs and the private schools are, in the context of the current book, self-managing by definition, but they are also self-transforming in the broadest sense of the term: they are transforming the lives of young people who seek to learn under the most distressing conditions.

Madhya Pradesh

Madhya Pradesh is a state with 138,500 public schools, 17 million students and 450,000 teachers. From 2006 to 2008, it adopted strategies to help raise levels of literacy. It tended to follow a fairly regimented approach, which is understandable given the size of the system and scale of the problem. McKinsey & Company described the major interventions in this state, which were common to those in Minas Gerais (Brazil) and Western Cape (South Africa):

> Closing the achievement gap also commonly required two further interventions. First, the students' basic needs were met so that they could focus on learning. To this end, the Madhya Pradesh, Minas Gerais, and Western Cape programs all offered free school meals to their undernourished students. Additionally, Madhya Pradesh provided free uniforms and bicycles to improve enrolment and attendance, while some schools in Minas Gerais provided bathing facilities for their students. Second, the improving systems sought to increase the instruction time for literacy and numeracy. In Madhya Pradesh the timetable was altered so that two hours a day could be devoted to the new literacy lessons.
>
> (Mourshed *et al.*, 2010: 40)

McKinsey & Company reported improvement in outcomes in Madhya Pradesh. The strategies that have been adopted fall into the general category of command-and-control in the model described in Chapter 3. It is an appropriate way forwards under the circumstances. Building capacity for self-management is further down the track for the great majority of schools, as is any plan to 'unchain' them, should the relatively low level of autonomy and the extent of central control be maintained for longer than necessary.

South Africa

The Republic of South Africa has a population approaching 50 million, increasing at the rate of about 1 per cent per year, with about 80 per cent African, 9 per cent white, 9 per cent coloured and 3 per cent Indian/Asian. There are nine provinces, with about half of the population living in the three major urban centres of Johannesburg–Pretoria, Cape Town and Durban. About 40 per cent of the population is 19 years of age or younger. GDP is growing at almost 5 per cent per year.

Building a national system of education is extraordinarily difficult given the history of the nation, as explained in the Preamble to the South African Schools Act (1996):

> This country requires a new national system for schools which will redress past injustices in educational provision, provide an education of progressively high quality for all learners and in so doing lay a strong foundation for the development of all our people's talents and capabilities, advance the democratic transformation of society, combat racism and sexism and all other forms of unfair discrimination and intolerance, contribute to the eradication of poverty and the economic well-being of society, protect and

advance our diverse cultures and languages, uphold the rights of all learners, parents and educators, and promote their acceptance of responsibility for the organization, governance and funding of schools in partnership.

(OECD, 2008a: 38–39)

Schooling is compulsory for all children from the ages of 7 to 15. There are very few private schools, with about 96 per cent, or about 26,000, being public schools. Student–teacher ratios across the country are about 32:1. Although the majority of students complete Grade 9, with many repeating a grade along the way, outcomes are of major concern, as reported by the OECD (ibid.: 21) in its country study:

> In 2002, Grade 3 students scored 68 percent for listening comprehension, but only 39 percent for reading comprehension, 30 percent for numeracy, and 54 percent for life skills. In 2004, Grade 6 students obtained averages of 38 percent for language, 27 percent for mathematics and 41 percent for natural science. Of the 12 African countries participating in the 1999 MLA project, South Africa scored the lowest average in numeracy, the fifth lowest in literacy and the third lowest in life skills.

The OECD highlighted the low quality of teaching:

> The 'returns to investment' in teacher education, or the quality of performance one might expect from learners in return for money spent on educators, is very low. Despite improvements in their qualifications, many educators are ill-prepared to teach the grades they are assigned to teach. Many come late to school, leave early, do not explain or provide feedback on homework and spend too much of their time on administrative tasks.

(ibid.: 23)

Education and the economy

According to *The Economist*, South Africa was not so long ago 'by far the most serious and economically successful country in Africa. At the turn of the millennium it accounted for 40 percent of the total GDP of the 48 countries south of the Sahara', but now, 'though still a treasure trove of minerals with the most sophisticated economy on the continent', South Africa 'is on the slide both economically and politically' (*The Economist*, 2012d: 11). Although the accompanying commentary cited many factors contributing to the decline, it drew on World Bank data to conclude that 'education is a disgrace', with it being ranked 132nd out of 144 countries for the quality of primary education and 143rd out of 144 in science and mathematics. However, there are bright spots, especially in Western Cape.

The country report of the OECD provided a more even-handed assessment in reporting that 'impressive progress has been made in education legislation, policy development, curriculum reform and the implementation of new ways of delivering education, but many challenges remain in many areas, such as student outcomes and labour market relevance' (OECD, 2008a: 3). As with counterparts for other countries, such reports are prepared by a team of international experts and take account of background papers prepared by officials in the country concerned, with funding for the review provided by that country.

Western Cape

McKinsey studied the richest province of Western Cape, which includes Cape Town, as one of a small set of systems that moved from poor to fair in its classification of journeys, joining Minas Gerais (Brazil) and Madhya Pradesh (India), whose strategies were described above. All three improved relatively quickly after adopting similar strategies in their common focus on literacy and numeracy. The three themes in these strategies were providing step-by-step guidance and motivation for low skill teachers and principals, getting students to school and into class, and bringing all schools to a minimum standard of quality. This improvement was achieved in Western Cape from 2003 to 2007.

Western Cape is a relatively large system organised into eight districts with a total of about 1,100 primary schools, 600,000 students and 17,000 teachers. It achieved a steady rise in achievement in reading for students in Grades 3 and 6 and narrowed the gap between low- and high-performing students. McKinsey described key strategies as follows:

> To achieve this improvement, the Western Cape Education Department (WCED) identified and developed strategies to support the lowest performers and raise the floor of outcomes. It combined data on school performance with geographic information in order to identify specific communities with performance challenges, understand the specific local needs of those communities and tailor its support accordingly. For example, in one district, district officers worked with illiterate parents to jointly write stories that they could memorise and recite to their children. It also asked the farm owners' association to allow farm workers (parents) time off to meet their children's teachers. WCED staffers spent three days annually with each of the eight districts in the state to review school performance data, speaking to the district leaders and parents, and visiting the highest and lowest-performing schools in the district.
>
> (Mourshed *et al.*, 2010: 40)

The WCED initially allowed a degree of flexibility in instructional approaches, subject to schools being required to devote 30 minutes per day to reading for pleasure. However, centrally determined requirements were tightened after several years, with eight areas for improvement specified for each district.

Governance and finance

Of particular interest are the governance arrangements and, especially, the fact that about half of the public schools are able to charge fees. There are few systems of public education around the world where this is possible. The OECD (2008a) country study summarised arrangements in the following terms:

- School governing bodies (SGBs), composed of the principal and elected representatives of parents, educators, non-teaching staff and (in secondary schools) learners, have powers to determine school admissions policy, recommend the appointment of staff and charge schools fees, subject to majority parental approval. (OECD, 2008a: 23)
- Effective this year [2008], the poorest two quintiles of schools have been declared 'no fee schools', i.e. 40 percent of schools nationally, ranging from 56 percent in the poor Eastern Cape to 14 percent in the richer Western Cape. During the 2007 academic year, over 5 million learners will be attending 13,856 no fee schools. (ibid.: 25)

Public schools in South Africa therefore have a capacity for self-management as far as determining the levels of fees is concerned.

Schooling 2025

The Department of Basic Education has prepared a statement under the title 'Schooling 2025' that describes the outcomes it would wish to see in 2025. This is, in effect, a statement of vision. It includes a commitment to monitor progress 'against a set of measurable indicators covering all aspects of basic education including amongst others, enrolments and retention of learners, teachers, infrastructure, school funding, learner well-being and school safety, mass literacy and educational quality' (Department of Basic Education [Republic of South Africa], 2012b). The vision includes the following:

- Learners who attend school every day and are on time because they want to come to school, the school is accessible and they know that, if they miss school when they should not, some action is taken.
- Teachers who have received the training they require, are continuously improving their capabilities and are confident in their profession.
- A school principal who ensures that teaching in the school takes place as it should, according to the national curriculum, but who also understands his or her role as a leader whose responsibility is to promote harmony, creativity and a sound work ethic within the school community and beyond.
- Parents who are well informed about what happens in the school, and receive regular reports about how well their children perform against clear standards that are shared by all schools.

- Learning and teaching materials in abundance and of a high quality.
- School buildings and facilities that are spacious, functional, safe and well maintained.

(adapted from Department of Basic Education
[Republic of South Africa], 2012b)

The Department of Basic Education has prepared a plan to realise the vision in 'Schooling 2025', with relatively detailed strategies and targets to 2014. Of particular interest are plans for Annual National Assessments (ANA):

- Each year, all learners in Grades 1 to 6 and 9 will write national tests in languages (home language and first additional language) and mathematics at the end of the year. The purpose is to establish an objective national benchmark by which to measure literacy and numeracy achievement levels in primary schools, so that improvement can be accurately assessed and appropriate interventions designed where additional support is required.
- Teachers will mark these standardised tests according to instructions provided by the department.
- Parents will receive the ANA results in learners' annual report cards at the end of the year.
- School Governing Bodies (SGBs) will receive a district-wide ANA report, which will be shared by other parents at the school, to allow them to compare their own ANA results with those of other schools in the district.
- The objective in making the results public is not to shame schools or create perceptions of 'winners' or 'losers', but rather to give schools and their parent communities an idea of how their achievements compare to those at other schools.

(adapted from Department of Basic Education
[Republic of South Africa], 2012b)

There are thus some powerful tensions in policies and practices in South Africa. On the one hand, there are self-managing School Governing Bodies with significant powers, including for about half of the schools determining the level of fees to be paid by parents. On the other hand, there is relatively low autonomy but high control (as illustrated in Western Cape) in approaches to learning and teaching that must be adopted. The need to establish benchmarks at various levels in literacy and numeracy, with a comprehensive assessment programme across the country, is understandable. However, there are elements in the plan for Annual National Assessments that are a perfect match with strategies in the GERM that Sahlberg (2011) believed have been dysfunctional in jurisdictions that have gone down this path. Although most of the actions on the scale now unfolding in South Africa are necessary, can these aspects of the GERM be bypassed?

Important messages for policymakers and practitioners

1   Governments in Brazil, India and South Africa realise the need to improve the quality of education in their schools, and strategies for improvement have been designed and implemented by national, state, provincial and municipal governments. These strategies are having an impact and are generally of the low autonomy, high control kind that provide limited opportunity for self-management. Much remains to be done if schools are to make a contribution to society and the economy in these countries that are expected to be, or have the potential to be, among the powerhouses of the twenty-first century.

2   The private sector has a critically important role in Brazil and, especially, in India. Support from social entrepreneurs is targeted at schools in highly disadvantaged settings and there is evidence of a positive impact.

3   Several of the strategies in these countries, especially in South Africa, are of a kind that have proved dysfunctional in other jurisdictions. An important issue is whether these can be bypassed, and if command-and-control approaches that are understandable in the improvement journey from poor to fair are maintained for longer than necessary, thus impairing a capacity for self-management and, beyond that, for self-transformation.

7 Contours of change

Chapter 7 returns to the big picture and addresses five inter-related issues, the resolution of which will give shape to the contours of the terrain that lies ahead for schools on the journey to self-transformation. These are (1) what assumptions underlie efforts to bring about change in schools and school systems; (2) what assumptions have been made about the role of innovation; (3) what is measured – what counts as performance; (4) how it is measured – the economics of transformation; and (5) how fast – the speed and scale of transformation. The way in which (1) and (2) are addressed has a powerful influence on (3), (4) and (5).

These accounts do not provide descriptions of what the terrain will actually look like in 25 years or details of how the journey will be experienced by those who participate. These are unknown, consistent with an important theme in Chapter 1, namely that it is not possible to predict the future in precise terms too far ahead, even though there are powerful trends – megatrends – that will influence the course of events. Rather, the focus in Chapter 7 is on critical issues and it is how these issues will be resolved in the short to medium term that will determine the contours. Policymakers face choices now and the choices that are made will determine the shape of things to come.

What assumptions have been made about change in schools and school systems?

It is possible that the dysfunctional aspects of the GERM described by Sahlberg (2011) may be the result of some governments and system authorities failing to draw from or respect classical change theory, updated to contemporary contexts, or the result of inappropriately adopting or persisting with aspects of this theory. Such actions will probably result in command-and-control or carrot-and-stick approaches, from which self-managing schools should be unchained, as described and illustrated in Chapter 3.

One classical change theory is that developed more than four decades ago by Chin and Benne (1969), who described assumptions underpinning efforts to bring about change in human systems. Drawing on examples from a range of settings, they described three sets of assumptions that are sometimes referred to as 'meta-strategies', that is they describe overarching approaches to change that shape particular strategies in particular settings. The three assumptions were designated rational-empirical, power-coercive and normative-re-educative. The terms may be complex but they may be described in simple terms (telling, forcing and participating, respectively).

Adopting a *rational-empirical* strategy assumes that people will respond to evidence that the change will lead to better outcomes. Self-interest comes into play because the strategy assumes that people will see it is in their own best interests to adopt the change. This does not always occur. Contemporary practice that is consistent with this approach is the commitment to evidence-based change, often associated with an unrelenting collection or presentation of data that is intended to make the case irresistible, and expecting that people will change accordingly.

The *power-coercive* strategy assumes that people will change only if they are forced to change, either in the harder sense in some circumstances, such as the use of force, or in the softer sense, as is the case in education, in which laws and regulations are passed and there is strict accountability for compliance or sanctions for non-compliance. A power-coercive approach is appropriate in some circumstances, for example in the requirement that schools can employ only teachers who meet certain certification standards, or in requirements to ensure that occupational health and safety regulations be obeyed. Requirements for implementation of a tightly prescribed curriculum may be an example of this strategy. So, too, is the requirement that a higher level of government will make funds available to a lower level of authority only under strict conditions, with the latter prepared to comply because they do not wish to miss out on the funds. An evidence-based approach, or certain contextual circumstances, could mean that the lower level of authority might act differently if compliance were not required. Miles and colleagues (2002) described this as the economic application of political power:

> Under the economic power strategy for change, the rewards (and sanctions) focus on the provision (or withholding) of financial incentives. Organizations can differentially reward members for their active implementation of new methods of management or new approaches to dealing with issues. Governments can dole out (or withhold) funding from organizations in return for their willingness to comply with new policy directions. This last example represents a combination of political power (the right to set policy directions) and economic power (the ability to fund the new directions and to withdraw funding from other practices now seen as outmoded).
>
> (ibid.: 8)

This is an accurate description of what is occurring in several countries, including Australia and the United States.

The *normative-re-educative* strategy assumes that people will make change when they have had the opportunity to be engaged in the process, often with an opportunity to shape the direction of change; their values about the process and the outcomes are changed through such engagement. New norms are established as a critical mass of people values the changes that ensue. There are many examples of this assumption in education, including stakeholder engagement at different stages of the process. There is fidelity with the normative-re-educative strategy under these circumstances, provided there is not a predetermined outcome, in which case engagement is a sham and it is really a case of a manipulative power-coercive strategy.

Each of the strategies or sets of assumptions, or a combination thereof, is appropriate in some circumstances and inappropriate in others. A common approach at present, in education and other fields of human services, is to commission an enquiry in which submissions are invited and evidence is gathered. Stakeholders may be engaged to help shape recommendations or shape the way recommendations should be adapted for implementation or included in legislation. This is a combination of all three sets of strategies. Developments in technology since Chin and Benne first described the strategies mean that the processes can be accomplished relatively quickly and with much wider involvement.

These strategies have been updated and augmented in both theory and practice. Quinn and Sonenshein (2008), for example, proposed a fourth strategy (*transforming*) that is consistent with the theme of this book. They give simpler labels to the Chin and Benne strategies: telling (rational-empirical), participating (normative-re-educative) and forcing (power-coercive). They are clear about the effects of a power-coercive approach: 'The main advantage of this approach is that it delivers results rapidly. However, the benefits come at the expense of damaging relationships, destroying trust, and forfeiting voluntary commitment' (ibid.: 69–70). This describes fairly accurately the achievement of modest improvement followed by flatlining in learning outcomes in some countries and the surliness of, if not resistance by, much of the profession. These phenomena are not apparent in other countries that are often described as 'high trust', for example, Finland (see Chapter 4).

The fourth strategy proposed by Quinn and Sonenshein calls for a different way of viewing the change agent, who, in the Chin and Benne strategies, is typically a consultant, an internal or external team, or even the government or system authority itself. Quinn and Sonenshein believed that these people, understandably and appropriately in most instances, have their own self-interest, which may arise from contractual remuneration, securing further contracts, or maintaining position power. In the transforming strategy, the concept of the change agent as being a person or group different from the target, who is expected to change, is shifted so that all are, in effect, change agents. Expressed another way, the change agent is as much a target for change as the traditional target: 'the change agent shifts from self-interest to the collective interest' (Quinn and Sonenshein, 2008: 75). This fourth 'meta-strategy' seems well suited to the self-transforming school or to a system that seeks to build capacity in self-managing schools so that they become self-transforming.

A fourth strategy emerged from the comparative international study of change in public sector organisations in Canada and China (Miles *et al.*, 2002). The study was framed by the three meta-strategies of Chin and Benne. It described the propensity in Canada to follow the approach described above for public enquiries, involving or followed by stakeholder consultations, essentially a combination of the rational-empirical and normative-re-educative. The Chinese component included a study of change in state enterprises and the researchers observed a pattern of rational-empirical approaches within a more dominant culturally determined power-coercive framework. They noted, however, that the success of the Chinese strategy was determined by another culturally determined strategy, namely the time invested in building trusting relationships ('banquet frequently'). The authors proposed a fourth meta-strategy (*relational*) that accommodates the Chinese approach and concluded with the challenge: 'Could it be that we can learn something so simple – and profound – as the power of "relationship" as a strategy of implementing change from the Chinese?' (ibid.: 21). The response fits comfortably with practice in the self-transforming school, if not a meta-strategy for the 'Asian Century'.

What assumptions have been made about the role of innovation?

The same meta-strategies may be employed in the design, delivery and analysis of approaches to innovation in a school or system of schools. An innovation that has proved successful may be presented to all as preferred practice, and evidence of its efficacy is the lever to induce change: a rational-empirical strategy. The organisation of seminars and workshops that provide participants with an opportunity to explore its merits or devise adaptations that suit their settings would add a normative-re-educative dimension. An outstanding example of how these two meta-strategies work together is the QEF in Hong Kong, described in Chapter 5. In summary, an initial capital of HK$5 billion in 1998 led in the first decade to the support of more than 7,000 projects at a total cost of about HK$3.5 billion. The fund continues; the capital is intact. There is regular showcasing or sharing of evidence and outcomes, either face-to-face or through an online facility. There is no compulsion for a school to adopt or adapt.

A policy that requires all schools to adopt an innovation when there is limited evidence to support its efficacy, or when it is inappropriate in some or even all settings, even if the intended outcome is universally agreed, is an instance of a power-coercive strategy. As observed earlier, there may be gains in the short term but they may be at the cost of trust or commitment.

Examples include the adoption of highly specified approaches to the teaching of reading, or the requirement that all schools follow a detailed model of school improvement, or insistence that principals of all schools participate in visits to other schools, often described as 'instructional rounds'. Each may have proved successful in other settings, and may prove successful again in some circumstances, but there is likely to be a cost if there is imposition on all. The use of power-coercive strategies along these lines has no place in the self-transforming school.

Dissemination of innovations, regardless of the meta-strategy that has been employed to design or develop them, will follow different pathways the further we go in the twenty-first century. Traditional ways of having 'the system' do this for schools may still have their place but they are likely to slow the process. An increasing number of schools are bypassing these ways and seeking their own sources of information, and this is a characteristic of the self-transforming school. Self-transforming schools are doing this through networking, be it face-to-face, digitally or through exchanges of information in a chain or chains of schools that have common interests. Information about innovations is moving faster now than ever and the phenomenon is aptly described by Malcolm Gladwell (2001) in *The Tipping Point*. He suggested that 'ideas and products and messages and behaviours spread like viruses do' (Gladwell, 2001: 7), the tipping point being 'that one dramatic moment in an epidemic when everything can change all at once' (ibid.: 9). David Hargreaves (2003) employed the same imagery in *Education Epidemic* to explain how change on the scale of an epidemic may be created in schools. Knowledge-based networks encourage change on this scale and are a feature of self-trans-forming schools. These networks operate faster than any system-designed, bureaucratically organised approach to delivery. Chapters 8 and 13 provide illustrations of how systems and schools can build capacity along these lines.

A major theme in Chapter 8 is that innovation should pervade every level of a system of schools. It is surprising that it is not presently so and that there is still reliance in some systems on central innovation units or one-size-fits-all approaches to innovation, given that every prescription for social and economic well-being in the twenty-first century calls for deeply embedded capacities for innovation. It is one of the so-called twenty-first-century skills.

Particular mention has been made of classical theories of change, such as the meta-strategies described by Chin and Benne, updated to contemporary conditions. What of other classical or seminal theories, such as that proposed by Everett Rogers as far back as 1962? Rogers conducted one of the first meta-analyses, in this instance of 508 studies of diffusion of innovations. He concluded that people or organisations adopt innovations at different rates and he came up with his famous classification of innovators, early adopters, early majority, late majority and laggards (Rogers, 1962). How relevant or useful is the Concerns Based Adoption Model (CBAM) developed for edu-cation by Hall and Hord (1987), who demonstrated seven stages of concern and eight levels of use in attitudes and adoption of innovations? Both models are highly relevant in contemporary contexts and they should be taken into account in designing and delivering approaches to the dissemination or diffusion of innovations in education. However, they were developed before the advent of technology that dramatically compresses the time frames for dissemination.

What counts as performance?

Public policy in education around the world is being shaped to a large extent by the performance of nations in international tests of student achievement, such as PISA or TIMSS, and within nations by the outcomes of tests that all students are expected to take at different levels of schooling. Reference has been made in several places to the gains and losses that accrue from a preoccupation with the results. The 'contours of change' in the years ahead will be shaped by how we maintain, respond to or move beyond this preoccupation.

The good news as far as the self-managing school is concerned is that evidence that has emerged from an analysis of PISA shows that nations with a relatively high level of authority and responsibility do better than those without, provided certain conditions are satisfied (see Chapter 2). However, conclusions about cause-and-effect are so hedged by these 'certain conditions', and there are such wide variations within nations, that it is fair to ask if PISA is yielding very much that is a helpful guide to the formulation and implementation of policy. In a similar vein, patterns of centralisation and decentralisation that were reported in the 2012 edition of *Education at a Glance* (OECD, 2012) were of limited validity, since they do not ring true to dispassionate observers. Canada, for example, is reported as being highly centralised when it comes to the proportion of decisions that are made at the school level, yet some of the outstanding practices in self-management may be found within its borders.

More fundamentally, it is fair to ask if PISA is measuring the capacities that are essential to learning in the twenty-first century. If it is not, or if the transition to more valuable measures is proving to be too slow, are the tests worth the effort, especially if the consequences are, on balance, dysfunctional?

Before proceeding, it is important to acknowledge the benefits of PISA. Some countries that were complacent about their performance in education were challenged to do better when the tests were first administered and the outcomes reported. The hundreds of journeys by system leaders to Finland in the early years of this century are potent testimony of this benefit. It did not mean that they necessarily copied what they had learnt, but at least hard questions were asked on their return. For example, two practices in Finland seemed immediately transferable after adaptation, one being the quality of initial teacher education and the other being the outstanding individualised support provided to students whenever they fell behind or needed other special support. A dysfunctional effect, consistent with Sahlberg's identification of the GERM (Sahlberg, 2011) that is 'infecting' some nations, was the introduction of unrelenting testing with public reporting of results to show how well or how poorly schools were doing, as illustrated in what transpired in Australia, England and the United States.

At the far end of the critique is a questioning of OECD itself. One such critic is Judith Sloan, who is a frequent commentator in the media in Australia but has senior experience and a high level of expertise in economics. She is a former Professor of Labour Studies at Flinders University in South Australia. In a provocative opinion piece in *The Australian* (Sloan, 2012), she identified important discrepancies in OECD reports in her area of expertise and posed the ultimate challenge: 'Is it time for Australia to pull out of OECD?'. She noted that the organisation employed 2,500 people with an annual budget of $450 million. She acknowledged that 'one potentially useful exercise is to benchmark various economic and social indicators across countries', as is done in education, but then questioned the comparability and validity of the data contained in its reports. She concluded that, 'at the policy level, its reports are mainly politically correct, bureaucratically written and excessively lengthy sludge' and that 'the value of OECD has come and gone over the years'. Illustrations of the limitations, if not of the doubtful validity, of parts of the annual *Education at a Glance* were cited above.

It is worth pointing out that Finland achieved its success without the stimulus of PISA; indeed, its policymakers were surprised by its results. Its reputation is well deserved but it should be noted that it did not do so well in the Trends in Mathematics and Science Study (TIMSS) when it participated prior to its switch to PISA. A report by Loveless (2011) for the Brookings Institution compared performance in the United States with other countries, citing results in PISA, 2009. It drew attention to other features of schooling in Finland and highlighted aspects of PISA that make it a worthwhile programme that is not widely understood:

> The emphasis on learner-centred, collaborative instruction and a future oriented, relevant curriculum that focuses on creativity and problem solving has made PISA *the* international test for reformers promoting constructivist learning and 21st-century skills. Finland implemented reforms in the 1990s and early 2000s that embraced the tenets of these movements. Several education researchers from Finland have attributed their nation's strong showing to the compatibility of recent reforms with the content of PISA.
>
> (ibid.: 11)

Loveless referred here to an important characteristic of PISA, namely its focus on creativity and problem solving; it does not involve simple tests of literacy and numeracy.

It is also important to note the critique of Yong Zhao about relative performance among nations that participate in PISA and measures of entrepreneurship, which he noted is 'fundamentally about the desire to solve problems creatively' (Zhao, 2009: 9). He drew on the findings of the 2011 Global Entrepreneurship Monitor survey (reported in Bosma *et al.*, 2012) to show a statistically significant negative relationship between scores on the 2009 PISA Mathematics Test and Perceived Entrepreneurial Capability in 23 developed countries that are 'innovation-driven' (Zhao, 2012: 12). For example, Singapore was the top-performing nation on this PISA test but had one of the lowest scores on entrepreneurial capability. Other high-scoring nations on PISA included Korea, Chinese Taipei (Taiwan) and Finland. Australia scored highly on PISA and higher than it is often given credit for in respect to entrepreneurship. The United Kingdom and the United States scored relatively poorly on PISA among this set of nations but relatively well on entrepreneurial capability. However, the observer would be puzzled by the relatively high scores for Greece and Spain on entrepreneurial capability, whereas their relatively low scores in PISA are well known. Both nations are struggling as far as their economies are concerned. Maybe it is this capability that is waiting to be deployed if Greece and Spain are to survive their current crises!

The central issue derives from the oft-stated maxims that we measure what we value or we value what we measure. If governments are giving priority to lifting their nation's performance in PISA, and policy settings give priority to curriculum and pedagogy that will deliver improvement, what will be lost in terms of knowledge and skill that are deemed to be so important for national success in the twenty-first century? More important politically and educationally, do the same considerations apply to national tests that are much better known to their communities, with governments likely to be more sensitive to community response to poor or declining performance in these tests than they are to the results in PISA, which usually fill the headlines for a day or so and then disappear from public consciousness for another 12 months? This is the case, for example, in Australia, with the high-profile annual release of the performance of every student in the nation at four levels of schooling in the National Assessment Program – Literacy and Numeracy (NAPLAN). The headlines appear at regular intervals and are reported on one of the most sophisticated websites to be found in education (My School is discussed in more detail below).

Policymakers face choices on how to proceed with international, national and sub-national tests and how they take into account the critiques of people such as Sahlberg and Zhao when they point to their dysfunctions. The choices they make now will shape the contours of the terrain for self-managing schools that seek to be self-transforming.

How is it measured?

Policymakers in several countries must be frustrated that so much additional money has been invested in school improvement with no change, or with decline, in the outcomes they seek to achieve. Examples include the dramatic increase in public funding for reform in schools under the Blair and Brown governments, and the accompanying decline in the United Kingdom's performance in PISA, or the contention of Seddon (2010b), cited in Chapter 3, that better outcomes are achieved in the United Kingdom by 'localism' than under a policy that assumed greater efficiencies from uniform, large-scale, system-wide change. Then there is the case of Australia, where there has been an increase in per student funding of 273 per cent in real terms over four decades, during which time there has been a flatlining or decline in achievement (Barber and Mourshed, 2007), most recently in results in both PISA and NAPLAN.

It may be that strategies that were funded in the reforms were poorly designed and implemented, or that there was an extraordinary change in social and demographic context, but the root cause may lie in the strict adherence by policymakers to a rational view of public policymaking that assumes that people, when confronted with empirical data about links between cause and effect, will change their strategies, or an assumption that practitioners, if offered powerful incentives to change their behaviour, will respond rationally in the manner intended. This was described in the first section of this chapter as a rational-empirical strategy. This 'rational' approach has been dominant:

> The dominant theory of decision making in economics and other social sciences has been the rational choice model. People are generally assumed to be self-interested, rational agents: they analyse the costs and benefits of various options and choose the option that maximises their utility. They have stable, consistent preferences and the options they face are comparable to one another. This model is also a common paradigm for analysing policy decisions. In choosing between various options, policymakers typically assume that people will respond rationally – and therefore predictably – to incentives. Consequently, the right policy is that which creates incentives for the desired behaviour.
>
> (Koh, 2012: 17)

Assumptions underpinning the rational choice model (rational-empirical with an overlay of power-coercive) appear to have been made in the adoption of policies that were criticised in such strong terms by Sahlberg (2011) and Zhao (2012). It seems that recent developments in behavioural economics have been bypassed:

> Behavioural economics can help policymakers *structure* choices and information for their citizens in ways that take into account their cognitive biases and complications. By offering governments a realistic understanding of how people decide under conditions of risk, uncertainty and complexity, behavioural economics provides governments with the means to design policies that are sensitive to people's psychology.
>
> (Leong, 2012: x)

Finland is an example of a country that has blended rational and behavioural economics in its policies on education. Account has been taken of fundamental values in Finnish society, anticipating the way a highly skilled profession will act, reflecting the values of trust and professionalism. There are good examples of behavioural economics in action in Singapore (as described by Low, 2012, from which source the above statements of Koh and Leong are drawn). In these cases policymakers have anticipated the pitfalls of rationality in the manner described by Koh: 'A primary function of policymakers is to anticipate the impact of their policies and assess the likelihood that their policies will yield the desired outcomes' (Koh, 2012: 17).

Apart from a disjunction in the culture of policymakers, who follow the rational choice model, and the culture of practitioners, whose preferences reflect a more personal response, there may have been what might be called 'confected consultation' in the approaches that have led to such disappointing outcomes (manipulative normative-re-educative). Leong expressed it this way: 'Good ideas in public policy are not developed in the laboratory. They must take into account how the ideas are translated into implementable, enforceable and accepted policies' (Leong, 2012: ix).

The manner in which policies are delivered and received is also an issue: 'We could make the broader point that how a policy is framed and presented to the public can have a significant impact on how it is received' (Koh, 2012: 27). Policies in education are often communicated in language that is received as 'blame'.

A powerful example of policymaking of the rational choice kind in school education is presented in proposals for merit pay for teachers based on various indicators of performance, including, in some instances, the results of their students in achievement tests. The assumption of policymakers is that teachers will respond in a positive way to financial rewards based on the performance of their students and will therefore do whatever it takes to improve that performance in order to receive their reward. As Koh (2012: 17) described it, 'the right policy is that which creates incentives for the desired behaviour'. However, the reality and the correct response are described by Michael Fullan: 'When common sense tells you it won't work, when no research exists that back up the claim for merit pay (save for small segmented examples where subgroups benefit while the system as a whole suffers), it is time to give up the ghost of merit pay' (Fullan, 2010: 84).

There is another perspective on why features of current efforts at school reform are proving dysfunctional in some jurisdictions. It was presented by Tomas Sedlacek, a Czech economist who served as an economics advisor to Václav Havel, the philosopher and playwright who became President of Czechoslovakia (and then of the Czech Republic) after the Velvet Revolution in 1989. In a tour de force on the development of economic thought (*Economics of Good and Evil: The Quest for Economic Meaning from Gilgamesh to Wall Street*), Sedlacek (2011) described how economics has lost its way and has been seduced by mathematical modelling, but acknowledged that this is not the fault of mathematics. He declared that 'Without a doubt, mathematics has become the main language of modern economics . . . In economics, we now find little of history, psychology, philosophy, or a wider social science approach' (ibid.: 285). He quoted the great economist Joseph Schumpeter, writing in the first issue of *Econometrica*: 'Much of what you want to know about economic phenomena can be discovered and stated without any technical, let alone mathematical, refinements upon ordinary modes of thought, and without elaborate treatment of statistical figures' (ibid.: 290).

Does this commentary not also apply to what we are attempting to do in setting expectations for schools and how we are measuring progress in achieving those expectations? Does this not also apply to how governments react when they see the latest results from PISA, or their own national or sub-national tests, and how they respond with policies of the command-and-control or carrot-and-stick variety that are intended to improve the outcomes? The fault is not with the mathematics (echoing Sedlacek), or with the importance attached to what the tests are attempting to measure. It is in the way we are reducing our sense of accomplishment in education, as we do in economics, to 'equations, graphs, numbers, formulas . . . well, mathematics' (Sedlacek, 2011: 285). The fault does not lie with mathematics (both authors are mathematicians and scientists by training). It is in the reduction of the worth of education to 'mathematics'.

An outstanding illustration of this reductionism is seen in how school performance is reported on the My School website (www.myschool.edu.au) of the Australian Curriculum, Assessment and Reporting Authority (ACARA). What is reported for every school in Australia, more than 9,000 in total, is arguably the most sophisticated, indeed elegant, presentation of data on school funding and, especially, student performance on national literacy and numeracy tests at Years 3, 5, 7 and 9 to be found in any nation. Schools are compared with 'like schools' on the basis of their scores on an Index of Community Socio-Educational Advantage (ICSEA), and with nearby schools. The graphical presentations of these comparisons are impressive. Determining the extent to which a school adds value to the learning of students is made possible by tracking the performance of the same students from one level of testing to the next, and this is shown graphically along with how like schools, schools with the same 'starting point' and all schools at the same grade level have performed. The reader in any nation is invited to access the site and select a school to gain an understanding of what has been accomplished. However, apart from 'the mathematics', there is just a single paragraph that the school provides to describe itself. Performance is limited to measures of literacy and numeracy in Australia's NAPLAN, which are important to be sure, but there is no information about student engagement and performance in other areas of learning. The ICSEA measure must be treated with caution, if not scepticism, in respect of the settings of 'like schools', for the communities and student demography are dramatically different in each set of comparisons. But the mathematics is impeccable!

My School is intended to assist parents who seek information to guide the choice of school for their children. Although parents are invariably counselled to obtain as much information as they can, not just from the My School website, the expectations for the facility are unrealistic. It is probable that few parents make use of it for this purpose. However, policymakers place great value on it in setting expectations for schools in their jurisdictions and the behaviour of schools is influenced accordingly.

Policymakers face choices on how performance is measured and reported and then taken into account in decision making, including decisions on the allocation of resources to schools and the distribution of rewards and incentives. The choices they make now will shape the contours of the terrain for self-managing schools that seek to be self-transforming.

How fast?

Transformation often carries the connotation of dramatic change that occurs at great speed. Is this necessarily the case for the transformation of schools? Is this what lies ahead for the self-managing school that seeks to become the self-transforming school? Does this set a far too demanding expectation for schools and those who work in them?

The answers to these questions may be framed by a famous statement by Peter Drucker in the oft-quoted opening lines of *Post-Capitalist Society*:

> Every few hundred years in Western history there occurs a sharp transformation . . . Within a few short decades, society rearranges itself – its world view; its basic values; its social and political structures; its arts; its key institutions. Fifty years later, there is a new world . . . We are currently living through such a transformation.
>
> (Drucker, 1993: 1)

Schools should surely be considered among the 'key institutions' that Drucker referred to. If his statement applies to schools then we would expect that, over the course of 50 years, schools have been or will be transformed. An important question is the starting point and end point of this period. A strong case can be made that we are roughly at the mid-point of this transformation, which may have begun in the mid-to-late 1980s (roughly about the time *The Self-Managing School* was published) and will continue for another 25 years (the time frame of *The Self-Transforming School*).

In Drucker's mind, the transformation of schools may have barely started in 1993, when *Post-Capitalist Society* was published, as suggested in the following statement:

> As knowledge becomes the resource of post-capitalist society, the social position of the school as 'producer' and 'distributive channel' of knowledge, and its monopoly, are both bound to be challenged. And some of

the competitors are bound to succeed . . . Indeed, no other institution faces challenges as radical as those that will transform the school.

(ibid.: 209)

1993 may be an important marker because it was also the year when Seymour Papert's book *The Children's Machine* (Papert, 1993) was published. Its opening paragraph was as striking as Drucker's. Many teachers are familiar with the imagery, although recognition is rarely given to Papert. He invited readers to imagine teachers and doctors of the 1890s transported in time to the classrooms and operating theatres of the 1990s; teachers would immediately recognise the setting, and could possibly take over the class, whereas doctors would not be able to operate, given the extraordinary array of technology they would see and the team of specialists and support staff who may surround them.

It is by no means clear that the teacher of the 1890s could do this in the 2010s, such has been the pace and scale of change since the early 1990s, especially as far as technology is concerned. A moment's reflection would make clear that schools in many countries have changed in profound ways and that a transformation is indeed under way, yet these schools are still by and large operating in a paradigm that has prevailed for a century or more.

There was an opportunity to explore the issue in a 'strategic think tank' conducted by Educational Transformations in association with the Australian Council for Educational Leaders (ACEL) (Victoria) in Melbourne in May 2012. Participants included about 40 leaders from schools affiliated with International Networking for Educational Transformation (iNet) or who were members of ACEL (Victoria). The question that was addressed was: 'Are current models of schooling sustainable?'. The starting point was acknowledgement that, in recent decades, there have been significant calls for the transformation of the 'industrial' models of schooling that had prevailed throughout the twentieth century and that rapid changes in society were having a significant impact on students. The question encouraged participants to think about these changes and assess whether current models were meeting the needs of individuals and society, or if more concerted and drastic actions should be taken to achieve transformation. 'Current models' referred to the way schools were built, owned, governed, operated, staffed and funded, and to the curriculum and how it was delivered, and to approaches to learning and teaching that were currently in vogue.

Theme-setting presentations were made by Brian Caldwell and David Loader, co-authors of *Our School Our Future* (Caldwell and Loader, 2010). The centrepiece of the think tank was a set of 'expert witness statements' from leaders in three public (state) schools that were self-managing (this being the context for state schools in Victoria) and that were undergoing change on the scale of transformation, that is they were making significant, systematic and sustained change that was securing success for all students at their schools, or were on the way to doing so.

Mount Waverley Secondary College is a large multi-campus secondary school in an eastern suburb of Melbourne, serving communities that are above average in respect of socio-educational advantage. The school had created 'learning neighbourhoods' with new international award-winning space for students on learning pathways that could be tailored to their individual needs, led and facilitated by teachers who could share expertise and workload to achieve differentiation that had previously been unattainable. The approach was based on two premises: (1) acknowledgement that discrete discipline-based learning is important for students at this stage of their schooling and (2) an understanding that students learn in three different modes and each of these modes has a place in a well-planned and effective curriculum: direct instruction, independent learning and practice, and cooperative and collaborative learning. It is on the way to transformation within the current model of schooling, but this transformation is at a pace that is consistent with what Peter Drucker described for years on either side of the turn of the century.

Wooranna Park Primary School is located in a suburb in south-east Melbourne in a community that is below average as far as socio-educational advantage is concerned. It has created 'collaborative learning environments', reflecting a belief that the environment is 'the third teacher'. Spaces are designed to promote collaboration, allow for differentiation and risk taking, and support the development of active enquirers willing to challenge what they know. Teachers use careful questioning to facilitate the development of ideas and concepts. One-to-one conferencing time assists students to not only set their own personal learning goals, but also determine how best to achieve them. Carefully planned provocations at each learning space invite children's imagination and curiosity. Much of the school consists of facilities that are at first sight long past their use-by date.

Port Phillip Specialist School is located in Port Melbourne not far from the centre of the city. It is what is generally known as a 'special school' for students with disabilities. It has been transformed over two decades (since the early 1990s) from a school of barely 20 students, in an ant-infested converted house, into one that is serving more than 150 students from several suburbs, in a refurbished former primary school that had been closed. The school now occupies state-of-the-art facilities that reflect a 'full-service' concept to support the needs of its students. It has gained an international reputation for using the arts, broadly defined, as a vehicle for learning (see James, 2012, for an account of its transformation). Millions of dollars of cash and in-kind support have been obtained from a range of public and private sources.

Participants in the strategic think tank were linked online to promising innovations around the world, several of which are described in Chapter 9 ('The transformation of learning'), and engaged in intensive group discussions to address the question, 'Are current models of schooling sustainable?'.

It was apparent that each of the schools for which 'expert witness statements' were provided, along with those whose practices were examined through online links, had been engaged in change that matched Peter Drucker's description of what occurs over decades. Transformation is occurring within the current model of schooling but, after a period of time, it is evident that profound change has occurred, with schools in charge of the process. These self-managing schools had become self-transforming schools.

Leadership was widely distributed at each school. Principals and others were in touch with what was happening in education, not only locally but elsewhere around Australia and internationally. They did not wait for 'the system' to tell them what to do and how to do it, but support or approval from 'the system' was required or sought on certain matters, especially in respect of the use of public funds to build new facilities. In general terms, however, the schools 'called the shots' and moved at a pace that made sense in their contexts, although the pace may quicken in the years ahead with developments in technology (each of the three schools is at the forefront in this respect). In terms of the imagery in Chapter 3, these schools have thrown off the chains, real or imaginary, and are fine examples of 'the self-transforming school'.

Important messages for policymakers and practitioners

1 Classical theories of change (meta-strategies), as updated to contemporary conditions, have been bypassed in aspects of policymaking in education. There is a preoccupation with the rational-empirical (telling), with an overlay of power-coercive (forcing). Classical models for dissemination of innovations continue to be relevant but advances in technology have compressed time frames and expanded the opportunities for stakeholder engagement.

2 Policymakers face choices on how to proceed with international, national and sub-national tests. Although these provide useful information to guide some kinds of decisions, they often have limited validity, especially where comparisons between and within nations are involved. There is a risk that a preoccupation with a narrow range of outcomes will impair the development of knowledge and skills that are needed in vibrant societies and successful economies in the twenty-first century. Policymakers also face choices on how performance is measured and reported and then taken into account in decision making, including decisions on the allocation of resources to schools and the distribution of rewards and incentives among staff.

3 Policymakers face choices on the extent to which they allow or constrain schools to use their capacities for self-management to become self-transforming. They should refrain from forcing the pace in the light of evidence that schools that have the necessary capacities are well able to succeed. A command-and-control or carrot-and-stick approach that tells them what to do, how to do it and with what resources, and who should be rewarded and in what fashion, has a dismal record of success.

8 Innovation everywhere

The crisis in education described in Chapter 1 will not be solved by working harder or even smarter in current approaches to schooling, even though some self-managing schools in some systems are now self-transforming. Incremental change has had disappointing outcomes in many nations, manifested more often than not in flatlining or in decline in achievement on international, national and sub-national tests. There is commendable improvement in some areas but it is rarely sustained, except in particular instances of schools or groups of schools that have transformed their practice, as illustrated in examples at the end of Chapter 7.

Working harder or smarter is, of course, an important if not necessary approach, but the key to sustained improvement on the scale of transformation is innovation in policy and practice that reaches the student, whose needs, interests, aptitudes, ambitions and passions are satisfied; improvement is sustained; and there is a contribution to social and economic well-being. Restructuring or restaffing the system will have little effect unless the changes that result have a direct impact on learning and teaching. There can be no doubt that innovation of a kind that has this 'direct impact' is a key driver, in a general sense, and is one strategy among many that help the self-managing school become the self-transforming school.

Anthony (Tony) Mackay, Chair of the Australian Institute for Teaching and School Leadership (AITSL), Deputy Chair of the Australian Curriculum, Assessment and Reporting Authority (ACARA) and Chair of the London-based Innovation Unit, is an impeccable authority on the topic of innovation. He considers it to be the 'defining driving force' in schooling:

> You hope that with appropriate research and development you're able to feel more confident about what works; and then after establishing that, you move to scale-up. Now at that point, I do think you need to get into experimentation. You do need to incubate; you do need to apply serious resources to that work. I'm only saying something which every other industry of course is engaged in constantly, and devotes huge R and D resources to. So if you ask the question 'should we innovate' – absolutely!
>
> (Caldwell and Loader, 2010: 87)

Overview

Chapter 8 provides descriptions and illustrations of the scope and scale of innovation that is required to achieve transformation. Reference is made to a statement in 2004 by Ricardo Lagos, former President of Chile, about the importance of developments around the Pacific, reinforced in *Oceans of Innovation* (Barber *et al.*, 2012). Ground-breaking conceptual work by Leadbeater and Wong (2010) is summarised, along with a useful adaptation in Australia (Wardlaw and Dawkins, 2010). Particular attention is then given to Finland which, despite its sustained success, recognises the need for new approaches. Some key questions are then addressed: How can capacity for innovation be embedded in a system? What capacities are required of system leaders? What capacities are required at the school level?

Innovation, reform and change

A definition of innovation should be the starting point. For example, the *Merriam-Webster Dictionary* defines innovation as 'the introduction of something new' or 'a new idea, method or device'. In drawing on this definition, context should be taken into account: what is an innovation in one setting may be routine in another. Everett Rogers, author of the seminal work on diffusion of innovations described in Chapter 7, defined an innovation as 'an idea, practice, or object that is perceived as new by an individual or other unit of adoption' (Rogers, 1962: 11). A related issue is the connection between innovation, change and reform. Innovation and reform are intersecting subsets in the broader domain of change, as illustrated in Figure 8.1. Expressed

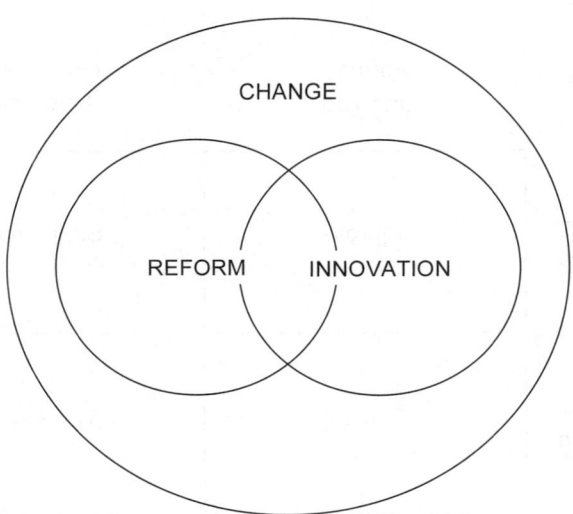

Figure 8.1 Relationship between change, reform and innovation.

simply, not all reform is innovation; not all innovation is reform; reform and innovation are both examples of change.

Global perspectives on innovation in education

Chile was host to the 2004 Asia–Pacific Economic Cooperation (APEC) meetings of leaders and ministers. Ricardo Lagos, then President of Chile, opened the series with these words: 'Civilizations have developed around the big seas, from the Mediterranean to the North Atlantic, and now it is the Pacific. It is around this ocean that the history of the 21st century will unfold' (cited in Bitar, 2004). The *Oceans of Innovation* report (Barber *et al.*, 2012) for the Institute for Public Policy Research in London took up the theme based on the contribution of the authors to the 2012 meetings of APEC in Russia (Vladivostok).

A helpful framework for understanding the relationship between improvement, transformation and innovation was developed by Leadbeater and Wong (2010), who proposed the 'Innovation Grid' illustrated in Figure 8.2. They drew extensively on their research in India and several developing countries but intended that the grid be universal in its application. The elements in the grid (improve, supplement, reinvent, transform) were described by Leadbeater and Wong (2010: 4) in these terms:

- *Improve* schools through better facilities, teachers and leadership.
- *Supplement* schools by working with families and communities.
- *Reinvent* schools to create an education better fit for the time.
- *Transform* schools by making it [education] available in radically new ways.

	Formal Learning	Informal Learning
Sustaining Innovation	Improve	Supplement
Disruptive Innovation	Reinvent	Transform

Figure 8.2 The Innovation Grid (Leadbeater and Wong, 2010: 4).

The particular innovations reported by Leadbeater and Wong were disruptive to the extent that they involved radically different forms of schooling or learning and new arrangements that gave rise to alternative schools (the idea of 'disruptive change' was popularised by Christensen, Johnson and Horn, 2008, as described in more detail later in this chapter). Leadbeater and Wong suggested that current transformations within a system result mainly from the efforts of mavericks that are 'disruptive', rather than from innovation in the mainstream:

> A band of disruptive innovators is emerging within school systems in many parts of the developing world. Yet radical innovation rarely comes from the mainstream. Most often it comes from renegades, mavericks and outsiders working in the margins. This report focuses on a potent source of such innovation: social entrepreneurs promoting learning in the slums of fast-growing cities in the developing world.
>
> (Leadbeater and Wong, 2010: 4)

The authors explained the lack of disruptive innovation in countries such as Australia, Canada, England, New Zealand and the United States:

> Disruptive innovation in education is too weak because state regulation, teacher union power, parental conservatism, and political micromanagement create high barriers to new entry. Creating diverse new ways for people to learn is still too difficult. Disruptive innovation needs more support and encouragement.
>
> (ibid.)

The Innovation Grid in Figure 8.2 may be interpreted in this way as far as improvement and transformation are concerned. School systems in many countries are focusing their efforts on improvement. The Australian government, for example, foreshadowed in 2012 the design and implementation of a National Plan for School Improvement. There will be innovation (top left quadrant in Figure 8.2), but it will be 'sustaining', emerging from within the mainstream, rather than being 'disruptive', and it largely applies to formal learning, which, in Australia, is embodied in the Australian Curriculum, the national curriculum that is taking shape through the efforts of the ACARA. For serious transformation to occur (bottom right quadrant in Figure 8.2), the innovation must be 'disruptive', generated for the most part from outside the system (as in the case of technology) and affecting, especially, more informal approaches to learning (which developments in technology make possible).

A refinement of the Innovation Grid was proposed by Chris Wardlaw, former Deputy Secretary, and Peter Dawkins, former Secretary of the Department of Education and Early Childhood Development in Victoria (Wardlaw and Dawkins, 2010), as illustrated in Figure 8.3. They suggested that

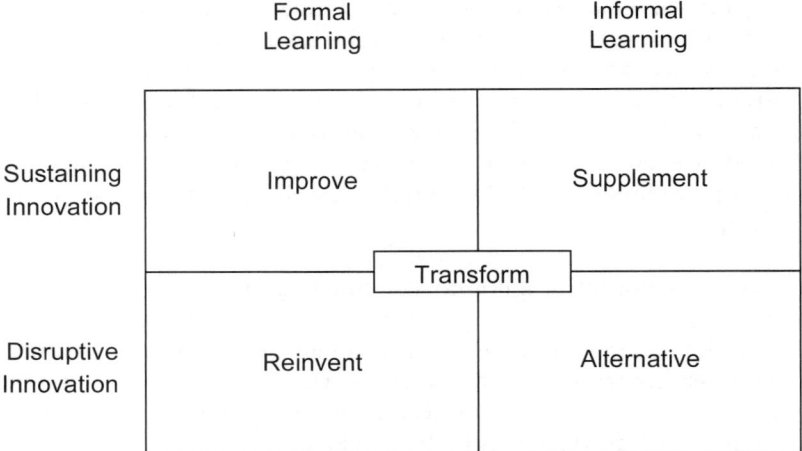

Figure 8.3 A modified Innovation Grid (Wardlaw and Dawkins, 2010).

transformation can occur in both formal and informal learning and can arise from sustaining innovation as well as disruptive innovation. Transformation can occur under the conditions illustrated in each of the four quadrants. This refinement is consistent with the findings in the workshop reported in Chapter 7: transformation can occur within the current model of schooling, that is innovation need not be disruptive to achieve transformation.

Focus on Finland

Finland provides an illustration at the national level of how innovation can occur in the mainstream, with examples of disruptive as well as sustaining innovation, and that formal and informal learning will be affected. The outcome is intended to be the ongoing transformation of an already successful system. What is occurring in Finland is consistent with the illustration in Figure 8.3.

An already strong track record

Finland has a strong commitment to innovation and technology across all sectors. In 2005, the World Economic Forum ranked Finland first in its Business Competitiveness Index, suggesting that it has 'one of the most innovative business environments in the world' (Lopez-Claros, 2006: xiv). The National Knowledge Society Strategy 2007–2015 (Information Society Programme, 2006) included a national vision and strategic intent to do more. The Ubiquitous Information Society strategy provided an overarching agenda for policy on innovation. It is coordinated by the Ministry of Transport and Communication as a joint initiative with the Ministry of Education and Culture and the National Board of Education (among other agencies). The Ubiquitous Information Society developed an Action Programme for 2008 to 2011 with education central to the effort through the provision of 'new kinds of learning environments that exploit information and communication technologies' (Ubiquitous Information Society Advisory Board, 2008: 15).

There has been policy on innovation in digital learning resources since at least 1995 (OECD, 2008b). A priority of the National Board of Education is the development of digital capacities across subjects in the national core curriculum through a 'learning environment' approach. The Ministry of Education and Culture increased its commitment to online teacher professional development through a 'Virtual Schools' programme and a partnership with the state broadcaster to develop a broad range of online content. There has also been enhancement of innovative resources through exchange and cooperation with other Nordic countries and a connection with European Union priorities and policies.

The 2008 *OECD Study on Digital Learning Resources as Systematic Innovation: Country Case Study Report on Finland* found that the policies and supports for Innovation in Digital Learning Resources have 'created an environment of grassroots and decentralised, "bottom-up" innovation. This is in part because of the autonomy of the local municipalities to interpret the national curriculum and central policy' (ibid.: 6).

Universities in Finland have produced high-quality research on digital learning resources and innovation in pedagogy. Through connections with schools and municipalities this research has resulted in many examples of school reform and pedagogical innovation (OECD, 2008b). The University of Jyvaskyla has developed and maintained Peda.net, an innovation tool that is used in over 100 municipalities. It is a platform for curriculum management and sharing information and resources. It also has a 'gate' facility that allows collaboration with parents and students (ibid.).

Funded jointly by Tekes (Finnish Funding Agency for Technology and Innovation), participating municipalities, the Ministry for Education and Culture, and companies such as Microsoft Finland, the InnoSchools Consortium developed the 'Future Schools Concept'. The Future Schools Concept is the result of research at several universities, pilot schools and municipalities. It was intended that the pilot schools work through their networks to gain support for innovative approaches to pedagogy, architecture, service and management. An outcome was *The Handbook of the Innovative School* (Tekes, 2007).

The City of Oulu provided an illustration of municipal commitment to innovation in schools when it opened the Ritaharju School in 2010–2011. Plans drew on the International Microsoft Innovative Schools Project and the InnoSchools Consortium. The school opened in a new area of the city which houses the University of Oulu and several technology companies. The need for innovation of this kind was described by a partner in these terms:

Local education officials in Finland who are involved in the planning of the Finnish Innovative School indicated that although the national curriculum offers 'good content', there are few examples of 'how to implement [the content] in a modern way'. They hope through the Innovative Schools Program 'to challenge the prevailing situation' and act as a model to other schools.

(Microsoft Corporation, 2008: 13)

Knowledge and Education in 2020: Board of Education Strategy (National Board of Education [Finland], 2011) described the strategies of the National Board of Education in seven areas, referring to an increase in sharing across municipalities and the use of 'electronic educational material and rich learning environments as a key part of learning and teaching' (ibid.).

Overall, it is evident that innovation in Finland is well supported by the government. However, the actual practices of innovation across individual schools and municipalities are decentralised, autonomous and varied. There is significant input from the university sector to municipalities and schools through research and the development of tools and resources. The Ministry of Education and Culture and the National Board of Education provide encouragement and support for innovation through high expectations expressed in policy and planning documents and by access to resources and professional development.

Why Finland needs even more innovation

Against this background of high achievement and dynamic innovation, it is remarkable that Finland acknowledges that it needs even more to remain strong both economically and socially. The case for further change was made in a paper (National Board of Education [Finland], 2011) prepared for the 2012 GELP held in Helsinki (see Chapter 1 for a description of GELP).

Its honesty is refreshing: 'students' satisfaction at school is at a lower level than the international average' (ibid.: 10), 'Finland is currently around the European average and the last of the Nordic countries in terms of educational use of information and communications technology' (ibid.: 10), 'Finland has the highest differences between girls and boys in terms of reading literacy among OECD countries' (ibid.: 11) and 'The number of students admitted to special needs education has increased in Finland during the 21st century' (ibid.: 13). The following were identified as priorities:

The priorities for development of education include: strengthening of reading and writing literacy, languages and communication; increasing scientific, technological and mathematical competence; increasing civic competencies, participation and influencing skills; strengthening artistic expression and production skills; and strengthening health and functional capacity.

(ibid.)

This list is remarkably similar to one that is often assembled for action in such countries as Australia, Canada, England, New Zealand and the United States, as described in Chapter 4. The international observer will therefore follow further developments in Finland very closely to see if a different package of reforms is produced. There seems to be a determination to maintain its current strengths: 'The new way of thinking that change is a continuous process requires flexible school organizations and working cultures that are based on trust and professionalism' (National Board of Education [Finland], 2011: 27). This is consistent with the culture of a self-managing school that seeks to be self-transforming.

Embedding a capacity for innovation across a system

Can large-scale innovation be energised from within a system of public education? The insider account of the dramatically expanding academies movement in England provided by Andrew Adonis might raise doubts: 'Promoting innovation was central to my work on academies . . . I was struck by how little local authorities engaged in such innovation, despite their commissioning and funding powers. Their bureaucratic and producer-interest mindset tended to stifle innovation rather than encourage it, and this mentality is changing far too slowly' (Adonis, 2012: 190). He described why he had to start small with academies. 'Only if they were considered a minor irritant, not a major reform, would they stand a chance of being tolerated by the forces of conservatism entrenched in the Education Department, the local authorities, and all three political parties' (ibid.: 60).

A contrasting and more optimistic view of what is possible was provided by Michael Fullan in his account of what has been achieved in Ontario: 'We have had good success in accomplishing whole-system reform in Ontario. Since 2003, we have taken a stagnant system and made impressive gains across the 5,000 schools in the public education system'. He referred in particular to improvements in literacy and numeracy in elementary schools and high school graduation rates, along with morale, capacity and ownership, which 'have become embedded in the schools, districts and government agencies' (Fullan, 2012: 3).

In general, there has been enough experience to question the expectation that a 'whole-system' outcome can be achieved through a 'centre-energised approach', where this is based to a large extent on early evidence of successful innovation in one or a few settings that can be scaled up and become the focus of a 'whole-system' strategy. Scaling up innovation in this manner is in many respects 'the holy grail' of improvement and transformation in a system of public education.

Successful innovations often arise in unexpected fashion when the right culture allows them to do so. Not all innovations need to be scaled up or can be scaled up. The efforts of a discrete unit within an education department may have little impact or be unnecessary because some innovations are 'disruptive' (Christensen *et al.*, 2008), for example the appearance of the tablet computer. An example of a centre-energised approach driven by a discrete unit was the decision in some systems to test through research the efficacy of the tablet computer with a sample of students in a sample of schools. Most schools took the matters into their own hands as parents and students provided the tablets, or schools purchased or leased them as teachers quickly saw their merit. A 'tipping point' (Gladwell, 2001) was reached very quickly. Events moved quickly in self-managing schools that had the authority to take action and aspects of learning and teaching were quickly transformed.

Apart from these considerations, selecting which innovations are to be scaled up can, on occasion, come close to 'picking winners' that do not work out in the long run, in which case needless expense and loss of trust are incurred.

Dyer and colleagues (Dyer *et al.*, 2011) built on the concept of 'disruptive change' (Christensen *et al.*, 2008) to describe 'the innovator's DNA'. Their work was an outcome of research over eight years in which leaders of the most innovative companies were interviewed to determine their personal attributes. The questions were penetrating to the extent that these attributes are quite fundamental in a personal sense, hence the idea of 'the innovator's DNA'. The companies were private, profit-making enterprises, but the authors made clear that the findings are more broadly applicable. There is no reason to believe that they are not pertinent to innovation in schools, with the authors identifying the following as the core skills: (1) associational thinking – innovative thinkers connect fields, problems, or ideas that others find unrelated; (2) questioning – innovators are consummate questioners who show a passion for inquiry; (3) observing – innovators are intense observers who gain insights into and ideas for new ways of doing things; (4) networking – innovators spend a lot of time and energy finding and testing ideas through a diverse network of individuals with different backgrounds and perspectives; and (5) experimenting – innovators are constantly trying out new experiences and piloting new ideas.

What capacities are required of system leaders?

Leadbeater phrased the question thus: 'What should a largely government-funded education system do to create the kind of innovation needed to make that kind of learning [innovation] possible, at scale, for perhaps millions of children, on a daily basis?' (Leadbeater, 2011: 4).

An example of centre-energised scale-up was described in the Boston Consulting Group report on *Unleashing the Potential of Technology in Education* (Bailey *et al.*, 2011). After reviewing exemplars such as Reasoning Mind (Houston and Dallas) and School of One (New York), each of which focused on personalising learning, as well as 'virtual labs' that expose students to world-class science (Brigham Young University and Pearson Education), the report settled on the Ultranet in Victoria, Australia, as its exemplar of best practice of 'educational technology on a large scale' (ibid.: 17). Through Ultranet:

Students and teachers can have their own online working space, as well as the ability to chat with other students and teachers about their goals and progress. Teachers can plan and develop learning sequences by drawing on a large content repository and the resources of their colleagues from other schools.

(ibid.: 15)

However, this positive assessment by a reputable consulting group should be contrasted with a devastating critique by the Victorian Auditor-General, who reports to the Parliament of Victoria. He reviewed two major initiatives in learning technologies that serve public schools in Victoria, one of which he assessed favourably but, with respect to the Ultranet, he concluded:

In contrast, the Ultranet, the Statement's key foundation plank and key enabler, was poorly planned and implemented. Six years after its announcement as a government priority, it is yet to achieve expected benefits for students, parents and schools. It is significantly late, more than 80 per cent over its first announced budget, has very low uptake by users, and does not have the functionality originally intended.

This audit identified a number of serious probity, procurement and financial management issues surrounding the Ultranet project. DEECD's tender process lacked rigour and was seriously flawed. There is little confidence in the costing and financial management practices around the Ultranet project, and limited assurance that the selected outcome represented value for money.

(Victorian Auditor-General, 2012: vii)

Apart from the issues raised in the second paragraph above, there is the broader issue of whether a system-wide scale-up of such technology is the most efficient way to proceed. The reader will recall that system-wide approaches along these lines are under way in such countries as Brazil (Chapter 6). It may be counter-intuitive, but perhaps schools should develop their own, or work with others in a chain to develop their capacities (see Chapter 13 for sharing resources in chains of schools). The Victorian Auditor-General concluded that the Ultranet had not delivered on its major objectives, which lie at the heart of transformation:

- to improve responsiveness to individual learning needs;
- to provide better information to parents, the school system and government;
- to improve the efficiency of the learning environment and school administration.

(ibid.: ix)

Christensen and Horn (2011) considered the advent of the personal computer as a 'disruptive innovation', but, since going to market with low-cost products, it became a 'sustaining innovation'. The sequence of disruptive innovation and sustaining innovation is consistent with the view of diffusion of innovations proposed by Malcolm Gladwell in *The Tipping Point* (Gladwell, 2001).

Innovations that use emerging technologies, such as the tablet computer, will be constrained if 'the system' attempts to control what is taken up by schools. 'The system' can assist by providing much of the infrastructure for a roll-out, for example, by helping schools obtain the bandwidth that is required for some innovations. The entrepreneurial efforts of schools and teachers will ensure much faster take-up and dissemination of particular technologies that can be utilised by students and teachers. It is striking that such an approach has been adopted in Hong Kong, Shanghai and Singapore.

There are implications for school and system leaders and managers.

1 Every leader in every unit should have the five capacities in the 'innovator's DNA' described by Dyer and colleagues (Dyer *et al.*, 2011) (see previous section); position descriptions and selection criteria should be changed accordingly.
2 Particular attention should be paid to the appointment of principals and, within schools, to the appointment of staff.
3 Mentors and coaches should have high levels of skill in these areas – coaches and mentors who help others reproduce the status quo may have limited value.
4 Changing the culture of schools will take time.

Leadbeater concluded that 'innovation in education should take place simultaneously – at different levels and in different settings from the daily practice of teachers and learners – through organizations, systems and platforms, to the social movements and the ideologies that inspire them' (Leadbeater, 2011: 4).

'Best practice' or 'next practice'?

Schools and school systems have been encouraged to search out and adopt 'best practice'. It seems straightforward to advocate such an approach. After all, considering class size, it seems to make sense that the smaller the class the more individual attention can be given to students, and the more manageable the already heavy workload of teachers. Some schools advertise their small class sizes and parents respond because it is assumed that small classes are 'best practice'. Yet evidence stubbornly fails to show the benefits once classes fall below about 25. Although controlled experiments to determine an evidence base for good practice should be encouraged, the fact remains that a range of different approaches seem to work well in different situations. The probable explanation is that practice in any classroom in any school is really a combination of approaches on many dimensions that are being implemented with a high degree of professionalism by staff that are able to make different mixes work well. Although every effort should be made to replicate the kind of clinical trials that are common in medicine, we cannot, either practically or ethically, isolate and control for clearly defined 'treatments'.

These shortcomings may explain, in part, the current interest in 'next practice'. One of the most frequently cited experts on leadership and change is C.K. Prahalad. He preferred the concept of 'next practice' to 'best practice'. He identified three characteristics of 'next practice': 'firstly, it is future-oriented; secondly, no single institution or company is an exemplar of everything that you think will happen; and thirdly, next practice is about amplifying weak signals, connecting the dots' (Hannon, 2007: 2). This summarises very neatly the limitations of 'best practice' and the merits of 'next practice'.

System-wide initiatives to identify 'next practice' are important, and individual schools would benefit from participating in these. The Innovation Unit has developed a Next Practice Innovation Model:

- Stimulating (analyze need, scan the horizon, seek innovators, and generate creative options) – system-wide reflection and intervention;
- Incubating (support the leadership of change, broker relationships and alliances, create communities of practice, and invoke power to innovate) – local level action;
- Accelerating (exploit knowledge management techniques, synthesise evaluation and research, accelerate diffusion with national agencies) – system learning.

(ibid.: 12)

Tony Mackay suggested that 'next practice' is concerned with 'disciplined innovation' over three to five years: 'I think the innovation timeframe, the next practice timeframe, has got to be three to five years. Now we've been talking about the future of schooling; well that's actually a 10, 15, 20 year timeframe' (Caldwell and Loader, 2010: 89).

Barbara Stone is former principal of MLC Sydney, a private school that was selected in Australia's Futures Focused School Project to illustrate outstanding practice. She described how a long-term perspective had been adopted, expanding the timeframe of planning in previous years. She addressed the issue of innovation by posing the question 'what's the next big thing?':

I find it's almost amazing to think that when we first did our 'Let's think about what the future might be' in 1995, we saw the future so clearly in terms of how instrumental, how absolutely important the technology would be. Our current 'next big thing' has been about global social responsibility. We saw that coming well before we had the tsunami and the recession; it is going to be so tangible in people's lives. So it's timely that our next review will be next year [2009] when we will be collectively – as many of us as we can – with our antenna, out there saying, 'So what's the next best thing?'

(ibid.: 89)

Embedding a capacity for innovation in a school

There is evidence that teachers and leaders at the school level are being 'unchained', enabling them to build capacities for innovation. They are to a large extent unchaining themselves, as illustrated in the example of MLC Sydney cited above, and Plato's image of prisoners in a cave is a helpful way to explain why some schools are not engaged in innovation and what should happen.

Plato's cave

Gareth Morgan (1997) used the image of Plato's cave to describe the challenge faced by leaders in understanding what is occurring outside the immediate work setting. He was referring to Socrates' allegory in Plato's *The Republic*, in which the reader is encouraged to imagine people chained to the wall of an underground cave. In the mouth of the cave is a fire, in front of which people go about their various activities, making sounds and moving objects. The cave dwellers can only see the shadows of these movements on the wall in front of them and they try to make sense of their cause and their relationship to the sounds.

Morgan used this allegory to suggest that organisations become 'psychic prisons', in which 'organizations and their members become trapped by constructions of reality that, at best, give an imperfect grasp of the world' (Morgan, 1997: 216). In schools and school systems, it is relatively easy to become trapped in this manner, leaving little opportunity to be directly involved in or gain a deep understanding of the wider workplace locally, let alone globally. The forces shaping the transformation of society have led to the most dramatic change in the nature of work since the industrial revolution, and unprecedented change in education has occurred in recent decades, and these developments can, quite understandably, appear like the shadows on the wall of Plato's cave.

Another part of Socrates' allegory concerns what might occur if one of the prisoners in the cave managed to escape and leave the cave to see and understand exactly what is happening out there. Should that person return to the cave, he or she could never live the same way again and, should they share with fellow prisoners what was discovered, it is likely that they would be ridiculed if not rejected for their efforts. Is this not the way some leaders have changed, and been received on return, when they have had the opportunity to experience at first hand what is occurring outside the world of school education? For example, when they had the opportunity to travel widely and frequently or when they had the good fortune to engage in an extended and challenging professional development programme.

The implication for the educational leader is to seek ways to escape the 'psychic prison' and provide every opportunity for colleagues to do the same. Globalisation, the knowledge society, the information revolution, the re-engineering of the public service and the new world of work will not be seen as shadows on the wall opposite which one sits chained and powerless. All should be unchained and empowered to engage with the realities of the remarkable events that are taking place at the dawn of the third millennium. The good news is that there is an unprecedented amount of travel by school leaders to see developments at first hand and the internet has achieved the same but on a much larger scale. YouTube and podcasts enable teachers to see, listen to and interact with thought leaders and outstanding practitioners, often in action in their work settings. Engaging in these activities is a prerequisite for innovation in schools and school systems.

A futures perspective

Complementing the need for deeply embedding a capacity for innovation in schools is the importance of gaining a 'futures perspective'. Caldwell and Loader (2010) adopted the metaphor of 'seeing' in describing a futures-focused school. A futures-focused school 'sees ahead', but it also 'sees behind', honouring and extending its accomplishments in the past. It 'sees above' in the sense of understanding the policy context. It 'sees below', demonstrating a deep understanding of the needs, interests, motivations and aspirations of students and staff. It 'sees beside' by networking professional knowledge to take account of best practice in other schools in similar settings. It 'sees beyond' by seeking out best practice in other nations and in fields other than education. It is consistent and persistent; it 'sees it through'. The metaphor of 'sensing' is also helpful, given that 'seeing' refers to what is already in place or is projected. A futures-focused school is alert to signals in its internal and external environment that may influence what may occur in the future and that may, subsequently, be 'seen'. These signals may be strong or weak and a high level of sensitivity is required to distinguish among them (Caldwell and Loader, 2010: 20).

The challenge for schools is to do well in what they are currently expected to do at the same time that they keep an eye on promising innovations and future possibilities, basically a 'split screen' approach. Each must be done well if a self-managing school is to also be a self-transforming school. As suggested in several places throughout this book, a chief cause of concern is that so much time and energy is taken up with what are proving to be the dysfunctional aspects of current demands, especially those concerned with the frequently excessive and unrelenting focus on testing and the seemingly endless and often unnecessary demands for accountability.

Strategic navigation

Strategic planning and operational planning continue to be important, but they need to be managed differently. Old-style strategic planning, with voluminous documents covering almost every aspect of school operations (invariably based on unmanageable, often data-free, analyses of strengths, weaknesses, opportunities and threats), should pass into history, as should similar efforts in school improvement planning. This kind of work can be fruitful only if there is a degree of stability and predictability in matters that may involve large commitments of funds over time. Examples include strategic planning for new facilities. The complexity and pace of change demand a different approach for most aspects of strategic decision making

One way of doing this is through a process Richard Hames called 'strategic navigation' (Hames, 2007), an approach adapted to the school sector by Caldwell and Loader (2010: 48–49), from whom this summary is drawn. Instead of generating a plan with dated and static intelligence, strategic navigation responds to real-time, current intelligence. Instead of leaders following directions and meeting deadlines, they are free to respond to the situation as they read it. Instead of an emphasis on the plan, the emphasis is on the navigation. The result is a more dynamic approach to strategy that is more inclusive of staff in both the assessment of the issues and the development of responses. Strategic navigation is more suited to the current turbulent times, when continuous corrections are necessary.

Strategic navigation calls into question the idea of strategy as a linear process which assumes that if strategy is implemented then the desired result will follow. Strategic navigation takes its strength from an ecological perspective. Strategy in this view is not the implementation of bureaucratic directions but the freeing of individuals to act in accordance with how they read the situation in the context of the strategic direction of the school or school system. At the same time, there is an emphasis on balancing the symbiotic relationships that exist within the organisation, discouraging individualism.

Strategic navigation challenges the idea that purpose and direction are determined solely by a few, the leadership team at the top. This is achieved by the sharing and gathering of ideas within the community. Before the social networking capabilities of Web 2.0 and the knowledge storing of web-based technologies, collective intelligence was more difficult and expensive. Today, listening to the community and harnessing its collective intelligence is much easier; it is a critical component of strategic navigation.

Strategic navigation is a systems approach to planning and operating. The organisation will live or die as a complete system, not as a collection of independent parts. The system is gathered together into a complex whole, members working with one another and the external environment. The members work towards a common overall objective, with an overriding moral purpose and a shared identity (moral centre). Values clarification is important. Good communication is critical.

Strategy is no longer a once-a-year task. For the school and school system leaders and their colleagues, it is the very core of their daily work and the essential lens through which they evaluate and prioritise that work. As a result, what schools and school systems need is a community of leaders who understand the social and political trends, who share a desire to deliver an agreed possible future and who are therefore able to be responsive and innovative within a strategic framework. The goal of strategic navigation is to engage the whole community in a continuous process that will address complexity and manage uncertainty.

Indicators of an innovative, futures-focused self-transforming school

Caldwell and Loader (2010) derived 10 indicators of a futures-focused school from their work in Australia's Futures Focused School Project, as listed below. These include a capacity for innovation and, overall, they describe important capacities of schools that seek to be self-transforming:

1 The school has clearly defined values and beliefs about life and learning that are used to balance past, present and future in the formulation of its plans.
2 There is a capacity and willingness for staff and other stakeholders to keep abreast of trends and issues, threats and opportunities in the wider environment, nationally and internationally.
3 There is a capacity and willingness for staff to respond to threats and opportunities anticipating their impact on education generally and on the school in particular.
4 There are structures and processes which enable the school to gather evidence and other intelligence, set priorities and formulate strategies which take account of likely and/or preferred futures.
5 School leaders ensure that the attention of the school's community is focused on matters of strategic importance, sharing their knowledge about these matters with the school's community, and encouraging other leaders to do the same in their areas of interest.
6 The school has an ongoing structured review process that facilitates the monitoring of the implementation of strategies as well as emerging strategic issues in the wider environment.
7 The school strategically positions itself for enduring success by skillfully balancing strategies that have succeeded over time with new strategies that take account of changing circumstances.
8 Ongoing informal conversations about future possibilities are encouraged as much as the more formal processes of strategic planning.

9   The school invests in innovation so that it becomes an 'incubator' of new ideas and new practices.

10 There is recognition that convergence of ideas is not always possible or even desirable, but every effort is made to develop a shared understanding of what is important to create and sustain success.

(Caldwell and Loader, 2010: 30)

Important messages for policymakers and practitioners

1   Although many innovations may be disruptive to the extent that they come from outside the system or arise from the efforts of mavericks within the system, transformation can occur in more orderly ways if the necessary capacities have been built at all levels across the system. Centre-energised innovation resulting from a scale-up of innovations deemed to be 'winners', or innovations designed in central units for dissemination across the system, might not be sustainable.

2   Systems that are performing outstandingly well at present must continue to be innovative if they are to sustain their success in the years ahead. Those who work in schools have the means to learn about outstanding innovations around the world on a continuous real-time basis. Advances in technology mean that no longer do they need to be chained to their workplaces, as was often the case in the past when it was difficult to travel to see new and successful practices at first hand.

3   Old-style strategic planning, with voluminous documents covering almost every aspect of school operations, should pass into history. Strategic navigation is the preferred approach. Instead of generating a plan with dated and static intelligence, strategic navigation responds to real-time, current intelligence and is more consistent with the need for innovation as schools seek to be self-transforming.

9   The transformation of learning

Transformation is considered in this book to be significant, systematic and sustained change that secures success for all students in all settings. The issue to be addressed in this chapter is how learning should change to secure such an outcome, namely 'success for all students in all settings'. Underpinning this issue is a series of questions: What is the purpose of learning? What should be learnt? How should it be learnt?

Furthermore, given that the book is endeavouring to look ahead to 25 years after publication, to at least 2038, as well as reflecting on the 25 years before publication, from 1988, it is important to provide a futures perspective on how learning is likely to change in response to these questions, assuming that the purpose of learning is to bring benefits to the student, to society and to the economy in a time of unprecedented change. It is sobering, if not daunting, to realise that a child entering school at the age of five in 2013 could still be in the work force at the age of 75 in 2083, so the time they spend in the years of formal schooling, as currently understood, sets an immediate context for learning over the next 12 years, that is to 2025.

A key theme in this chapter, as in the book as a whole, is that schools should 'take charge', indeed must take charge, if transformation is to be achieved. This does not preclude the need to have a national, sub-national or system perspective or framework, but any expectation that a command-and-control approach to achieve a uniform or one-best-way outcome is doomed to fail as far as meeting the needs of the student, society and economy are concerned. A high level of self-management is a prerequisite for self-transformation and these capacities are as important to achieving a transformation in learning as they are in any other aspect of school and school system operations.

There is clearly a link between what has been addressed in Chapter 8 ('Innovation everywhere') and Chapter 9 ('The transformation of learning'). Indeed, the authors had to make a choice on what matters were to be addressed in one rather than the other. Levin's distinction between innovation and transformation proved helpful:

> A main distinction between innovation and transformation is scale. Innovations are changes in discrete elements of schooling – a new program or a new pedagogy or a new organizational format – but transformation

implies changes in all of these. A corollary is that most innovation in education presently occurs in schools or classrooms but that transformation is system-wide change.

(Levin, 2011: 170)

A major theme in this book is that school transformation is a prerequisite for system transformation but the 'main distinction' in Levin's view is accepted, that innovation tends to be concerned with 'discrete elements' and transformation is concerned with holistic change.

The chapter is organised as follows. First, the work of Milton Chen is taken up to describe the 'leading edges' of innovations that align to achieve transformation in learning. A mechanism for mapping the progress a school is making is proposed. The terminology of Cisco is employed to describe the overlapping sequence of Education 1.0, Education 2.0 and Education 3.0. The harms that accrue from staying too long in Education 1.0 and Education 2.0 are recognised. Questions are raised about approaches that are sometimes presented as transformations but which are really adaptations, including virtual learning, blended learning and 'the flipped classroom'. At the same time, however, there is still a place for direct instruction. Attention is then turned to curriculum and more questions are asked: in this instance, whether all of the effort and cost involved in creating a national curriculum are worthwhile when a global curriculum of sorts is likely to emerge, with choices made by the self-transforming school as far as design and delivery are concerned.

As acknowledged from the first pages of this book, it is not possible to predict the particular ways in which learning will be transformed, even in the short term, such is the pace of change. A book is no place to list current breakthroughs, for these are increasing exponentially, and the list will be far behind by the time it is read. Professional networking and regular access to online digests are much better. This does not prevent a school from understanding how the broad field of policy and practice will change and making plans accordingly.

Framing the possibilities

Milton Chen is former executive director of The George Lucas Educational Foundation and one-time director of research at Sesame Workshop, working on Sesame Street. He is well placed to frame the possibilities for the transformation of learning. Writing in *Education Nation: Six Leading Edges of Innovation in our Schools* (Chen, 2010), he described six 'leading edges' that are giving shape to the transformation of learning.

At first sight, Chen is concerned with innovation, which, in the distinction provided at the start of the chapter, is more concerned with 'discrete elements' whereas transformation is more holistic. However, the 'six leading edges' he describes give a sense of coherence to the many domains in which change may occur. The following is a synopsis:

- The thinking edge: 'the most basic prerequisite to creating an Education Nation is changing our thinking about the enterprise itself – the learning process, the role of students, teachers and parents, and what is possible given the opportunities afforded by technology' (ibid.: 11). An illustration of 'the thinking edge' is to turn 'either/or' debates into 'both–and' syntheses. Chen lists 10; for example, rather than teacher-centred instruction or student-centred learning he offers a synthesis: 'teachers are vital in a student-centred classroom, but they play a different role when technology is the platform for content and collaboration' (ibid.: 23).
- The curriculum edge: 'the curriculum edge represents the growing trend of transforming and reorganising the most fundamental educational activities; what students are taught and how their learning is assessed. This edge recognises that today's curriculum has not kept up with the rapid pace of change in every discipline. The very definition of what a course is, how it is organised, and what it covers needs to be reconceived for advances in twenty-first century knowledge' (ibid.: 35).
- The technology edge: 'until every student has his or her own computer, the benefits of using them on a regular, ongoing basis are undercut' (ibid.: 87). Although he documented the extraordinary growth in the number of school students taking online courses, he is careful to acknowledge that attending a 'bricks-and-mortar' school will continue to be important. He has reservations about the position taken by writers such as Christensen, Johnson and Horn (2008) in *Disrupting Class* that online learning is a competitive force 'that finally will challenge the dominance of bricks-and-mortar schools relying on teachers in physical classrooms' (Chen, 2010: 111).
- The time/place edge: this 'represents the destruction of the old view of education happening within the four walls of the classroom' (ibid.: 139). Noteworthy are the illustrations provided by Chen of the benefits for those who do not or cannot attend school and who have benefited from learning after school and in summer programmes. He referred to one study 'in which law enforcement officials chose the expansion of after-school programs over hiring more police by a 4-to-1 margin to reduce youth-related crime' (ibid.: 149).
- The co-teaching edge: Chen acknowledged that teachers are the most important resource in securing the success of students, but described partnerships with others who can support the effort, including parents, professionals in other fields, and students.
- The youth edge: today's students 'are marching through our schools, carrying a transformational change in their pockets in the form of powerful handheld devices. Yet this generation, 95 percent of the stakeholders in education and the ones who stand the most to lose from a poor education, are often left out of the conversation about how to change it' (ibid.: 213). Chen provided the following description of the twenty-first-century learner:

In the traditional classroom, a student's main job is to sit, listen, take good notes, do the homework, memorise facts, figures, and formulae, and repeat this information back in quizzes and tests. The twenty-first century student uses technology to actively seek out reliable and high-quality information, analyse these sources, and utilise them in producing a product of his or her knowledge. In the traditional classroom, the teacher works hard and the students rest. In classrooms emulating the modern workplace, the students should be the ones working the hardest.

(Chen, 2010: 237)

Figure 9.1 illustrates the continuum of possibilities for each of the leading edges. How far a school or classroom or learning experience has moved along the continuum for each of the leading edges may be mapped, as illustrated in the three lines that connect each continuum. The dotted line at the left illustrates the traditional classroom in the traditional school: there is only one way in which knowledge is transmitted (either/or); the curriculum is traditional and largely discipline-based; few students, and probably few teachers, are empowered with current technology; formal learning occurs in the classroom

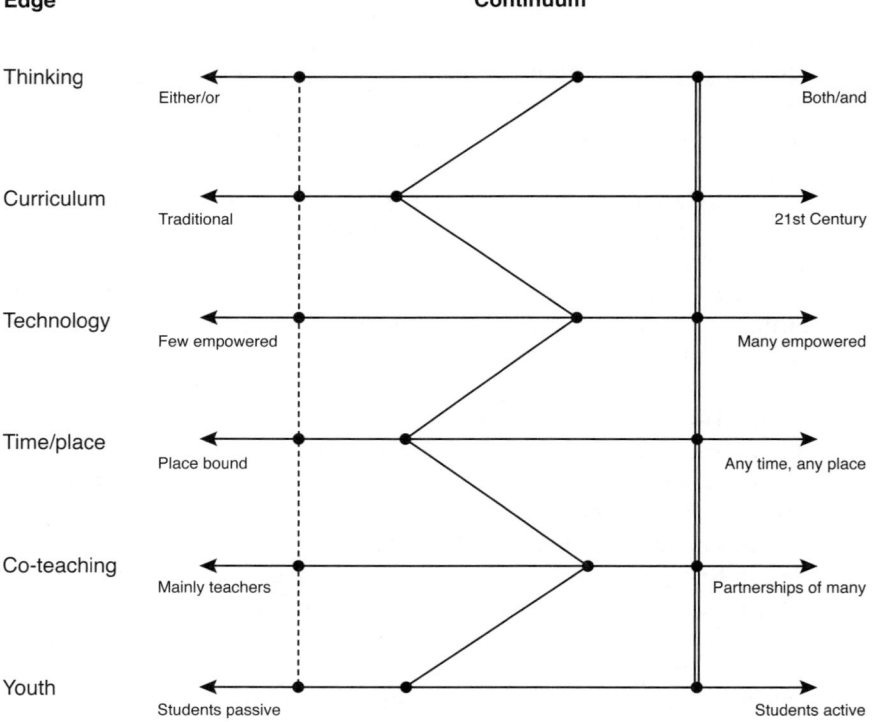

Figure 9.1 Mapping the leading edges of innovation (devised by the authors using classifications proposed by Chen, 2010).

and is delivered by the teacher alone; and students are largely passive recipients in the process, with teachers doing all the work.

The central solid line, which moves backwards and forwards across the various continua, illustrates a school that has moved some way towards developing a 'both–and' way of managing knowledge, but does so in a fairly traditional classroom where about half the students have access to up-to-date technology: most, but not all, of the formal learning occurs at the school site; the teacher is not the sole source of knowledge; those who work in other settings are brought in as experts on some occasions, either face-to-face or online; students are gaining their voice, they are not passive, but teachers still do much of the work; this classroom has made a modest start to the transformation of learning.

The double line at the right represents a school where learning has been transformed. Schools and students that have drawn on the resources of the Khan Academy and other organisations like it have moved in important ways towards the journey represented by the double line. More information about the Khan Academy is contained in a later section of the chapter but it is sufficient to note at this point that Salman Khan and others who have prepared for online access thousands of videos on a range of subjects, but especially mathematics, have joined the classroom teacher as co-teachers (Khan stresses that he does not replace the class teacher), with access at any time and at any place.

These illustrations do not convey the depth of knowledge and skill required to move from left to right across Figure 9.1. We know far more than ever before about how young people learn and the efficacy of different approaches to learning and teaching, and the support of learning and teaching. Building the capacity of the profession on these matters is critically important, as addressed in Chapter 13.

It is neither possible nor desirable for a school system to command and then control the rate of movement of schools along these continua. It can provide a lot of support, ranging from building the capacity of teachers to investing in the necessary infrastructure. It may conduct trials and pilots but these should give way to school decisions about the speed of change. The school should be self-transforming in the domain of learning.

The Department of Education and Early Childhood Development in Victoria has encouraged and supported developments that are consistent with the 'leading edges' described by Chen. For example, $2.35 million was invested in three programmes from 2006 to 2009: the Emerging Technology Program (58 projects in more than 200 schools), the Knowledge Bank (75 schools), and the Innovating with Technologies Research Program (30 schools). An evaluation of the initiative listed the impacts on learning and teaching:

- A shift from teacher-centred learning to student-centred learning, enabling teachers to develop more authentic tasks and accommodate different learning styles;

- More meaningful assessment, including peer review and publication to authentic audiences – both of which encouraged students to present higher quality work;
- Increased student engagement, as students were encouraged to construct new knowledge with teachers as coaches and mentors;
- More collaborative learning, with student connections formed with experts, parents and peers;
- Mitigation of disadvantage to geographically remote locations and students with special needs through assistive devices, virtual classroom technologies and gaming.

(Department of Education and Early Childhood Development [DEECD] [Victoria], 2010: 5)

Good work along these lines in Victoria and other systems has its limitations when an innovation is 'seriously disruptive'. An example is the appearance of the tablet computer, for example, the iPad. Formal trials or pilots were organised or contemplated in some systems but these proved unnecessary, if not futile, as schools quickly took charge of the agenda. They had no choice, as children arrived at schools with their own.

What are the implications for leaders at different levels of a school system? Chen provided a helpful starting point, building on the six leading edges of innovation:

[M]any education change agents, from thought leaders and policymakers to principals, teachers, and parents, as well as students themselves, are creating the types of schools and other learning environments that will equip today's students to become future leaders, citizens, and lifelong learners. Their work at the edges of the current school system is gradually moving to the centre. Yet progress has been slow to achieve scale, especially compared with the pace of technological and global change.

(Chen, 2010: 242)

The Cisco framework

A touchstone for considering these matters is presented in the Cisco report entitled *Equipping Every Learner for the 21st Century* (Cisco, 2008), which referred to three sequential but overlapping stages described as Education 1.0, Education 2.0 and Education 3.0. Some may not warm to the terminology but the descriptions attached to these designations and what change may entail are broadly accepted. Education 1.0 refers to learners and learning in the traditional school and this may generally correspond to the dotted line illustrated in Figure 9.1.

Education 2.0 refers to recent developments in which there has been a preoccupation with curriculum, teaching, leadership and accountability. There may be progress in the transformation of learning, as illustrated in the solid line in Figure 9.1. Education 3.0 refers to what has changed or should change in the twenty-first century, with a focus on so-called twenty-first-century skills, nurtured through a twenty-first-century pedagogy, enabled at least in part by technology. Education 3.0 is intended to achieve 'holistic transformation' (ibid.), as illustrated in the double line at the right in Figure 9.1.

The twenty-first-century skills are normally understood to include communication, teamwork, problem-solving, innovation and creativity. The designation is contentious because there is a good, if not irrefutable, case that good teaching and good learning in the traditional school (Education 1.0) nurtured these skills. The great achievements of humankind in any field one cares to name were underpinned by the nurturing and application of these skills.

Cisco summarised the major features and the challenges of Education 3.0 in the following terms:

> Our education systems continue to reinforce traditional approaches to teaching. Changing this will require leaders to develop a compelling vision of 21st century learning, communicate it with passion, and ensure that it is translated into action at all levels of the system. The transformation will need to be holistic; from government ministries to principals and classroom teachers. It will also require a holistic reform of education delivery, to align incentives and provide resources for teacher training, curriculum development, accountability, and assessment. The Education 2.0 pillars of system reform will need to be adapted significantly for Education 3.0.
>
> Teachers: Great teaching is at the heart of successful learning. Great 21st century teachers will weave 21st century skills into core subjects through new pedagogy, enlivened by collaborative technologies. New and proven instructional approaches and digital resources will become a core toolkit for 21st century teachers. This transformation will require new forms of teacher training and professional development.
>
> Curriculum and assessment: In the future, curricular reform will most likely be required to balance core subjects and new 21st century skills. This will also require fresh thinking about performance measures to overcome legitimate concerns that there has been limited progress toward recognising and rewarding skill development that cannot be detected in an end-of-term assessment.
>
> Accountability for outcomes: Accountability will be more essential than ever in 21st century education systems. School leaders will be accountable to students; questioning if school is staying relevant to their lives. Policy leaders will be accountable to employers and citizens; questioning if the system is effectively preparing young people to help meet national aspirations. It will also be important to measure accurately the impact of new skills and pedagogy in the classroom to bring about new and improved outcomes.

(Cisco, 2008: 15)

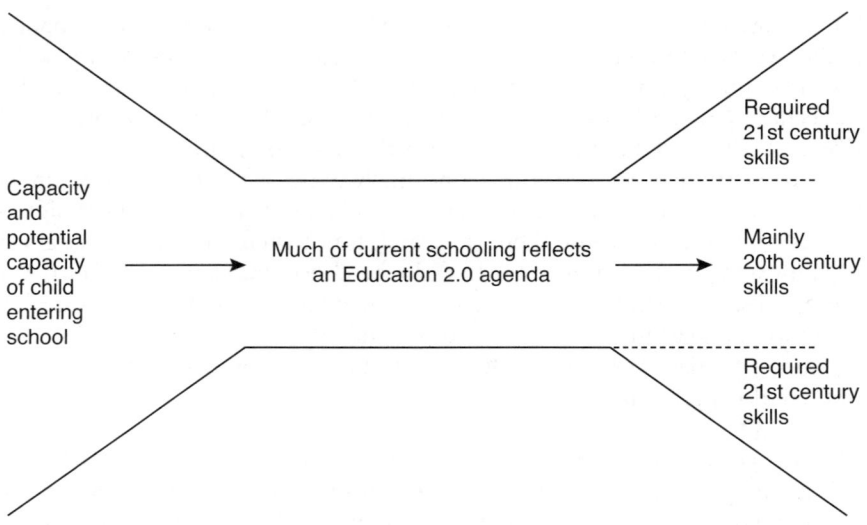

Figure 9.2 The constraining effects of Education 1.0 and Education 2.0 (adapting Zhao, n.d.).

Yong Zhao illustrated the constraints of Education 1.0 and Education 2.0 in the manner suggested in Figure 9.2. He described the capacities of young children in the early years of their development and then the narrowing effects of schooling that are slow to move to Education 3.0. They come out of the experience with mainly twentieth-century skills, into a world that requires twenty-first-century skills.

Zhao's illustration of the narrowing effects of Education 2.0 can also be applied to the consequences of the unrelenting focus on high-stakes, narrowly focused testing. There is distressing evidence that important aspects of the curriculum are being sidelined, especially the arts, as described in *Transforming Education through the Arts* (Caldwell and Vaughan, 2012). Caldwell and Vaughan reported research in highly disadvantaged settings in Australia, where it was found that students in upper primary school gained as much as one year in literacy as a consequence of their engagement in the arts, compared with their counterparts in an identically matched set of students in other schools in the same communities, who were not engaged in the arts. The arts programme was offered by a not-for-profit organisation (The Song Room) that provided the services of teaching artists free of charge to schools in communities that had made the decision to participate. In this respect, they had made a self-transforming decision. Details are contained in Chapter 12.

Michael Fullan raised doubts about what has been accomplished so far with the twenty-first-century skills. He and Nancy Watson assessed progress with the Cisco formulation and related projects in several jurisdictions and drew the following conclusion:

No matter how you cut it, we are not making progress on this agenda. By and large the goals are too vague, having a glitzy attraction. When we start down the pathway of specificity, the focus is on standards and assessment (which does help with clarity), but the crucial third pillar – pedagogy, or fostering actual learning – is neglected. And aside from its use in assessment schemes, which is a contribution, technology plays little role in *learning*, surely the main point of all this highfalutin fanfare.

(Fullan, 2012: 36)

Transformation or adaptation

Some changes are often presented as transformations but it is fair to ask if they are not adaptations of current approaches or examples of discrete innovations on one or a small number of 'edges' in the classification provided by Chen. Three examples are 'virtual learning', 'blended learning' and the 'flipped classroom'. These are of particular interest for another reason in countries where funds are limited or cutbacks are required. Can costs be reduced in a time of limited resources when these are adopted? Can funds be redeployed to other purposes? The summaries below include comments about costs.

In *virtual learning*, all instruction takes place online. Students continue to interact with teachers in real time, listen to lessons, do homework and complete activities but these are all conducted at a distance. Students may engage in virtual schooling part-time or full-time.

In *blended learning*, students attend a bricks-and-mortar school, where there is a mix of online and face-to-face learning. There are two models of blended learning: 'rotational' and 'flex'. Under the rotational variant, online learning is a fixed part of the school day within which students receive personalised technology-enabled instruction. A well-known example is Rocketship Education, a charter school network in California. Its features include parent empowerment, teacher development and individualised instruction.

> The Rocketship model generates approximately $500,000 in cost savings per school of 450 students, which can then be reallocated toward higher teacher salaries and professional development, among other things. Additionally, as a result of these cost savings, Rocketship schools are able to operate sustainably on traditional school funding and without additional philanthropic funds.
>
> (Battaglino *et al.*, 2012: 1424 of 3120)

With the flex variant of blended learning, students follow their own pathway, checking with a teacher when they seek answers or assistance. This means that it is difficult to estimate costs. An example of this model is the Flex Academy in Florida (K–12) where the educator-to-student ratio is about 1:25, with class sizes typically in the range five to eight.

Battaglino, Haldeman and Laurans (ibid.: 1451 of 3120) provided estimates of costs for the traditional model (excluding central administration costs averaged across the United States for all levels of schooling) ($10,000), virtual model (full-time high school students) ($6,500) and blended model (middle school) ($8,900). Estimates are standardised to a school of approximately 500 full-time students. These estimates were prepared from public documents and conversations with experts and vendors. They reflected a wide range of costs; for example, costs for the virtual model range from about $4,000 to about $9,000 per student.

Battaglino and colleagues make clear that there are uncertainties when it comes to costing variants of these models.

> Amidst the excitement and promise of new virtual- and blended-school models, it is easy to lose sight of the fact that online learning is an immature, still-developing sector. No discussion of the economics of online learning is complete without acknowledgement of the changes the field has experienced over the past decade – and the changes that are undoubtedly on the way over the next decade and beyond.
>
> (ibid.: 1677 of 3120)

Michael Horn, co-founder of the Innosight Institute (a non-profit think tank on education and innovation) and a co-author with Clayton Christensen of *Disrupting Class* (Christensen *et al.*, 2008), joined with his colleague Heather Staker to provide a well-balanced statement on the costs and benefits of blended learning:

> Our own view is that blended learning will and should help schools – and ultimately the public – save money. But the overriding reason to adopt a blended-learning model isn't because of its cost savings, but instead because of the benefits for students that can result. Ultimately blended learning should help schools and policymakers move our education system to a student-centric one that educates children both more effectively and efficiently. And just as there is no one-size-fits-all way to educate a child, there will be no one-size-fits-all way to implement blended learning.
>
> (Horn and Staker, 2012)

There is growing interest in the 'flipped classroom', originating in the United States (Bergmann and Sams, 2012) but with early adoption by some schools in other countries. The flipped classroom is:

> a reversed teaching model that delivers instruction at home through interactive, teacher-created videos and moves 'homework' to the classroom. Moving lectures outside of the classroom allows teachers to spend more 1:1 time with each student. Students have the opportunity to ask questions and work through problems with the guidance of their

teachers and the support of their peers – creating a collaborative learning environment.

(TechSmith Corporation, 2012)

There do not appear to be cost savings in this model. There are increased costs associated with the preparation and delivery of content. There will be economies in the longer term, especially if the flipped classroom is combined with either virtual or blended learning.

There are no costs for the school, teacher and student in drawing on the resources of the Khan Academy, referred to briefly in an earlier section of the chapter to illustrate the transformation of learning. They are typically used in the flipped classroom style. Salman Khan started in modest fashion in 2004, providing support from a distance for his cousin using the 'Doodle' function in Yahoo!. At the time of writing, he and his colleagues have produced more than 3,000 videos on a range of subjects, with take-up by hundreds of thousands of students and teachers on an 'any time, any place' basis. Khan was supported in the early stages by the Bill and Melinda Gates Foundation with a grant of $1.7 million. Bill Gates described Khan as 'a true education pioneer' whose impact 'might be truly incalculable' (Cummings, 2012). Khan has relinquished his role as a hedge fund analyst to work full-time on this initiative, with an expanding team based in Silicon Valley. *The One World School House: Education Reimagined* (Khan, 2012) describes the transformation of learning that is now unfolding. A capacity for school self-transformation is a prerequisite.

Michael Fullan suggested that the Khan Academy does not involve the transformation of learning: 'Khan has not invented a new way to teach math, but has improved the delivery of the old way'. He praised the approach to delivery: 'Khan is an incredibly great 20th century pedagogue using 21st century technology (and not the most advanced at that)' (Fullan, 2012: 38). Fullan provided an account of several projects in Ontario that have promise of successful system-wide scale-up.

The Khan Academy is capturing the headlines but there are other players including the non-profit edX, and Udacity and Coursera, which are for-profit. The field is certain to flourish in the years ahead and be irresistible for schools and students.

Is there still a place for direct instruction?

Where does direct instruction fit into the leading edges described by Chen? At first sight, this will probably be found at the left of the continua in Figure 9.1, especially time/place, co-teaching and youth. This is not necessarily the case. John Hattie's description of direct instruction is helpful in this regard. His findings on direct instruction illustrate the importance of balance. He set the scene by describing a stereotyped, if not misleading, view of direct instruction:

Every year I present lectures to teacher education students and find they are already indoctrinated with the mantra 'constructivism good, direct instruction bad'. When I show them the results of these meta-analyses, they are stunned, and they often become angry at having been given an agreed set of truths and commandments against direct instruction. Too often, what the critics mean by direct instruction is didactic teacher-led talking from the front; this should *not* be confused with the very successful 'direct instruction method'.

(Hattie, 2009: 204–205)

It is helpful to draw on Hattie's description of the processes of direct instruction: (1) specification of learning intentions; (2) delineation of success criteria; (3) building commitment and engagement among students; (4) describing how the teacher should present the lesson; (5) guided practice by students; (6) closure by the teacher; and (7) independent practice by students (ibid.: 206).

In a nutshell: The teacher decides the learning intentions and success criteria, makes them transparent to the students, demonstrates them by modelling, evaluates if they understand what they have been told by checking for understanding, and re-telling them what they have been told by tying it all together with closure.

(ibid.)

An example of evidence provided by Hattie that arose in his meta-analyses is the following:

In only one approach, the Direct Instruction (DI) model, were participating students near or at national norms in math and language and close to national norms in reading. Students in . . . the other 8 approaches – discovery learning, language experience, developmentally appropriate practices and open education – often performed worse than the control group. This poor performance came in spite of tens of thousands of additional dollars provided for each classroom each year.

(ibid.)

It takes only a moment of reflection to realise that a richer form of direct instruction can be part of most of the leading edges of innovation described by Chen, including any time, any place learning.

Is there still a place for a national curriculum?

Some countries have invested in developing a national curriculum when none had existed before. An example is Australia, which, until recently, was in a set of three out of 23 jurisdictions around the Pacific that had not done so (the others are Canada and the United States). There was a sense of achievement because agreement had to be reached among federal and state governments and this occurred more than two decades after the first efforts were made. The outcome is a national curriculum which is too large to print; it is an online curriculum, which, if printed, would run to thousands of pages. There are some impressive features of the Australian curriculum, including the way in which resources for learning and teaching have been developed to match it, and these are also available online.

The United States has not been able to do the same, although there has been general agreement on Common Core State Standards. In other countries that have laboured to gain such agreement, the general trend is to reduce compliance requirements and allow schools more discretion. England is a good example. Finland, on the other hand, has been able to perform outstandingly well with a very broad curriculum, which in its printed form is no more than a few hundred pages in length for all subjects across all levels of schooling.

It is fair to ask if the effort has been worth the cost, especially in the case of Australia. On balance, the answer is likely to be in the affirmative but further change is inevitable if the country is to have a first-class system of education in an era of globalisation. A school in inner Melbourne, a metropolis of about 4 million, will probably have more in common, as far as curriculum is concerned, with a school in a city such as London than it has with a school in a remote location, such as Alice Springs. In this respect, it is worth reviewing what has been accomplished in efforts to create an international curriculum, the best known being the International Baccalaureate (IB).

The International Baccalaureate Organisation (IBO) is a non-profit education foundation headquartered in Geneva. It was founded in 1968 at the International School of Geneva. It was initially designed to offer a single programme to serve the needs of internationally mobile students preparing for university. The IBO now offers three programmes worldwide: in 2012, at 3,567 schools in 145 countries for 1,098,000 students. The three programmes are the Primary Years Programme (PYP), established in 1997 for students aged 3 to 12; the Middle Years Programme (MYP), established in 1994 for students aged 11 to 16; and the Diploma, established at the outset in 1968 for students in the final years of secondary school.

The number of schools in programmes offered by the IBO is increasing rapidly. Data are available for enrolments across the world in February 2010, as summarised in Table 9.1, and these show a global increase over 12 months across all three programmes of 12.18 per cent, with the highest rate of growth (24.28 per cent) being in the PYP. The number of offerings exceeds the number of schools, since some schools offer more than one programme.

Of the 2,822 schools offering programmes in 2009, by far the largest number (1,072) was in the United States, followed by Canada (290), the United Kingdom (217) and Australia (127). The total of 1,706 schools in these four countries represents 60.45 per cent of all IB schools worldwide.

Table 9.1 Increase in the number of schools in programmes of the IBO from 2009 to 2010

Programme	2009	2010	Increase (%)
Primary (PYP)	495	615	24.28
Middle (MYP)	679	748	10.16
Diploma	1873	2055	9.72
Total	3047	3418	12.18

Although the first IB schools were predominantly international private schools, the IBO reports that more than half of all schools across the world offering its programmes are now public schools. In the United Kingdom, for example, of the 132 schools that offered the IB Diploma in 2008, 56 per cent came from the state sector whereas 44 per cent came from the private sector. Australia remains an exception to this pattern, as most IB schools in this country are in the private non-government sector. It is only recently that state governments have permitted public schools to offer an IB programme.

In general terms, IB programmes are intended to 'help develop the intellectual, personal, emotional and social skills to live, learn and work in a rapidly changing globalizing world' (IBO, 2012). Its mission is more specific: 'to develop inquiring, knowledgeable and caring young people who help to create a better and more peaceful world through intercultural understanding and respect' (IBO, 2012).

Students taking the Diploma must choose six subjects. There must be one subject from each of Groups 1 to 5: Language, Second Language, Individual and Societies, Experimental Sciences, and Mathematics and Computer Science. The sixth subject may be chosen from Group 6, which is the Arts group, for which five subjects are available – Dance, Film, Music, Theatre and Visual Arts (Dance is currently being piloted by the IBO) – or it may be another subject from Groups 1 to 5. Subjects are offered at either standard or higher level. Students are normally required to undertake at least three subjects at the higher level. In addition to these six subjects, students are required to successfully complete three core elements: Extended Essay (EE); Theory of Knowledge (TOK); and Creativity, Action, Service (CAS).

National curricula and the IB will continue to have important roles to play in the immediate future, but it may be that schools should now develop their own curricula, choosing or adapting from what is on offer around the world. A capacity to do so is likely to be important over the next 25 years as self-managing schools become self-transforming schools. Yong Zhao warned of the dangers of a narrowly constructed curriculum in *World Class Learners* in his criticism of the core curriculum that has been adopted in the United States whereby 'the floor, that is the basic essential knowledge, becomes the ceiling'.

At best all these exercises will be a futile waste of resources and opportunities. At worst, these actions will lead to irreversible damage. This is because our children will face a society that has been fundamentally changed by globalization and technology while the efforts to develop and implement nationally and internationally homogenised curriculum are working on fixing an educational paradigm that has outlived its utility

(Zhao, 2012: 42)

Setting the stage for a focus on funding

Several adaptations of approaches to learning were briefly described earlier in the chapter and the issue of whether these constituted a transformation was raised. The issue of costs was also introduced. Chris Dede and John Richards addressed both issues in their conclusion to a comprehensive collection of articles on the possibilities of customising classroom learning for each student. In *Digital Teaching Platforms* (Dede and Richards, 2011), they concluded that 'educational transformation is coming not only because of the increasing ineffectiveness of schools in meeting society's needs – though that is certainly a good reason – but even more due to the unaffordability of the current classroom model' (ibid.: 208).

What Dede and Richards described as 'the current classroom model' continues to pervade the scene in most systems of public education. It is therefore critical that such systems develop optimal models for allocating scarce funds to their schools. Such models have been developed for public schools in Victoria in recent years. Chapters 10 and 11 provide detailed accounts of these developments in this system of self-managing schools.

Important messages for policymakers and practitioners

1 The 'leading edges' of innovation that will cohere to enable the transformation of learning to occur have been identified. Schools can make plans accordingly and map their progress, though the details may not be known, even in the short term.
2 The narrowing effects of an unrelenting focus on high-stakes testing are pernicious, leading to the sidelining of critically important areas of learning, especially the arts. There is still a place for direct instruction but how it will be implemented will change as learning is transformed.
3 Despite the large effort and substantial costs involved, a national curriculum or a core curriculum will soon give way to a global curriculum of a kind that the self-transforming school can choose from or adapt, or it can develop its own.

10 Financial capital and transformation

This is the first of four chapters that are framed by the concept of capital, referring to the rich range of resources that a self-managing school may draw on to become a self-transforming school. The use of capital in this sense was explained in Chapter 3, based on findings in the International Project to Frame the Transformation of Schools. The four chapters are organised in this way: financial capital (Chapters 10 and 11), social and spiritual capital (Chapter 12) and intellectual capital (Chapter 13).

Chapters 10 and 11 were written by co-author Jim Spinks, hence the use of the first person in several places. Much of his work in recent times has been conducted in Victoria, Australia, which has been at the forefront of efforts worldwide to develop a student needs-based approach to the allocation of funds to schools. This is the fourth co-authored book by one or both of the current authors that have included detailed accounts of developments in Victoria, the others being *The Future of Schools: Lessons from the Reform of Public Education* (Caldwell and Hayward, 1998), in which the former minister Don Hayward described his oversight of higher levels of autonomy for public schools and the introduction of student needs-based funding; *Beyond the Self-Managing School* (Caldwell and Spinks, 1998), which summarised research on the links between higher levels of autonomy and outcomes for students; and *Raising the Stakes: From Improvement to Transformation in the Reform of Schools* (Caldwell and Spinks, 2008), in which Jim Spinks described and illustrated how models for needs-based funding can be designed and implemented at the system and school levels. In each book, developments in Victoria were set in the context of global trends in self-management.

The reader will note the change of pace, so to speak, in Chapters 10 and 11, with the sharp focus on funding and the relatively detailed attention to criteria for allocating funds to schools. This is a major issue in public education around the world and governments in many countries are being challenged to distribute scarce resources through effective student needs-based funding mechanisms. The authors intend these two chapters to be a guide to policy-makers and practitioners alike, to the former because they are challenged to design the best approaches and to the latter because they should expect, indeed insist, on the best – these chapters provide evidence to strengthen the case. Optimal approaches are prerequisites for success in self-transformation.

Closing the gap

If there is to be success for all students in all settings, transformation calls for closing the achievement gap between students in low-performing schools, mainly serving lower socio-economic families, and those in high-performing schools, mainly serving their affluent counterparts. Schools do not produce the gap in achievement. It is already there when students begin school. Students destined for lower outcomes arrive at school with lesser language capabilities (vocabularies of 3,000 words as opposed to 8,000–10,000 words), lower expectations and values that do not necessarily translate into the pursuit of school learning.

With life chances closely related to school success, it becomes the role of the school, together with the family, the community and the nation, to gain success for every student irrespective of circumstances. 'Closing the achievement gap' is easy to say and an attractive concept but difficult to do. It can be done and has been done by many schools in different countries but can it be done systemically across whole groups of low-performing schools? The task is not just to achieve a rate of improvement equivalent to the rate of the average school. The rate of improvement must be significantly above those of other schools for the gap to close. It is essential to accelerate the rate of achievement for these low-performing students so that three years' worth of learning is achieved in any two-year period. With this achievement comes transformation.

Given the nature of the task, is financial capital a factor in the equation? It is acknowledged that the critical factors in transformation are teacher quality, relevance of learning and teaching strategies, and leadership. However, the recruitment of talent and the maintenance of quality in relation to teachers and school leadership, as well as relevant curriculum development, are going to cost money, particularly when these factors are required in abundance to accelerate the rate of improvement beyond the realm of the average school. No football team in a premier league is going to succeed if dependent on local raffles or other low-revenue approaches to secure additional funds.

To be fair to governments across the world, where significant increases in resources have failed to close the achievement gap, there must be recognition that popularly motivated but unsuccessful solutions, such as reducing class sizes, have to be resisted. Advocacy groups operating within the political arena are sometimes misguided in this respect. On one occasion, I was asked to consult with an organisation advocating greater expenditure on primary education in a very large system of schools. The premise was that 17 per cent of students transferring from primary schools to secondary schools lacked sufficient language skills to succeed. No one disagreed with this premise. However, there had to be concern over their proposal to deploy the additional resources equally across all primary schools, in relation to enrolment. No cognisance was taken of the fact that the majority of the students in the 17 per cent were concentrated in a minority of schools. The proposal failed.

In addition, there is a need to be able to quantify the level of resourcing required for transformation, and how it should be deployed in relation to student characteristics.

What level of resourcing is sufficient to achieve transformation?

Unfortunately, no system of schools has yet achieved the distinction of success for all irrespective of circumstance, although some come close. However, many systems are addressing the issue and, within such systems, success is being achieved by significant numbers of individual schools. These occurrences provide the opportunity to identify and measure the cost of success and the factors underpinning the success. This exercise has been attempted by many but usually through a small sample of schools. In addition, there is always the impossibility of quantifying the cultural factors that provide the context. As a young principal in the late 1980s, I visited Japan, beguiled by the fact that 80 per cent of students in that country met the entry criteria for Australian universities. I was to be utterly astonished by the innovation in Japanese education for that year: on one Saturday in each month there was to be no school, but tutoring outside school hours was to continue! How could my students compete on 25 hours of scheduled learning per week for 40 weeks a year? The old adage that 'it is the quality of the learning and teaching and not the time spent learning that counts' is seriously flawed. Recent visits to high-performing schools in Shanghai and Chengdu were very impressive and the time spent learning equally so. Even visits to schools in Finland found the learning day being extended for underperforming students in primary school. Parents could choose: before school or after school.

Measuring the sufficiency of resources to close the achievement gap cannot ignore the cultural context. Published expenditure data by country are of little value in establishing funding models for specific systems. Best practice requires any system to measure sufficiency levels through its own research with its own schools that have been transformed, or have made the most progress towards transformation. Such research also needs to address the contributing factors of leadership, teacher quality and the relevance of the learning and teaching programmes to the learners.

Issues constraining the research effort

Several issues contribute to the difficulty of undertaking research to identify sufficiency of resources to close the gap in all schools. First, there is the problem of measuring achievement to identify acceleration of the learning rate. Second, there is the problem of identifying all the resources contributing to success. Some schools are more able than others to access funds from 'other' sources, and authorities are reluctant to include these resources in publications and analyses. Even in high-performing public schools in Australia serving affluent communities, families often voluntarily contribute up to $2,000 per student. This represents an approximate increase of nearly 30 per cent over the resources available from government sources to fund the operation of the school. This additional support overshadows additional government funding to other schools to address high needs.

A third issue in identifying a sufficiency of resources to underpin transformation is isolating and quantifying the relative significance of each factor, including levels of funding. Schooling is not an activity where controlling, isolating some factors to measure the impact of others is an ethical possibility. Whoever said that 'reforming education is like re-designing and re-building an aircraft in flight' knew their subject. Compare the use of placebos in medical research.

A fourth issue is the realisation that, contrary to an often expressed popular opinion, high-performing schools serving affluent communities do not necessarily provide the learning and teaching programme and leadership models to transform the underperforming schools serving low socio-economic communities. Students in the former case bring to school a backpack of values, expectations, capacities, motivations and strategies geared to success. Students in the latter also carry a backpack but the contents are very different. A successful school operation and curriculum require constructs that are contextually derived. This situation was vividly demonstrated on my visit to a number of schools with high proportions of indigenous students in the outback of the Northern Territory in Australia. On any measure, indigenous students seriously underperform and attempts to rectify the situation over many years have not succeeded. The visit demonstrated that this situation could be changed by abandoning attempts to find 'the solution' and instead recognising that solutions could be found by empowering local communities and school leaders to work together and that solutions could be unique to each community. For example, attendance is a critical school issue so why not change the organisation of school days to fit the local culture and environment? The monsoon-derived 'wet season' (approximately six months) confines families to their home location, whereas the 'dry season' (the other six months) enables travel. Traditionally, families travel in the dry season to visit relatives and to participate in cultural activities. Traditionally, schools operate across all seasons but with the major summer school break within the wet. Some more innovative communities have chosen to concentrate school operations in the wet season, with consequent improvement in attendance. They have even moved to extend school hours and days for those students unlikely to achieve a 90 per cent attendance rate through cultural circumstances. School provision is following culture, not conflicting with culture. It is so obvious, but school systems are often locked into set modes of universal provision.

The case of Victoria

These four issues confounding the research possibilities need to be addressed if levels of sufficiency in government funding of public schools are to be identified. The state of Victoria in Australia provides an opportunity across a system of 530,000 students and 1,550 schools. For the past 30 years, successive governments have been endeavouring to close the achievement gap between low- and high-performing public schools with little success. A search for a model of how to govern, fund and operate schools has accompanied, if not always driven, the agenda for excellence and equity. Recent developments have intensified the agenda for system transformation, including the search for and development of specific strategies to transform schools for students who have traditionally underperformed.

A past problem in researching funding sufficiency to achieve excellence and equity of outcomes in Victoria, as elsewhere, has been the application of universal funding models across all schools. Although there has been differentiation on funding need, the overall level of equity funding has been low and insufficient to drive transformation. The input of commonwealth government funding to high-needs schools has changed this situation to some degree. The National Partnership Program (NPP) has significantly increased equity-based funding in some high-needs schools, at least for a four-year period. It provided the opportunity to assess the extent to which increased support results in transformation. It is also opportune that new measures of student outcomes are becoming available, as well as the identification and implementation of specific strategies that are successful in high-needs schools.

The possibility of systems now being able to ascertain the cost of transformation across a system of schools is explored in the case of Victoria. The context is first established by referring to the Victorian public school funding model and its development, together with ways of measuring its effectiveness in underpinning school transformation.

Funding public schools in Victoria

In the mid-1980s, steps were taken in Victoria to devise a school funding model that was fair (students with equal needs received equal support), equitable in terms of outcomes (students with greater needs received additional support) and transparent. It was the public demand for transparency that probably most drove the initiatives for a systemic funding model that was ethical and defensible in the public arena. Previous distribution of education resources certainly did not stand up to this increasing scrutiny. The Victorian situation at the beginning of these initiatives was no different from the situation in other states and territories across Australia.

The first attempts to develop a coherent model centred on an enrolment and school-type based staffing entitlement or quota (teaching and non-teaching) plus an operational grant. There was some recognition of socio-economic need as well as location and school size. Support for students with disabilities was on an individual student basis and outside the school budget. Many jurisdictions in Australia have still not progressed very far past this initial situation.

Through successive steps, marked significantly by the development of the School Global Budget in the mid-1990s, Victoria has now developed a school resourcing model known as the Student Resource Package (SRP). The model and its development were described in *Raising the Stakes* (Caldwell and Spinks, 2008). The SRP is generally recognised as a world leader in school resourcing and is frequently studied by jurisdictions pursuing coherent systemic improvement. Strengths of the SRP are that it is entirely student-focused; that is, it addresses the nature and needs of the students within each school in determining a global budget. Staff selected are an actual cost against the school budget. Many systems claim to have global budgets but, in reality, allocations remain as quotas of staff plus an operations budget. The cost of staff is expressed as an average and, when translated into real costs, schools with the same enrolments and student profiles can have very different actual costs dependent on the staffing profiles. As teachers almost invariably move to lower-needs schools as their salaries/experience increase, not only expertise but also resources concentrate in schools with the least need.

The Victorian and English models of school funding focus entirely on the student profile, and the staff profile does not become the 'elephant in the room' when trying to address equity of student outcomes as well as excellence. At this point it must be remarked that, although Victoria and England have advanced models for funding schools, the jury is still out on determining sufficient allocations based on equity of outcomes to drive school transformation system-wide.

The nature and development of the Victorian school-funding model has always had to meet the test of transparency and is therefore very well documented and in the public domain (www.education.vic.gov.au/management/srp/guide/studentbased).

The development of the Victorian SRP was accomplished in close association with the development of higher levels of school autonomy. Victorian schools exercise autonomy on a scale unparalleled in other Australian states and territories.

The degree to which the Victorian SRP meets its purpose to fund schools in general, and high-needs schools in particular, is addressed in Chapter 11. The following section specifically addresses endeavours to calculate the level of additional funding required to support the successful transformation of high-needs schools.

Determining sufficiency of equity funding to underpin transformation

The implementation of the National Assessment Program – Literacy and Numeracy tests (www.nap.edu.au/naplan/naplan.html) across Australia provided an opportunity to assess the success of endeavours to transform schools. NAPLAN is an initiative of the Australian government in cooperation with the states and territories to assess the ongoing capacity of students in the essential skills to progress through school and to successfully participate in post-school life. Assessments are conducted and reported through an independent body called the Australian Curriculum, Assessment and Reporting Authority (www.acara.edu.au).

All students across Australia in Years 3, 5, 7 and 9 are assessed annually in reading, persuasive writing, language conventions (spelling, grammar and punctuation) and numeracy. School outcomes are reported annually on the My School website (www.myschool.edu.au). Reporting does not involve league tables, although comparative data on 'like schools' in an Australia-wide context are readily available. Data on any school are also readily available and an intention is to provide information to families when making a choice of school. More comprehensive data are provided to governments and schools to inform progress in learning programmes.

Correlation of school NAPLAN data, with additional provision for high-needs schools through the NPP, enable exploration of the improvement/cost relationship in situations where schools are required to construct new approaches to learning and teaching that lead to improvement.

Doubt can be (and is) cast on any endeavour to measure student learning progress across schools and educational systems. NAPLAN has received its fair share of this treatment. However, NAPLAN is the only national measure currently available. It was developed under the leadership of outstanding international experts, including Professor Barry McGaw, Chair of ACARA and former head of the education division at OECD, and Dr Peter Hill, former Chief Executive Officer of ACARA. The efficacy of NAPLAN data has been greatly improved by the availability of matched cohort data for the 2009 to 2011 period. Matched cohort data for any school eliminates students who have left the school during that period and those who have newly enrolled during the period. Measurement of improvement is confined to those students attending the school for the whole of the period.

The challenge of transformation, or closing the achievement gap across Australian schools, is well illustrated in Figure 10.1, presented in the Gonski Report, drawing on data from ACARA (Australian Government, 2011: 114).

Figure 10.1 demonstrates achievement in Years 3, 5, 7 and 9 reading across Australia in relation to defined levels of parent education, which are good predictors of student potential achievement. Within the Victorian public school system, potential achievement is predicted by the Student Family Occupation (SFO) index. The SFO and levels of parental education are equally acknowledged as good predictors of student achievement.

The data clearly show the learning gap existing in the first years, which is maintained throughout the years of schooling. The pattern does not change. It is of some comfort to educational providers that the gap in Year 3 does close fractionally by Year 9, if the scale of measure can be considered to be consistent throughout the range. However, the challenge for educational jurisdictions is to significantly close the gap and this requires a transformation in student learning in high-needs schools in particular.

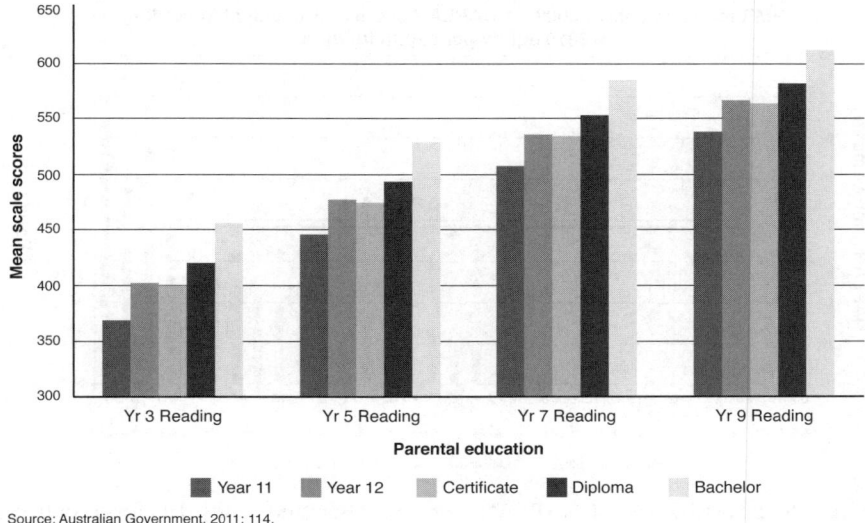

Source: Australian Government, 2011: 114.

Figure 10.1 Achievement in NAPLAN 2010 Reading by parental education.

Transformation of student achievement in high-needs schools can be achieved only if the rate of learning is accelerated for these students; that is, students are required to achieve three years of learning during each school period of two years. This is no easy task and requires the highest quality of teaching. The acceleration of the rate of learning is being pursued particularly by National Partnership Schools in receipt of significant increases in needs-based funding. NAPLAN-matched cohort data enable the measurement of learning rates achieved in comparison with other schools.

Figure 10.2 depicts NAPLAN and equity funding data for the Northern Metropolitan Educational Region (NMR) secondary colleges in Victoria. NMR provides school education for 82,500 students in 206 schools and colleges. NMR serves the northern suburbs of Melbourne and encompasses an extraordinary diversity of cultures. There is a high proportion of high-needs schools.

The NMR secondary colleges are shown in SFO index order and this index is critical to funding allocations. Table 10.1 contains the relativities among occupational groups that are used to construct measures on the SFO index.

The SFO index order of the NMR colleges in Figure 10.2 commences with the lowest on the left (affluent communities) and progresses in index order to the right. College names are not included.

Colleges labelled 'BM' on the horizontal axis have an SFO index below the state median of 0.05036 in 2012 and do not receive equity funding. Colleges labelled 'AM' are above the state median and do receive equity funding, shown as a column for eligible colleges which represents the equity allocation per enrolled student. The allocation consists of three components with each

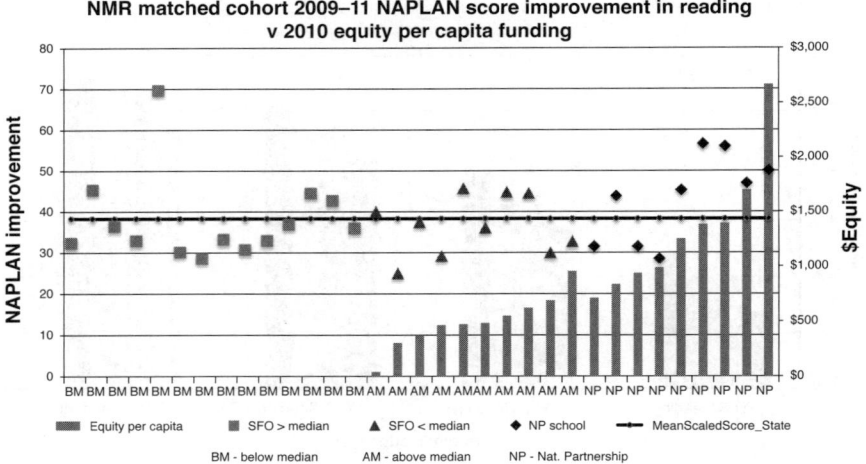

Figure 10.2 NMR 2009–11 NAPLAN-matched cohort and equity data for secondary colleges.

Table 10.1 Relativities among occupational groups in the SFO index (the school SFO index is the average of the weightings for all students)

Category	Occupational group	Weighting
A	Senior management and professionals	0.00
B	Business managers and associate professionals	0.25
C	Skilled workers	0.50
D	Unskilled workers	0.75
E	Long-term unemployed and pensioners	1.00

being driven by the SFO index, and other data (student age/outcomes) in two cases. Colleges labelled 'NP' on the far right are above the state median and receive NPP equity-based funding in addition to the equity funding that is an entitlement for all schools above the median. The horizontal line at just below 40 on the vertical axis represents the state average in NAPLAN reading improvement for matched cohorts of students from 2009 (in Year 7) to 2011 (in Year 9).

The scattergram indicates the rate of improvement for each college on the matched cohort NAPLAN data; also for 2009 and 2011. The improvements for BM colleges not entitled to equity funding are depicted by box symbols whereas those for AM colleges entitled to equity funding, but not NPP funding, are depicted by triangle symbols. Improvements for NP colleges receiving NPP equity funding as well as other equity allocations are depicted by diamond symbols.

Points of interest

It is emphasised that the NAPLAN scores that form the basis of comparisons in Figure 10.2 indicate the units of improvement for students from 2009 to 2011. Actual scores (not shown) follow the pattern of a direct relationship between low SFO indices and higher achievement scores.

The improvement rates for the advantaged colleges (not in receipt of equity funding) are clustered around the state average, as expected. The one outlier with exceptional improvement was previously underperforming. Seven out of 10 of the AM colleges receiving equity funding, but not the additional NPP equity funding, are maintaining their position in relation to the state average (horizontal line) or are falling further behind – the achievement gap is increasing. Only 3 out of 10 of the AM colleges are closing the gap.

The improvement rates of the NPP colleges receiving the higher equity allocations through the addition of the NPP funding are of most interest. Six of nine are improving beyond expectations and closing the achievement gap. Three of nine remain below the state average and their additional NPP equity funding was at a lower level. Given that the normal expectation is that the gap between low and high SFO index schools will be maintained, the acceleration rate in improvement of two-thirds of the NPP colleges is above expectations. All NPP, and many of the other, colleges had access to a regional programme for improvement but the best gains are among those colleges with the higher rates of equity funding.

The data suggest that the additional equity funding provided by the NPP was sufficient to make a difference and enabled an estimate to be made of the level of equity funding required to close the achievement gap. It is probable that equity funding should be in the order of at least $1,200 per enrolled student in high-needs schools. This represents an additional equity allocation of 17 per cent above the standard student rate across all students in Victorian secondary schools.

Although the NMR data are encouraging in establishing an estimate of the required equity funding rates, it now requires up-scaling to include the same data from the other Victorian educational regions. However, care needs to be exercised in the selection of data to be included to ensure that all the data comes from the same context. NMR has developed and pursued a rigorous and systematic improvement programme for at least five years. All regions have accessed NPP funding but have followed different improvement paths.

Transformation in relation to incremental improvement requires not just more money but high-quality teaching and leadership and specifically designed learning and teaching programmes sustained over a significant period. This has been the case in NMR, where Wayne Craig, then Regional Director, had a strong aspiration to create not only the possibility of individually transforming schools but, more importantly, a system of transforming schools.

Documenting the journey to transformation

Craig was joined by Professor David Hopkins, an international expert in school improvement (Hopkins, 2007), who served successive Secretaries of State for Education in England, and Associate Professor John Munro, an Australian expert from the University of Melbourne, to edit and contribute to *Powerful Learning* (Hopkins *et al.*, 2011) that documented the processes and outcomes of interventions in the region. There were contributions from other leaders in the field. Hopkins also documented the journey in 'Powerful learning: Taking education reform to scale in the Northern Metropolitan Region' (Hopkins and Craig, 2011). *Curiosity and Powerful Learning* (Northern Metropolitan Region, n.d.) included a guide for schools in implementing the approach. The following 'coda' for powerful learning was offered:

> It is not just an accurate description of a strategy that focuses directly on enhancing the learning of all students in the region; it is also an idea that is capturing the imagination of teachers, parents and young people around the world. It is an idea that has its roots in the best practice of the teaching profession, and it has the potential to make every young person's learning experience stretching, creative, fun and successful. It reflects the current drive to tailor schooling to individual need, interest and aptitude, so making it increasingly personalised.
>
> (Hopkins *et al.*, 2011: 37)

Case studies of strategies for transformation

John Fawkner and Glenroy colleges are among those in NMR transforming the learning outcomes and life chances for their students. Both are exemplars of powerful learning in practice.

The strategies of these two colleges to address the issue of teacher quality are of particular interest. Both colleges have high-needs students from very diverse backgrounds. Student outcomes were low and both colleges could be described as being 'in decline'. Enrolments were falling, community perceptions were not encouraging and they were not attractive to staff in the competitive staffing environment of the highly autonomous schools of Victoria.

New principals were appointed to both colleges in 2008–2009. 'Project Excellence' was created by Wayne Craig to work in conjunction with the Powerful Learning initiatives to transform these two colleges. Teacher quality was a critical issue for progress. Powerful Learning focused on high-quality learning and teaching, and on the continuing improvement of learning and teaching through professional training, but it was decided that both colleges needed an initial impetus to enhance teacher quality, with an emphasis on passion and commitment. A bold decision was made for both colleges to be closed by the Department of Education and Early Childhood Development (DEECD) and new colleges created. Existing staff were able to apply for a position in the new schools and, if they were unsuccessful, the region undertook to provide assistance in finding alternative appointments.

Although similar endeavours have been used in England and the United States to give an initial impetus to the transformation of low-performing schools, this approach to changing the nature of the staff in John Fawkner and Glenroy colleges is a first for public schools in Victoria and, probably, in Australia. It required an alignment of a number of critical stakeholders, including the college councils, DEECD, NMR, staff and the Australian Education Union (AEU).

John Fawkner retained 60 per cent of staff and recruited the remaining 40 per cent. Glenroy retained 80 per cent. Both colleges expressed general satisfaction with the outcome. The stakeholder agreement prior to implementation included the requirement of an evaluation before similar strategies would be adopted in the future.

Principals sometimes express interest in this approach to initiating transformation. However, the Principal and Assistant Principal of Glenroy College recommend caution. First, there is the issue of recruitment of new staff from the same limited, general pool of potential staff as before, in a context of which the school is not 'a preferred location'. They stated that it has taken three years of reform and improvement to turn the non-preferred perception around. The advertisement of a science position in 2012 attracted 52 applicants from Victoria, nationally and internationally. In 2009, Glenroy would have been lucky to attract even one science applicant.

Leaders at Glenroy also offered the opinion that the biggest contribution to recruiting quality staff had been participation in the Teach for Australia programme, which has provided a supply of graduates (designated as associate teachers during their preparation for ongoing appointment) with high levels of knowledge and skill in their subject areas and with passion and commitment to working with disadvantaged students. Retaining these young, inspiring teachers when they completed their associate years was a high priority for Glenroy.

Glenroy and John Fawkner placed the highest priority on teacher quality through ongoing professional learning and cooperative teaching practices. However, they both point to Victorian staffing practice that can impede progress. All schools experience some degree of staff turnover and these two colleges are no exception. When vacancies are advertised, it is possible, and it often occurs, that staff declared surplus to requirement in other schools are given preference for appointment to the vacancy, if they meet the position criteria. All schools face this problem, but Glenroy and John Fawkner were exempt for their first year as new schools. The loss of this advantage has the potential to compromise their successful pursuit of the highest possible quality in teachers.

Systems of public schools invariably face this problem of how to place teachers declared surplus to requirement because of decreases in school enrolment and curriculum changes. There is an industrial obligation to assure placements. Sometimes these staff are known to be very good teachers in their field, but there is a perception to the contrary. Systems do have obligations to employees, as well as obligations to ensure that every school achieves good outcomes for its students. Perhaps schools in the process of transformation could be exempt from the referral process until an acceptable learning outcome level has been achieved.

The strategies adopted by DEECD, NMR and these two colleges illustrate how it is not just additional money that is required to move to transformation; it is how these funds are deployed. In both instances, priority was placed on building intellectual or professional capital, but it required external intervention to help build this capital through the replacement of some staff, as well as internal intervention within the region, to design and deliver an impressive programme of professional learning.

The work described in this chapter is ongoing. What has been accomplished to date is largely within current models of schooling. New models are emerging, including new approaches to learning and teaching, especially those that utilise advances in technology. Some of the cost implications of developments, such as blended learning, were explored in Chapter 9. There are certain to be more far-reaching changes in the years ahead.

Important messages for policymakers and practitioners

1   The transformation of underperforming schools is no longer just an option, or even a preferred option. It has become an imperative for systems of public schools as they respond to social and economic forces. There is a substantial body of knowledge about how schools may be transformed. System support is desirable, perhaps even necessary in some circumstances, but, fundamentally, transformation is a task for the school. With so many schools in many educational jurisdictions not gaining success for every student irrespective of circumstance, the question remains how schools can develop the capacity to transform.

2   The level of additional funding to support the process of transformation of high-needs schools is critical. Traditionally, equity-based funding has been less than sufficient, and it is recognised that increased funding is no guarantee of success. Strategic and evidence-based deployment of all resources is a prerequisite. The connection between financial capital and intellectual (professional) capital must be strong.

3   System-wide testing and differential equity-based funding are providing opportunities for educational jurisdictions to investigate the relationships between transformations, strategies for success and levels of funding. These relationships are contextual and appropriate additional funding levels will vary across different jurisdictions.

11 Funding models and their fitness for purpose

Funding models to allocate money to schools differ widely across nations and often between different jurisdictions within nations. There is usually a belief within any jurisdiction that they have it right. There is nothing wrong with diversity, and there may well be many successful approaches, but can a set of criteria be established to assist policymakers in improving their approach? There is usually a common starting point in purpose, with funding being deployed in the best interests of student learning. How does this intention translate into action?

Some systems still insist that centralisation of allocations and expenditure is more efficient, but most of those seeking improved learning outcomes are devolving some if not all funding to the school level for strategic deployment within the school in relation to the best interests of the student, taking into account system-wide priorities as well as local priorities and circumstances. For many systems, the allocation to the school is for materials only and staffing is allocated centrally as named appointments or as a number or quota of staff to be selected locally. Other systems make no distinction between materials and staff and base allocations entirely on the student profile, with the school making decisions about types of resources and relativities. The funding models used by the eight state and territory public education systems across Australia vary greatly across the spectrum described above.

In an environment of increasing accountability at the school level for student outcomes and pressure for improvement, the question is raised whether the school can be held accountable if it does not have the authority and responsibility for the ways and means, including key resources.

In this chapter, co-author Jim Spinks continues his description and analysis of approaches to needs-based funding in Australia, with detailed attention to preferred 'architecture', illustrated in the case of the Student Resource Package (SRP) in Victoria that was introduced in Chapter 10. Pioneering practice in the Edmonton Public School District in Alberta, Canada, is summarised and compared with that in Victoria.

Assessing the merit of needs-based funding models

School funding models in Australia are under scrutiny as never before through an initiative of the Australian government to drive educational reform to achieve a top five ranking in PISA by 2025. A key component of the reform agenda is to devise a student-focused and needs-based funding model to be applied across all sectors (government, Catholic and independent) in all states and territories, with introduction commencing in 2014 and reaching completion in 2020. Questions still remain on detail and the sources of the additional funding (estimated at $6.5 billion per annum) but no one can doubt the overall intention even if the time scale is problematic to say the least.

The proposed Australia-wide funding model is an outcome of the Gonski Report (Australian Government, 2011) commissioned by the commonwealth government and undertaken by an independent panel of experts. As part of the initial study by the panel of experts, Deloitte Access Economics (DAE) was commissioned to assess existing funding models. A key outcome of the DAE assessment was the identification of the features that characterise 'optimal funding model architecture'. The nine characteristics in the model (Deloitte Access Economics, 2011) are as follows:

1 Optimal funding models are designed with direct reference to public policy objectives. [Overarching optimality]
2 Funding is based on the efficient cost of meeting students' educational need, given the characteristics of the school they attend. [Efficiency; adequacy]
3 Empirical research underpins funding rates and their variation across student cohorts and schooling settings. [Effectiveness; equity; adequacy]
4 Funding formulae are reviewed – and as appropriate recalibrated – on a periodic basis and in a systematic fashion, drawing on cost and outcome data (noting the limitations on the use of these data in this context). [Effectiveness]
5 Funding is designed to keep pace with both increasing enrolments and efficient growth in service-delivery costs. [Adequacy; efficiency; certainty]
6 Trade-offs among adequacy and efficiency; simplicity and specificity are shaped by policy priorities and in light of improvements in the quality and availability of data. [Overarching optimality; simplicity]
7 The basis for funding allocations (i.e. funding formulae) is publicly available, except in instances where there is a privacy or other public interest case against such openness. [Transparency]
8 Mechanisms are in place to both support schools in their deployment of resources and to ensure that deployment is consistent with the policy intent (i.e. the underlying funding rationale) – especially in

devolved models, and particularly where potential for gaming exists. [Flexibility; accountability]

9 Optimal funding models incentivise private contributions where this is socially acceptable and not at odds with the underlying philosophy; and at the very least do not create barriers to schools procuring private funds in appropriate ways. [Incentive]

The DAE work in establishing the optimal funding model architecture provided a unique opportunity to test the efficacy of any funding model against an independently established framework. On the release of the DAE paper, the Victorian Department of Education and Early Childhood Development (DEECD) commissioned a critique to test the alignment of the SRP to the DAE framework. The outcomes of this test are reported in the following section.

The DAE architecture was based on the assumption that 'adequate, appropriately allocated funding underwrites the capacity of school systems to deliver high quality education programs' (Deloitte Access Economics, 2012). This position was developed from acknowledgement of the complexity of factors impacting on student learning, including teacher quality, socio-economic background and school autonomy, and the fact that these factors can be influenced by the nature of funding models. There was also recognition that optimal funding models are a necessary but not sufficient condition for high-quality outcomes for all students.

Initially DAE developed a set of 10 key public policy principles that generally relate to the development of school funding models and a set of indicators for each. An additional five principles relating to school funding models from a system perspective were also identified. The 15 principles are contained in Table 11.1.

The list of principles is comprehensive and most educational systems would find their own modelling principles as a subset. However, comparison with a similar set of guiding principles provided by Spinks in *Resourcing Schools for the 21st Century, 2: Models* (Spinks, 2006) points to a possible omission,

Table 11.1 Principles for development of school funding models (Deloitte Access Economics, 2012)

Funding model principles		Funding system principles
Equity	Effectiveness	Neutrality
Adequacy	Efficiency	Fairness
Incentive	Certainty	Sustainability
Flexibility	Transparency	Choice
Accountability	Simplicity	Coherence

although DAE may well have included it within other principles given the complexity and inter-connections of these issues.

Spinks (2006) included the principle of 'Learning' as a guide to the development of school funding models aimed at achieving excellence and equity for all students. This principle is stated as 'within the purposes of researching and redesigning a school resource allocation model, pre-eminence will be given to educational considerations for students' (ibid.: 23). In essence, this principle is emphasising that models should be focused on students and their learning. This may well be considered a given in designing education funding models. However, past and some current models are focused on funding schools, whereas the paradigm shift is to fund students and their learning. The movement from funding schools to funding students and their learning is of necessity evolutionary but aspects of school-focused funding can sometimes be retained and distort the intention. The significance of this issue is examined later in the chapter.

Analysis of the performance of funding models across Australia in relation to their identified set of guiding principles enabled DAE to propose optimal funding model architecture with the features listed above. It should be noted that the correlations of each feature to specific principles are shown in square parentheses at the end of each feature description. It is recognised that other principles may also have some degree of impact given their inter-relationships.

The optimal funding model presented by DAE provides a sound basis for educational jurisdictions to assess the performance of their funding models with a view to improvement. In undertaking this task for DEECD in Victoria, it was considered desirable to include one additional feature relating to the pre-eminence of students and their learning in model design. In DEECD documentation, this feature is usually given significance by reference to 'student-focused' or 'student-centred' modelling. This additional feature (labelled as No. 10) was described as 'pre-eminence will be given to educational considerations for students' (ibid.).

Assessment of the Victorian Student Resource Package (SRP)

The modified optimal funding model architecture of 10 features provided a strong basis for testing the efficacy of the Victorian government's models for resourcing public schools through the SRP. Table 11.2 summarises the major features of the SRP in 2012, included here as a point of reference in the assessment that follows.

The SRP was designed in 2003–2004 as an initiative of *The Blueprint for Government Schools* (Department of Education and Training [DET] [Victoria], 2003). A key public policy objective was for '90 per cent of students to successfully complete year 12 by 2010'. This objective was pursued on the basis of the moral, social and economic imperatives to ensure that all students optimise learning potential and that no student fails to achieve the minimum standards required for successful and positive participation in society.

Table 11.2 Components of the Student Resource Package (SRP) in Victoria

Component	School type	Basis for allocation
Core student learning allocation		
Per student funding P–12	Primary/secondary	Different rates for different levels (P–2, 3–4, 7–12)
Enrolment linked base	Primary/secondary	Flat base, reducing above enrolment threshold
Small school base		
Primary under 80.1 students Secondary under 400 students	Primary Secondary	Reducing base
Rural size adjustment factor Primary less than 201 students Secondary less than 501 students	Primary/secondary	Non-metropolitan, non-provincial
Equity funding		
SFO Middle years equity (Years 5–9) Secondary equity (Years 7–9) Mobility	Primary/secondary Primary/secondary Secondary Primary/secondary	SFO index with eligibility based on school's median SFO density
Special-needs funding		
Students with disabilities	Primary/secondary	Based on student disabilities index of 5 levels with sharply escalating rates per student
English as a Second Language (ESL)	Primary/secondary	Based on 3 SFO weightings across 5 levels of per student funding

Note: SFO, student family occupation.

1. Optimal funding models are designed with direct reference to public policy objectives

From this standpoint, equity was viewed no longer as equal access or opportunity but rather as equal outcomes. The pursuit of equity became and remained central to funding allocations to schools, even to the extent of the SRP significantly redistributing funding between schools to remove historical inequities and advance the optimal learning of all students. Prior to the SRP, 72 per cent of public schools received equity funding. It was initially proposed to redistribute the available funds to 25 per cent of schools but eventually redistribution to 50 per cent was agreed.

The current government has, in principle, strongly endorsed high-quality learning outcomes for all students by placing a robust emphasis on 'every Victorian child is given the best possible start in life' and providing a 'unique and personal education for every student' (Liberal Victoria, 2010: 2).

2. Funding is based on the efficient cost of meeting students' educational need, given the characteristics of the school they attend

Historically, school funding models have been designed on the basis of good intentions and within available resources, as determined politically. 'Good intentions' were based on the best available evidence but often this evidence was limited. Increases to funding were most often driven by political imperatives rather than hard evidence on how to improve the learning outcomes for all children.

The Victorian SRP was a breakthrough in designing school funding models. It not only sought empirical evidence on which to base design but specifically sought to address the feature of efficiency. An objective was to identify the efficient cost of effective provision but not through comparisons with international and other Australian jurisdictions. Evidence was sought directly through cost analysis in Victorian schools to take account of local circumstances as well as the different characteristics of the schools and their students. Seeking Victorian evidence was critical to gaining credibility, particularly with school principals and communities.

Evidence was sought from a school sample reflecting the diversity of schools in relation to stages of schooling, size, location and the learning needs of students. The evidence was obtained by the analysis of how learning occurred. The efficient optimisation of learning was a key factor in sample selection. The student rates in the SRP are firmly based on the efficient cost of provision to optimise student learning.

3. Empirical research underpins funding rates and their variation across student cohorts and school settings

(i) Cost analysis informs base rate funding rates and variance based on differences in service delivery costs (e.g. remoteness or size)

Empirical evidence is fundamental to the design and ongoing review of the SRP. The number and diversity of public schools provides a sufficient database to investigate the relationships between costs and outcomes, always considering that teacher quality, family circumstances and autonomy are the critical factors influencing outcomes rather than raw cost inputs.

All SRP core student rates and bases are derived from empirical evidence gained directly from schools. It has previously been explained how data were gathered in order to take account of efficiency. At the same time, effectiveness was also considered in sample selection. Victorian schools had been funded for all known factors for success in the past but on an uncertain basis. The SRP research reviewed the efficiency and effectiveness of these historical allocations and called for redistribution based on evidence from schools where both effectiveness and efficiency were in evidence.

Evidence included the effects of remoteness and size. Economies of scale are very evident in schools, particularly in relation to the capacity to optimise the size of every class. This is a more significant problem in secondary schools than primary, as the necessity to provide a broad curriculum in specialist subject areas can impact adversely on maintaining optimum class size.

Enrolment-linked bases were included in the SRP core to compensate schools for diseconomies of scale. Such provision is flawed by the introduction of enrolment thresholds. This was overcome by the design of enrolment-linked sliding bases as economies of scale developed.

All small schools incur additional costs due to diseconomies of scale; this is doubly so for small schools that are rural or remote. Smaller metropolitan schools can specialise to some degree and attract students with a related interest but remote schools must be 'all things to all students'. Effectiveness measures, as well as those of efficiency, assisted the SRP derivation of rural bases and student rates.

(ii) Performance data (broadly defined) inform assessment of educational need and the associated funding rates for equity

The SRP does not directly use performance data to inform assessment of educational need and associated funding rates. Initially, there was controversy over the reliability and validity of measures available. Instead, predictors of risk to successful learning associated with specific need were assessed and a selection made to drive equity formulae.

Prior to the SRP, a multiple index of need was in use but SRP research demonstrated the inadequacy of this index as relativities between perceived needs were not evidence-based because of a lack of availability of data at that time. SRP research demonstrated that family background was the greatest influence on student success. It was also demonstrated that family income was not the best predictor. The education level of the mother was slightly ahead of family occupation in reliability for predicting student success. On that basis, the student family occupation (SFO) density index, described in Chapter 10, was used as a key driver in all equity-based funding, except for students with disabilities.

A shortcoming of SFO implementation relates to the total funding available. Initially, the SRP research proposed that available funding would be sufficient to 'close the gap' only if funding was directed at the highest SFO quartile. It is also recognised that there is a relationship between degree of need and quantum of funding and that the relationship is more exponential than linear. However, available funding was directed to half the schools that exceeded the state SFO mean. Subsequent equity-based funding was directed to the highest quartile.

Directing funding on the basis of SFO density is problematic. It is based on the notion that the outcomes of any student are impacted by SFO density, that is a high-needs student will probably succeed in a low-density school and vice versa. Schools also tend to direct SFO funding across the school as a whole rather than targeting students with the highest needs. If the SFO funding were targeted at the student rather than the school then it could be more effective and low-need schools might be more inclined to enrol high-need students, knowing that additional support would be available. Targeting the student rather than the school could lead to more inclusive schools and decrease the tendency for residualisation. Residualisation is an impost on school improvement. The possibility of supporting the student rather than the school in general is the next step in the development of the SRP.

(iii) Targeting equity groups is underpinned by increasingly granular data and information (in preference to broad proxy measures), as data quality and availability increase

The implementation of the National Assessment Program – Literacy and Numeracy (NAPLAN) provided a more robust basis than previous state-based data and classroom-based teacher assessments had used in the past for allocating funding to support underperforming students. The current debate about schools manipulating participation in NAPLAN for their own purposes is more than academic. Before NAPLAN data can reliably be used to target underperformance, it will require minimum participation rates to be observed. Of course, this could well occur of its own volition if funding follows underperformance.

The question of whether funding is allocated as a reward for performance or to alleviate underperformance is contentious. Increasing data quality and availability are fundamental to this issue but a more granular approach is currently restricted.

4. Funding formulae are reviewed – and as appropriate recalibrated – on a periodic basis and in systematic fashion, drawing on cost and outcome data

A design parameter introduced into the SRP from its inception was the guarantee to schools that base and student rates in core and needs-based allocations would be recalibrated on a triennial basis. The SRP was designed in 2003–2004 and first implemented in 2005. The first recalibration was undertaken in 2007 and implemented in 2008. The second recalibration was in progress in 2012. The Centre for Post-Compulsory Education and Lifelong Learning at the University of Melbourne was commissioned to undertake each of these major projects.

A development of note in the recalibration for 2008 was the transition from differential relativities within secondary years (between 7–10 and 11–12) to a uniform index for all secondary years. In 2004, the evidence was clear that efficient and effective schools were favouring the senior years in expenditure, whereas recalibration in 2007 indicated that strategies to pursue effectiveness and efficiency had shifted to ensuring that learning problems were identified and addressed in the earlier years of secondary to optimise eventual success. Data also indicated that effective schools were not deploying the most experienced (and costly) teachers to the senior years but forming teams of teachers with ranges of experience at all years.

5. Funding is designed to keep pace with both increasing enrolments and efficient growth in service delivery

Base and student rates within the SRP are not recalculated annually to ensure that increased enrolments are incorporated within a budget ceiling by decreasing rates. Increased enrolments are accommodated by increased government funding. Rates are also indexed annually to maintain value with salary agreements and consumer price increases.

Efficient growth in service delivery costs is measured on a triennial basis by rate recalibration. However, Victorian public schools are the most efficient in Australia at cost delivery and less attention has been given to this aspect since the initial calculation of SRP student rates for 2005. The high cost of small schools contributes significantly to overall cost inefficiencies. There are 363 primary schools with fewer than 100 students; 45 are in metropolitan areas and some are very close to each other. There are 318 rural primary schools of fewer than 100 students, 67 of those with fewer than 20. The retention of small schools is a social issue and not driven by measures of efficiency.

6. Trade-offs among adequacy and efficiency; simplicity and specificity are shaped by policy priorities and in light of improvements in the quality and availability of data

Trade-offs of this nature are evident in the SRP, particularly in the determination of equity-based funding rates. The determination of core student rates to ensure adequacy of support for agreed standards of achievement for students without learning imposts is made relatively easy by identification of highly effective schools. However, identifying adequacy in needs-based rates has been more difficult in Victoria and elsewhere given ceilings on equity funding and a shortage of schools where all students, including those with very high needs, achieve success. It is also a complex situation, given that funding is but one of the factors impacting on outcomes, with teacher quality particularly critical. This issue is again considered later in the chapter as new possibilities are emerging to remove this trade-off.

7. The basis for funding allocations (i.e. funding formulae) is publicly available, except in instances where there is a privacy or other public interest case against such openness

Since implementation in 2005, the guidelines and funding formulae of the SRP have been freely available to all interested parties and are updated annually (www.education.vic.gov.au/management/srp).

Information is presented in a relatively simple and easy-to-understand format. The focus on core student-based funding and types of equity reduces the complexity often found in the funding models in other jurisdictions, where complexity often increases with the inclusion of the many specific purpose-type funding allocations. Transparency of school-level SRP allocations is provided to the council of each public school in Victoria.

8. Mechanisms are in place to both support schools in their deployment of resources and to ensure that deployment is consistent with the policy intent – especially in devolved models, and particularly where potential for gaming exists

From the total SRP budget, schools are responsible and accountable for financial planning and the management of all resources, including all staffing in terms of numbers, configuration and costs. The actual cost of any staff member, rather than an average cost in relation to a staff classification, is debited against the school budget in accordance with the budget allocation being student-centred.

The SRP allocation is directed to schools as both credit (90 per cent) and cash (10 per cent). The credit allocation is administered centrally to pay staff salaries in accordance with the staffing decisions of the school. The cash component is paid into school-administered bank accounts to cover all other operational costs. Any surplus held by a school at the end of a school year is automatically carried forward to the next year without penalty.

Centralised support arrangements provided to schools include administration of staff salary payments, with fortnightly reports to schools in relation to each staff member and likely surpluses/deficits to be accrued by year's end.

Other centralised support arrangements focus on the provision of an internet-based financial planner, which assists schools in considering the longer-term budget implications of staffing decisions. This provision ensures that schools 'mix and match' staff to ensure that they stay within budget. Rarely do any of the 1,550 schools run a deficit but workforce bridging can be made available to assist schools when circumstances are beyond their control.

Central systems have also been devised to assist schools with the management of their budgets and to provide continually updated financial reports. These reports indicate trends in expenditure and forewarn schools of possible deficits. The priority is on assisting schools to effectively manage their financial affairs rather than identifying mistakes retrospectively.

Support and accountability frameworks to enhance school effectiveness in budget planning and management need to be balanced against maintaining flexibility at the school level to cost-effectively deploy resources in the best interests of students within local as well as state-wide parameters. The SRP support and accountability frameworks have been continually developed since 2005 to optimise this balance. Local Administration Bureaus (LABs) were established to provide administrative support to small schools to assist with recording and reporting without diminishing their capacity to make the key decisions.

9. *Optimal funding models incentivise private contributions where this is socially acceptable and not at odds with the underlying philosophy; and at the very least do not create barriers to schools procuring private funds in appropriate ways*

Private contributions (locally raised funds – LRF) need to be distinguished between those provided by families and those emanating from sponsorship, partnerships and provision of services or facilities (rentals). The following does not in general apply to the rapid growth in philanthropic, not-for-profit and corporate contributions that are almost entirely focused on supporting high-needs schools (these are considered in Chapter 12).

Victorian government schools have increasingly developed their entrepreneurial capacities since the introduction of self-management in the 1980s. Contributions from families have also increased. Public schools in Victoria are among the least regulated government schools in Australia in relation to LRF and amongst the most benefited.

Total LRF per student can exceed $1,600 in primary schools and $2,500 in secondary, equivalent to an SRP rate 'increase' of approximately 30 per cent and 38 per cent respectively. These figures are exclusive of costs of fundraising but include costs of student excursions. Cost inclusion has been made on the basis of whether the associated activity was intended to enhance learning. Unfortunately, the per student LRF contributions are not evenly or randomly spread across schools. There is a direct relationship between contribution and the school SFO density index.

Victorian public school policies and regulations on LRF certainly provide an optimal funding model in relation to incentives according to this feature. There is no impact on the SRP allocation because of capacity to raise funds locally, nor is there any compensation where capacity to do so is low. The inequities of this situation provide the system with a considerable challenge and no practical resolution has been forthcoming.

It is questionable whether this optimal architectural feature is indeed 'optimal' when an outcome is to exacerbate an already uneven playing field. The resolution of this issue is not to prevent private and family provision but to ensure that sufficiency for all schools is addressed through equity provision.

10. *Additional feature: student-centred funding giving pre-eminence to educational considerations for students (Spinks, 2006)*

Fundamentally, a student-centred funding model is based on the belief that every student can learn and that all students can succeed, irrespective of family background or circumstance. Multiple pathways may be required to match curriculum and pedagogy to the individual student with appropriate support. Equity of outcomes is the objective, with every student achieving or exceeding state or national goals. It follows that funding support is dovetailed to the individual nature and needs of every student, even to the extent of taking into account the student's aspirations or lack thereof. Fairness is achieved when all students with the same level of need receive the same level of support, and students with higher needs receive higher levels of support to ensure equity of outcome.

The school budget becomes the sum total of the student-centred allocations, with some modification for diseconomies of scale and support issues to be addressed by every school. The role of the school is to deploy the totality of funding or the global budget to best address the needs of all students.

All funding models in Australia and most other countries would claim congruence with the above ideals but closer inspection often reveals serious deficiencies. In these cases, the underpinning of modelling is the nature and needs of the staff rather than the needs of students. This occurs through the common practice of allocating a global budget but then charging the cost of staff at an average cost, depending on staff category (e.g. teacher, principal). This practice is only a small advance on allocating a staffing quota and a separate cash component.

It is generally recognised that staffing processes tend to concentrate the most experienced and most expert staff in the lowest-needs schools, irrespective of whether staffing is centrally controlled or staff are locally selected, but at no financial impost to the recruiting school. The outcome is to distort the real funding to schools by the payment of a 'hidden' higher salary cost, mostly in lower-needs and smaller schools. This hidden higher cost can amount to approximately $1,250 per student or 20 per cent of the core student rate.

The significance of this distortion, embedded through charging average salaries to school budgets, is most obvious in the debates that arise when charging actual salaries is proposed for a school system. Education unions tend to oppose 'actuals' as it limits the capacity of highly sought-after schools to accommodate as many high-cost staff as possible. Similarly, principals and councils of low-needs schools are usually vociferous in opposing the proposal.

Charging staff costs as actuals to school budgets provides high-needs schools with the capacity to attract/retain highly expert and committed staff as well as possibly increase staff numbers to provide multiple pathways for student learning.

Charging actual salaries to school budgets was implemented in public schools in Victoria in 2002 and has remained a cornerstone of equity and fairness in school funding. It is to Victoria's credit that it successfully managed this change, given its controversial nature. England similarly introduced actuals in 1988. New Zealand intended this direction in 1989 but the proposal was opposed by education unions and others and has yet to be revisited. Most Australian states have not considered the possibility, responding to a view that rural and isolated schools would suffer in not being able to attract staff anyway, and have tried a 'points' system instead. There has been limited success and the issue of appointments to 'difficult-to-staff' schools has not been solved. Victoria may not have the remoteness factor of some other states but the concept of actuals has assisted in levelling the field to a significant degree. It is surprising that the DAE report did not identify the charging of actual salaries to school budgets as a feature (or part thereof) of the optimal funding architecture.

The development of student-centred funding is the ideal and a corollary is that the funding should follow the student if the family decides to change schools through necessity or choice. Funding following the student is a fundamental aspect of student-centred funding and needs to apply irrespective of sector (public or private). It mostly applies to equity funding for additional needs, as core funding is usually covered by 'swings and roundabouts' in enrolment changes.

An anathema to the concept of 'funding following the child' is the practice of imposing thresholds on schools as an eligibility criterion for particular types of needs-based funding. Thresholds apply in SFO funding where funding is only allocated to those schools where the index exceeds the state mean. Again the threshold was an outcome of a policy/availability trade-off but with an adverse effect on the integration of students into desirable environments.

The Victorian SRP is highly regarded worldwide as a student-centred funding model and it compares very favourably with the optimal features proposed by DAE. The outcome of the Gonski Report (Australian Government, 2011) is a proposal by the Australian government for a national approach to school funding on a similar basis to the Victorian model. Implementation would require an additional provision of $6.5 billion per annum, with uncertainty as to the level of contributions to be made by the different levels of government. Meanwhile, a pressing need for Victoria is to address the issues of determining the level of equity funding required to ensure that all students in all settings are successful learners. This development becomes an imperative if the Baillieu coalition government is to achieve its goal of Victorian education becoming a top-tier system within the next 10 years.

The Edmonton model

Victoria provides a school funding model that has evolved over 20 years and continues to change to better match the needs of students. The Edmonton Public School District in the province of Alberta in Canada also provides a student-focused system that has evolved over an even longer period, and again in association with the development of self-managing schools. The Edmonton model is briefly outlined below and assessed in the light of the DAE optimal funding model architecture and contrasted with the Victorian approach.

What has transpired in Edmonton is noteworthy as it has had continuous experience with needs-based funding in its highly decentralised system for more than 30 years. Its funding mechanism became a model in other jurisdictions in Canada and some school districts in the United States. It was especially significant in Victoria following the Schools of the Future initiative in the early 1990s and there are similarities between the structure of the formula underpinning the SRP and the factors included in the Edmonton approach. Victoria's approach to systematic annual surveys of students, teachers, principals and parents was directly modelled on the Edmonton experience. However, as in Victoria, Edmonton's schools are self-managing but not self-governing and its schools operate within a system-wide set of policies and priorities and clear lines of accountability. Practice in Edmonton shaped developments in other school districts in Alberta as far as school autonomy is concerned and this, together with its robust school improvement framework and the quality of initial teacher education, professional development and encouragement of innovation, is usually cited as the factor explaining why Alberta was second to Finland in several iterations of PISA.

Edmonton Public School District is located within the boundaries of the City of Edmonton in the province of Alberta. The population of Edmonton is approximately three-quarters of a million. There are two systems of education in Edmonton, the other being the Edmonton Roman Catholic School District. Both systems are funded on the same basis from the public purse, being a mix of local revenue from property taxes and provincial revenue (the federal government does not contribute except for small allocations to support indigenous students and children of defence personnel). Edmonton has an increasingly diverse population.

Although the detail of the approach has changed over the years, Edmonton has maintained the same structure in its funding mechanism over three decades. The 2011–2012 budget, for example, was based on the premise that all resources should be distributed equitably in accordance with responsibility for results. Approximately 80 per cent of the district's budget is planned directly by the schools with input from staff, students, parents and the community. Each school receives an allocation of dollars with which to plan the number of staff and the supplies, equipment and services they need to provide the best possible programme for all students. The remaining 20 per cent of the district's budget includes school board and central services, district-level fixed costs and district-level committed costs.

The budget was designed to support all students in an inclusive education system that provides choice while still addressing the increased cultural diversity and unique learning needs of the student population (Edmonton Public School Board, 2011).

The focus on choice and cultural diversity is common to the context for schools in Victoria. Being a city system, it has no allocations in the budget to take account of remoteness or rurality. Table 11.3 lists the resource allocation levels, ratios and rates for the decentralisation of funds to schools in Edmonton's equivalent of the SRP.

Additional allocations are made to schools with particular operating needs, including Aboriginal education; schools with unique operating needs; Alberta Initiative for School Improvement (AISI) and Alberta Small Class Size Initiative (initiatives of the Alberta government); educational services to which the formulae are not applicable; community use of schools; students attending designated schools from neighbourhoods where there is no local

Table 11.3 Student resource allocation levels, ratios and rates in the Edmonton Public School District, 2011–2012 (adapted from Edmonton Public School Board, 2011)

Category	Descriptors	Ratio	Rate (per student)
Level 1	Elementary, Junior High, Kindergarten	1.000	$5,145
Level 2	Senior High (General)	1.003	$5,160
Level 3	English Language Learners (Div II–IV) International Baccalaureate (Div IV)	1.108	$5,702
Level 4	Amiskwaciy, Awasis, Rites of Passage	1.204	$6,194
Level 5	Communication Disability ELL Foreign Born Refugee Background Learning Disability Mild Cognitive Disability Moderate Emotional/Behavioural, Hearing, Multiple, Visual, Non-verbal Learning Disability	1.842	$9,476
Level 6	Moderate Cognitive, Physical or Medical Disability Moderate Pervasive Developmental Disorder	2.057	$10,583
Level 7	Blindness or Deafness Severe Cognitive, Emotional/Behavioural, Multiple, Physical or Medical Disability Severe Pervasive Developmental Disorder	3.585	$18,442
Level 8	Blindness or Deafness Severe Cognitive, Multiple, Physical or Medical Disability Severe Pervasive Developmental Disorder	5.024	$25,846

school; the introduction of selected new programmes in a school or for the establishment of learning resources and supplies in new schools; professional development; literacy intervention funding; primary schools to support literacy intervention programmes; schools with small enrolments; information technology services; costs associated with custodial salaries; teacher aides to primary schools; and schools operating in two locations.

Noteworthy is additional funding to address High Social Vulnerability, being allocations to reflect the characteristics of a school's student population based on an index of nine indicators of social vulnerability for the community in which the student resides.

Levels 1–3 provide for core student learning with little differentiation between stages of schooling. In this respect, it should be noted that Edmonton teachers have the same contact hours per week, whereas secondary teachers in Victoria have fewer weekly contact hours than primary teachers and hence the ratio of secondary-to-primary funding has to be increased. Unlike Victoria, Edmonton does not increase funding rates in the early years in line with research on the importance of these years to overall school achievement.

Equity funding in the Edmonton funding model is limited mainly to disability provision. Additional funding for vulnerability based on socio-economic circumstances is provided outside the model to reflect the characteristics of a school's student population, based on an index of nine indicators of social vulnerability for the community in which the student resides. The Victorian model is the reverse, with socio-economically based provision within the model and provision for students with disabilities in a separate model of six levels, similarly based on degrees of severity.

Edmonton and the optimal funding model architecture

The Edmonton model is designed with reference to public policy objectives which are being achieved within an efficient cost structure. It is surmised that the rates and ratios are based on empirical evidence, although reference to publicly available research cannot be located. Reviews are conducted annually, based on community and professional opinions that underpin recommendations to the District Board. Increased enrolments are funded by increasing the overall budget and not by decreasing existing rates, although disability rates are contained within the proportional limit of the overall budget for schools. If the proportion of students with disabilities increases then rates must fall. This contrasts with Victoria, where disability rates are fixed and indexed irrespective of changes in student numbers. Transparency is very evident with the Edmonton model with individual school budgets available on the internet.

The major distinction between the Edmonton and the Victorian model relates to the focus on the student. In the Victorian model, the entire focus is on the student profile and the achievement of outcomes. The configuration and selection of staff are school decisions, and actual salaries with on-costs are debited directly to school budgets. The same applies to Edmonton, except that the costs of staff are debited to school budgets as averages. This practice means that a school with an inexperienced and/or less expert staff will cost less in overall real terms than a school with experienced and expert staff. Given the phenomenon of staff moving to schools in more affluent communities as their careers progress, the funding on the basis of averages can exacerbate the problem of attracting the best mix of staff to every school. Of course, if every teacher is of equally high quality then it is not an issue, but this is rarely the case.

Important messages for policymakers and practitioners

1   Planned, triennial school funding model reviews against credible criteria ensure that school budget allocations remain targeted on changing priorities. During reviews, opportunities are provided to eliminate thresholds and replace them with continuous allocation functions. An examination of the funding model of one jurisdiction identified so many stepped formulae that it was possible for a school to increase its staff quota by five

FTEs by enrolling eight additional students in the right age groups. In another jurisdiction, 301 students was the 'perfect' enrolment to optimise resource entitlements. Enrolments should be based on rights and choice and not on whether the school can see a threshold advantage.

2   Student funding rates, relativities or ratios should be based on empirical evidence. This evidence can be difficult to generate and needs to come from schools within the jurisdiction to ensure that culture and context are considered. Techniques for data collection from schools on the basis of how learning takes place are available and allow the costs of learning in effective and efficient schools to be compared with a random sample.

3   Jurisdictions are often reluctant to factor into their modelling the contribution of parents and other external sources to school funding. There is evidence that, in some public schools in affluent communities, external funding can amount to 30 per cent of government funding and exceed any additional equity-based funding provided for schools in less affluent communities. The search for empirical evidence of the cost to achieve success for all students in affluent communities needs to encompass external funding to ascertain the real cost of success. Additional equity-based funding for schools in disadvantaged communities needs to exceed the real cost in advantaged communities if the learning gap is to be closed.

12 Rediscovering social and spiritual capital

'Social capital' is a new field for many researchers, policymakers and practitioners in education, but this should not be the case. The first use of the term appears to have been in the context of education nearly 100 years ago, when a rural superintendent in Virginia used it to refer to the advantages that a rural school had over its urban counterparts. The networks of community support for the school seemed to be stronger in the former (Putnam, 2000). Now, it is central to efforts to create a self-transforming school.

Social capital refers to the strength of formal and informal partnerships and networks involving the school and all individuals, agencies, organisations and institutions that have the potential to support and be supported by the school (Caldwell and Harris, 2008: 10).

This is a broad view of social capital. Some experts provide a sharper focus. For example, Andy Hargreaves and Michael Fullan (A. Hargreaves and Fullan, 2012) considered 'professional capital' to be a form of social capital. They were referring to the knowledge and skills of teachers, which Caldwell and Harris described as 'intellectual capital', considered in more detail in Chapter 13. Differences in terminology are of no consequence, provided context and usage are explained. There is no question that strong professional or intellectual capital is a form of social capital which the profession brings to the task of transforming a school, and it may be strong or weak.

David Hargreaves (D. Hargreaves, 2012) offered another view of social capital, which he defined in terms of values, bringing the concept into the domain of spiritual capital, defined by Caldwell and Harris as 'the strength of moral purpose and the degree of coherence among values, beliefs and attitudes about life and learning' (Caldwell and Harris, 2008: 10). For Hargreaves, 'social capital consists of two connected elements: trust and reciprocity'. He posed three questions in relation to trust: 'How do individuals come to be optimistic enough to risk the cooperation that leads to trust?', 'How do they initiate trust relationships with others?' and 'How do they maintain trust relationships once they have started?' (D. Hargreaves, 2012: 13).

The four forms of capital introduced in Chapter 3 (intellectual, social, spiritual and financial) overlap, as illustrated in the work of Andy Hargreaves and Michael Fullan (social capital and intellectual capital) and David Hargreaves (social capital and spiritual capital). There is also an overlap of social capital and financial capital, and describing and illustrating policy and practice in this overlap forms the major part of Chapter 12. The overlap is also evident in the 10 indicators of social capital, each of which was confirmed in most of the countries participating in the International Project to Frame the Transformation of Schools (Australia, China, England, Finland, the United States and Wales):

1   There is a high level of alignment between the expectations of parents and other key stakeholders and the mission, vision, goals, policies, plans and programmes of the school.
2   There is extensive and active engagement of parents and others in the community in the educational programme of the school.
3   Parents and others in the community serve on the governing body of the school or contribute in other ways to the decision-making process.
4   Parents and others in the community are advocates of the school and are prepared to take up its cause in challenging circumstances.
5   The school draws cash or in-kind support from individuals, organisations, agencies and institutions in the public and private sectors, in education and other fields, including business and industry, philanthropists and social entrepreneurs.
6   The school accepts that support from the community means a reciprocal obligation for the school to contribute to the building of the community.
7   The school draws from and contributes to networks to share knowledge, address problems and pool resources.
8   Partnerships have been developed and sustained to the extent that each partner gains from the arrangement.
9   Resources, both financial and human, have been allocated by the school to building partnerships that provide mutual support.
10 The school is co-located with or located near other services in the community and these services are utilised in support of the school.

Particular attention is given in the pages that follow to policy and practice in Australia, where there is much greater recognition of the importance of social capital than is often acknowledged by the profession and the public. Brief comparisons are offered with policy and practice in other countries. Particular attention is given to philanthropic, not-for-profit and corporate contributions to schools, which are focused on efforts to close the gap in achievement between low- and high-performing students, which is essential in the transformation of schools. Two exemplars of schools that have drawn on their social capital to become self-transforming schools are described, one in Australia and one in Hong Kong.

Funding arrangements for public and private schools

The framework for the governance of schools in Australia was described in Chapter 3. There was brief reference to the roles of different levels of government and to distinctions between public and private schools. The following provides a much sharper focus on sources of funding for schools and, especially, the way in which money and other kinds of support are drawn from sources other than government, that is from private sources, consistent with indicators of social capital listed above, notably 5: 'The school draws cash or in-kind support from individuals, organisations, agencies and institutions in the public and private sectors, in education and other fields, including business and industry, philanthropists and social entrepreneurs'. It is in this respect that Chapter 12 differs from matters considered in Chapters 10 and 11, which were related to the public funding of public schools.

Public schools are owned and operated by the states and territories and receive most of their funds from government, with the smaller proportion of public funding coming from the federal government. The portion of their public funding is determined on a needs basis. They may not charge fees to cover the costs of core learning and teaching. Private schools receive funds from state and federal governments, with most of their public funds coming from the latter. They may charge fees. Public funds for private schools are determined according to a formula based on capacity to secure support from their communities. The formula for federal support of public and private schools is revised every four years, with the next revision to take effect from 2014.

The Gonski Report

The federal government commissioned a far-reaching review of funding for public and private schools to help shape the next revision. The report (Australian Government, 2011) is generally known by the name of the chair of the review committee (David Gonski): the 'Gonski Report'. Implementation depends on agreements being struck with state and territory governments as well as with authorities and organisations representing Catholic and independent schools. Reference has been made to the report in several chapters thus far.

Gonski recommended a dramatic increase in funding for all schools (about $6.5 billion per year), with the total of funds to be allocated on a needs basis to public and private schools in such a way that no school will lose funds. Significantly, as far as Chapter 12 is concerned, the report also recommended action in relation to philanthropic, not-for-profit and corporate contributions:

> *Finding 26* The panel notes the Australian Government's response to the recommendations in the Realising potential: Businesses [see below] helping schools to develop Australia's future report, particularly those aimed

at building capacity in schools to develop partnerships with community and business.

Recommendation 41 The Australian Government should create a fund to provide national leadership in philanthropy in schooling, and to support schools in need of assistance to develop philanthropic partnerships.

(Australian Government, 2011: 205–206)

Philanthropic, not-for-profit and corporate contributions

Corporate contributions

The Australian government, through its Department of Education, Employment and Workplace Relations (DEEWR), commissioned a report on connections between business and schools. A Business–Schools Connection Roundtable was established with leaders from the business sector. There were extensive consultations throughout the country and surveys were conducted to determine the extent of current and past associations. It was clear that partnerships were more numerous than generally understood. The report (Business–School Connections Roundtable, 2011) described these associations in terms of transformation and the support of the wider community.

> Our education system has embarked on a bold transformation to ensure that all our young people have access to a high quality 21st century education, regardless of where they live, their gender, cultural background or socio-economic status. In combination with the development of a national curriculum, physical infrastructure, new technology and other reforms, school-based partnerships – with business and the wider community – promise to deliver effective outcomes for our young people. Such partnerships have flourished over the past two decades. In many cases, business involvement in education has seen marked increases in the quality and extent of engagement of students, parents and whole communities in their schools. Nevertheless, there is much to be done to ensure that all schools can benefit from business connections.
>
> As the world has become more complex, so have the community's expectations of schooling. Contributing to this is a growing recognition that educating our young people is the responsibility of the entire community, not just schools. This has led to an increasing focus on schools developing partnerships with the broader community – including parents, community organizations, businesses, and other education institutions.
>
> (ibid.: 1)

An important initiative in Australia is the Schools First project of the National Australia Bank (NAB), Australian Council for Educational Research (ACER) and the Foundation for Young Australians (FYA), for which NAB allocated $15 million over three years (2009–2011) to recognise and reward outstanding school–community partnerships (the programme continued in 2012 and 2013). In the first two years of the programme, 195 awards were made from 2,432 applications with funding totalling $10.15 million. Schools First offers an online Partnership Matching Service that helps schools, businesses and community organizations find a partner. Public and private schools are eligible to apply for these awards.

Mapping philanthropic and not-for-profit contributions

Tender Bridge is a national subscription-based research and development service of the Australian Council for Educational Research (ACER) that is available for schools and not-for-profit entities in education. The organisational subscription in 2012 was $200 per year. It maintains a database of more than 1,000 funding sources that can support schools directly or in partnership with an eligible organisation. Details of education-related grants, scholarships and sponsorships from business, philanthropy, government (all levels) and universities are updated weekly and made available to subscribers.

More generally, Tender Bridge offers four services: (1) accessing funds (as described above); (2) professional learning to assist subscribers and non-subscribers; (3) personalised guidance and project idea clarification; and (4) an editing service to assist subscribers prepare applications for support. Cases of subscriber success are shared every few months through the publication *Tender Bridge Quarterly*. These services are provided to public and private schools.

Leading Learning in Education and Philanthropy (LLEAP) is a three-year project partnership of ACER through its Tender Bridge project, The Ian Potter Foundation and the Origin Foundation. The project was described by Michelle Anderson, Project Director of Tender Bridge, in the following terms:

> As a new research project, Leading Learning in Education and Philanthropy (LLEAP) aims to address these issues by exploring whether the full potential of funding and partnerships available to Australian schools is being achieved. The project aims to find ways to improve the quality of grant seeking and grant making in Australia, with a focus on identifying better ways for the philanthropy and education sectors to connect and collaborate.
>
> (Anderson, 2011: 56)

A survey of a representative sample of schools, not-for-profits and philanthropic organisations was conducted in 2011. There were 302 responses from every state and territory: 138 schools, 84 philanthropic organisations and 80 not-for-profits. Case studies were conducted. Hands On Learning (HOL), for example, was initiated in 1999 at Frankston High School in Melbourne but in 2012, 13 years later, it extends to 18 schools across Victoria and

Queensland. This programme is the exemplary school-based initiative chosen from Australia for more detailed attention later in the chapter.

Illustration 1: The Song Room (TSR)

Two national programmes are selected at this point to illustrate the harnessing of social capital across the nation and their positive impact: The Song Room (TSR) and Social Ventures Australia (SVA). A third illustration describes slow progress in engaging the non-public sector in the governance of public schools.

TSR is a Melbourne-based not-for-profit that offers free music- and arts-based programmes for children in disadvantaged and other high-needs settings. Approximately 20,000 students participate in its programmes each week. According to TSR, 700,000 students in public primary schools in Australia have no opportunity to participate in programmes in the arts. TSR is supported by grants from federal and state governments but with substantial funding from foundations, other not-for-profits and the corporate sector.

The impact of the programme was confirmed in research in 2010 by Educational Transformations, commissioned by TSR and funded by the Macquarie Group Foundation. The findings were published in *Bridging the Gap in School Achievement through the Arts* (Vaughan *et al.*, 2011), launched by Peter Garrett, Australia's Minister for School Education, Early Childhood and Youth. A detailed account is contained in *Transforming Education through the Arts* (Caldwell and Vaughan, 2012).

The research was conducted against a background of international research in both primary and secondary schools in all sectors. The research team examined the performance of students in 10 schools in highly disadvantaged settings in western Sydney. Three schools offered a longer-term programme over 12 to 18 months and three schools offered an initial short-term programme of 6 months. In each instance, the programme was conducted for Grade 5 and 6 students for one hour on a single day per week. A control group of four schools did not offer The Song Room programme. The three groups of schools were a matched set. At the time of the study, they scored roughly the same on the Australian Curriculum, Assessment and Reporting Authority (ACARA) Index of Community Socio-Educational Advantage (ICSEA), as calculated in 2009. An even closer match was evident when 2010 ICSEA scores were used. The study is a rare example of quasi-experimental design in educational research.

Important differences were found in favour of students that undertook the TSR programme. The findings have national and international significance. First, related research in other countries is confirmed. Second, there appears to be a direct association between the arts and outcomes in other areas. Third, the wisdom of including the arts in the Australian curriculum is confirmed. The key findings were as follows:

1   Participation in TSR is associated with a gain of approximately one year in Year 5 NAPLAN scores in reading and approximately half a year in science and technology when compared with outcomes for students in matching schools.
2   Participation in TSR is associated with higher levels of social and emotional well-being (SEWB) on every dimension of the ACER SEWB scale compared with measures for students in matching schools.
3   Although there was no implication that students in TSR in participating schools had a propensity to engage in juvenile crime, the findings are consistent with worldwide research on factors that mitigate such engagement.

Although caution must always be exercised in drawing cause-and-effect relationships, these differences in comparisons in matched sets of schools were statistically significant. Moreover, the longer the students were in TSR programmes the greater the differences.

It was noted above that 700,000 students in public primary schools in Australia have no opportunity to participate in programmes in the arts. Students in public schools in low socio-economic settings appear to be at a comparative disadvantage to their counterparts in schools in more affluent communities and in private schools. An explanation may be that large numbers of private schools have, at least in the eyes of parents, a more holistic view of the curriculum and have well-developed programmes in the arts that have withstood the narrowing effect of high-stakes testing. There are notable exceptions, of course, especially for public schools of long standing or where the arts are a 'protected' specialisation. An associated reason that takes account of socio-economic status in the public sector, as well as in the private sector, is that these schools have more financial resources to draw on or have higher levels of social capital from which they can secure support for the arts.

Illustration 2: Social Ventures Australia (SVA)

Social Ventures Australia (SVA) is a non-profit organisation established in 2002 by The Benevolent Society, The Smith Family, WorkVentures and the AMP Foundation. As noted in its 2011 annual report, revenue in 2011 grew by 18 per cent to $11.17 million. The organisation raised over $45 million to fund innovative social ventures and strengthen the non-profit sector more broadly. For example, its efforts as part of the GoodStart syndicate helped to provide early learning services for 72,000 children in 660 centres. Over the past five years, the consulting team within SVA has worked with over 160 organisations on more than 350 projects.

SVA has demonstrated its commitment to the school sector in many ways, including the organisation of two 'dialogues' of what it calls 'an uncommon alliance'. These were one-day events in Sydney in 2011 and 2012, which brought together representatives of major philanthropic organisations, not-for-profits and senior leaders in systems of public education. The focus in 2012 was on the contribution of teachers to schools in securing improved outcomes for students in disadvantaged settings, with the theme being 'Great teaching in tough schools'. The event was supported by the AMP Foundation, the Bryan Foundation and the Robertson Family Foundation.

SVA (Social Ventures Australia [SVA], 2013) has identified four change levers that have a significant impact on outcomes for students with disadvantaged backgrounds, which it describes as:

- Early learning: Ensuring low socio-economic status [SES] children attend a high-quality early education program.
- High-performing schools: Developing high-performing schools in low SES neighbourhoods through improving teacher effectiveness and quality leadership.
- Engaged parents and communities: Supporting parents, businesses and the wider community to engage with schools and support students.
- Effective pathways: Supporting low SES students to access effective pathways from school to further learning or work.

SVA directly supports a number of what it calls 'Bright Spots' within its venture portfolio by providing funding, expertise and access to networks. In the education arena, it supports the Australian Indigenous Mentoring Experience, Teach for Australia and The Song Room.

The organisation is showcasing Bright Spots that effectively train and prepare teachers for low-SES schools or offer induction, mentoring and professional development to new teachers in low-SES schools, working in partnership with governments from all jurisdictions. SVA is also exploring, together with schools and philanthropists, how it can provide flexible financial support and guidance to Bright Spots and disseminate information about associated innovations.

Illustration 3: Disengaged youth

Educational Transformations was commissioned to conduct a study of education in Local Learning Organizations (LLO) in the Southern Metropolitan Region (SMR) of the Department of Education and Early Childhood Development (DEECD) in Victoria. SMR covers suburbs in south-east Melbourne. LLO serve youth who are disengaged from regular schools and generally have low levels of literacy and numeracy. Disengagement is associated with issues such as learning disabilities, mental health challenges, substance abuse and family background. The study was significant for several reasons. First, it revealed that the number of young people served by the 63 LLO was 70 per cent higher than previously understood. Second, all providers of LLO services are not-for-profit, ranging from small Neighbourhood Houses, with fewer than 25 young people undertaking educational programmes, to large youth-focused organisations serving up to 356. Third, the funding of the programmes is complex, with funds from the Higher Education Skills Group (HESG) of DEECD providing support for those 16 years of age or older, and funds from the Student Resource Package (SRP) of the school a young person less than 16 years of age would normally have attended (SRP funding is described in Chapters 10 and 11). The amount of SRP support is agreed between the provider and the school in a Memorandum of Understanding.

Programmes of this kind are noteworthy. Public education is valued because it serves students from across the spectrum of educational needs. For these programmes, the services are administered and funded by a public authority but delivered by a private provider. Important issues are the adequacy of funding from the sources described above, given the complexity of the services provided, and the extent to which it is possible for partnerships with schools to be maintained. Who has formal responsibility for the individual being supported?

Illustration 4: Governance

The least adventurous aspect of the involvement of the private sector in public education is governance. In broad terms, Australia still has the same governance arrangements that it has had for more than a century. Public schools are built, owned, funded and operated by governments but with a steadily increasing injection of funds from the philanthropic, not-for-profit and corporate sectors, as described in the previous section.

Some states provide schools with more autonomy than they have had in the past, notably Victoria (self-managing schools) and Western Australia (a minority are self-managing independent public schools). Attendance zones have been loosened. The federal government is implementing, in association with the states and territories, the Empowering Local Schools programme over the next eight years but, in most instances, governments as well as Catholic and independent schools are choosing to use the associated funds to build capacity within current levels of autonomy, rather than increase the level of autonomy.

Only a few public schools have become specialist schools along the lines developed in England over the last two decades. After a slow start in the Thatcher years, specialist secondary schools grew rapidly during the Blair and Brown years to the point that virtually all secondary schools became specialist secondary schools, offering one or more specialisations for which they received additional public funding that effectively doubled the extra cash or in-kind support they received in partnership with public or private entities. The specialist programme was abandoned with a change of government in 2010.

There are no counterparts in Australia to charter schools in the United States. There are no proposals in Australia for what are arguably the most significant of initiatives in England, namely the creation of academies, which were an initiative of the Blair government to replace low-performing secondary schools in areas of severe disadvantage in cities around the country. Private sector contributions in cash and membership of governing bodies were required in the early stages.

The developments reported in this section of Chapter 12 were not evident to any significant extent at the start of the twenty-first century. National frameworks have emerged in the last five years and, although there may be ongoing debate about their structure and scope, there is bipartisan support for their uniform application across the public and private sectors in school education. Similarly, philanthropic, not-for-profit and corporate contributions to public schools, especially to support efforts to close the gap between low- and high-performing students, were very much at the periphery until recently. Contrary to an often-held view, private effort in support of public education is almost certain to reduce rather than increase inequality, and thereby build the capacity of schools to be self-transforming. Other measures may be more important and have greater impact, for example improving the quality of teaching and ensuring that all students no matter what the setting have access to it, but the private sector is making a significant and growing contribution.

Australian Exemplar: Hands On Learning (HOL)

Reference has been made earlier to the HOL programme that commenced at Frankston High School in Frankston, a suburb in south-east Melbourne, in 1999. It was selected as an exemplar in the case study phase of LLEAP (Anderson and Curtin, 2012) and a summary is provided here.

HOL is a one-day-per-week early intervention programme in which students work on creative building projects intended to benefit the school and community. Notable is the number of supporting partnerships, which included the Education Foundation, the Myer Foundation and the Sidney Myer Fund, the AMP Youth Boost Fund and SVA. The SVA role was described in these terms:

> In 2005, SVA invested $40,000. They saw that the program was a way to deal with the huge issue of student disengagement. But they did not provide the funds. That's not their remit. Instead, SVA removed the burden from Russell [Kerr] (the founder of HOL) alone to seek supporters. SVA sought support on the school's behalf. That was a crucial value-add in terms of time, knowledge and networks.
>
> (ibid.: 5)

SVA increased its support to $300,000 from 2005 to 2008 and sourced $1 million for the programme. The impact was demonstrated in a report entitled *The Socio-Economic Benefits of Investing in the Prevention of Early School Leaving* that was commissioned by HOL:

- Real retention rates for HOL students have been above 95 per cent each year for the 10 years to 2009.
- Real retention rates in schools which use the HOL method have been approximately 10 per cent higher than the State average for the 10 years to 2009. Both this point and the previous one directly support the COAG [Council of Australian Governments] objective of 90 per cent Year 12 or equivalent attainment for students across the country by 2015.
- Unemployment rates amongst former HOL students averaged 2.2 per cent in 2006, compared to 10.8 per cent for Australians aged 15–24 in the same period.
- In 2011, more than an 80 per cent reduction in school detentions was reported amongst HOL students who joined the program in 2010.
- In 2008, HOL partnered with the Education Queensland Indigenous Schooling Support Unit to implement the HOL program in the Northern Peninsula Area State College Bamaga. By the end of the first term, the College had achieved a 650 per cent increase in student attendance, as well as a significant reduction in school suspensions. The HOL program, through engaging the Indigenous community, directly contributes to the second of the COAG's key goals for supporting students at disadvantage.

(Deloitte Access Economics, 2012: 14)

It is noteworthy that the cost of supporting students in the HOL pro-gramme is approximately $2,300 per student. This is how the Deloitte Access Economics study reported on the matter:

Between 1999 and 2012, over 30 schools used the HOL method to support 3082 students. The estimated cost of providing this support, in 2012 dollars, is approximately $2300 per HOL student. To date, schools have funded the delivery of the program out of their own budgets, that is they have received no additional public funding to provide the program.

(ibid.: 16)

The conclusion of the report is particularly striking:

Between 1999 and 2012, 3,082 students have participated in the HOL program. The modelling results indicate that for this cohort, the benefit of program participation, calculated as improvements in average lifetime earnings, equates to $1.8 billion in net present value terms. Measured against the cost of HOL program provision and consequent costs of schooling reengaged students, $154 million, the net benefit of program provision to this cohort of students is $1.6 billion in net present value terms. This represents a benefit to cost return of $12 per $1 invested in reengaging and schooling disengaged students where these assumptions hold.

(ibid.: 21)

Frankston High School became a self-transforming school for its disengaged students through the adoption of HOL, with the support of public funds augmented over time from the philanthropic, not-for-profit and corporate sectors. HOL commenced as a single-school initiative but in barely a decade it had become a multi-school initiative in two states in what was, in effect, a chain of schools that succeeded in transforming learning for disengaged students. This illustrates another indicator of social capital, number 7: 'the school draws from and contributes to networks to share knowledge, address problems and pool resources'.

Hong Kong Exemplar: Fresh Fish Traders' School (FFTS)

Social capital is particularly strong in Hong Kong, where the majority of public-funded schools are owned and operated by churches, trusts and foundations, as described in Chapter 5. Social capital and spiritual capital may have powerful interactive effects when they are both strong, as they are in Hong Kong.

The Fresh Fish Traders' School (FFTS) is selected as an exemplar of how a school in Hong Kong draws on its social capital. Any number of schools could be chosen but the distinguishing characteristic in this instance is the way it illustrates one of the indicators in the list presented earlier, namely number 4: 'parents and others in the community are advocates of the school and are prepared to take up its cause in challenging circumstances'. There is evidence that the school would have had to close several years ago were it not for this support. The Education and Manpower Bureau (EMB) has determined that schools where enrolments fall below a certain base may have to close. Any shortfall in funding to keep a school open must be drawn from other sources and this has been achieved in remarkable fashion at FFTS.

Brian Caldwell visited the school on two occasions (2009 and 2012) and this account was drawn from his observations in 2012, as confirmed by Principal Leung Kee-Cheong. The school was nominated for these visits by a senior scholar with extensive knowledge of schools in Hong Kong as one that had been transformed and sustained a high level of performance. The focus in the account that follows is on matters pertaining to social capital and how the school has been able to survive under particularly challenging circumstances.

FFTS is owned and operated by the Fresh Fish Traders' Association. Like the majority of schools in Hong Kong, it is subsidised. It opened in 1969 and serves a disadvantaged community in Tai Kok Tsui on the Kowloon side of Hong Kong. There is considerable poverty in the community. It had 222 students and 18 teachers in 2012. It has been at risk of closure for at least a decade, with EMB normally requiring a minimum of 18 classes. FFTS has capacity for 12, but in 2012 there were only eight. An application to establish a new school in a community where these requirements would be satisfied was unsuccessful. The determining factor is demographic rather than educational. About 20 per cent of students have Special Education Needs (SEN). Overall, its students do well against key indicators. For example, in 2012, 7 of 33 graduating students enrolled in English as the Medium of Instruction (EMI) in secondary school. Its students learn three languages: Cantonese, English and Mandarin.

The principal is a former official at the EMB. He raised more than HK$13 million in private support in the decade after his appointment to FFTS in 2002, not only to help the school continue operations but also provide its students with opportunities that would not normally be available to them. For example, 12 students travelled to Singapore, 30 iPads were privately donated at a time when the EMB was still undertaking trials of the tablet computer, and all students have very smart uniforms. There are no school fees. Students are provided with breakfast each morning if one is not provided at home, and receive a boiled egg from parent volunteers at morning recess on Tuesdays and Thursdays.

The principal has mastered the media and there are many stories about the school in newspapers and on television. For example, Fortune Pharmaceutical met the cost of a 45-second advertisement for the school. The principal donated his HK$115,000 'actor's fee' to the school. He teaches media and community relations at the Chinese University of Hong Kong and the Hong Kong Institute of Education and donates his fees to the school. He developed media skills when he was a union leader at the EMB, an experience that also enabled him to develop networks in the media. It is clear that FFTS is a strong brand name in the wider community and this is an important factor in securing private support for the school.

Other examples of private support include counselling services provided by the Baptist church which has a room at the school, even though the school is secular; Studio 13, where art classes are taught by an artist after school each Wednesday, with costs met by an advertising agency that supports this kind of programme under the title of 'Room 13'; and donations of books to the school library. Parent volunteers assist in the reading programme on two days in each week.

The school also builds social capital. Many of the students come from single-parent homes. Regular seminars are conducted for parents on topics such as communication with students. Noteworthy is the practice whereby a number of parent volunteers come from 'other schools', that is they do not have children attending FFTS. The principal has published a letter to parents every week since he came to the school and, more recently, a letter to students (a total of 172 and 56 respectively at the time of writing). He had a selection of letters published as a book. Past students regularly visit the school.

Transformation has been defined in this book as significant, systematic and sustained change that secures success for all students in all settings. An important issue is succession and whether the leadership of the principal in creating and drawing on social capital will be sustained after his retirement in 2015. Although there will be an 'open competition' for the appointment, he is playing his part internally in building leadership capacity among current staff. He has a passionate commitment to helping alleviate poverty in the FFTS community, extending to the personal support he provides to parents in need.

Social and spiritual capital in context

Principal Leung's commitment to, and direct action in, helping alleviate poverty, as well as other themes in the approach at FFTS, suggests that the school has strong spiritual capital. Caldwell and Harris (2008: 10) noted that 'for some schools, spiritual capital has a foundation in religion; in other schools, spiritual capital may refer to ethics and values shared by members of the school and its community'. FFTS is a secular school but it is evident that it has strong spiritual capital. Most of the indicators of spiritual capital are evident in practice:

1   There is a high level of alignment between the values, beliefs and attitudes about life and learning held by the school and members of its community.
2   The values and beliefs of the school, including, where relevant, those that derive from a religious foundation, are embedded in its mission, vision, goals, policies, plans and curriculum.
3   The values and beliefs of the community are taken into account by the school in the formulation of its mission, vision, goals, policies, plans and curriculum.
4   The school explicitly articulates its values and beliefs in publications and presentations.
5   Publications and presentations in the wider community reflect an understanding of the values and beliefs of the school.
6   There are high levels of trust between the school and members of its community.
7   Parents and other stakeholders are active in promoting the values and beliefs of the school.
8   The values and beliefs of the school are evident in the actions of students and staff.
9   Staff and students who are exemplars of the values and beliefs of the school are recognised and rewarded.
10 The values and beliefs of the school have sustained it or are likely to sustain it in times of crisis. (Indicator 10 has stood the school in good stead, as it has weathered several crises that have threatened its existence.)

The connection between social and spiritual capital holds up when different contexts are examined, as in Finland, where social capital is particularly strong in both the broad sense adopted in this chapter and the more focused sense of Andy Hargreaves and Michael Fullan (A. Hargreaves and Fullan, 2012) ('professional capital'). The values placed on learning and teaching and the importance of education shine through in explanations of why Finland does so well in international comparisons. It seems that everyone trusts schools and their teachers, with trust seen by David Hargreaves (D. Hargreaves, 2012) as one of the two elements of social capital. The other is reciprocity, illustrated well in the two exemplars in Chapter 12 (HOL in Australia and the FFTS in Hong Kong).

Important messages for policymakers and practitioners

1   Philanthropic, not-for-profit and corporate contributions to public schools are more extensive than often recognised by the public and profession. In most instances, they are supporting strategies that are intended to close the gap in achievement between low- and high-performing students, especially in schools in challenging circumstances.
2   There is evidence in different national settings that these contributions are having a positive impact. They should be added to the repertoire of strategies that help build the capacity of schools to become self-transforming, but not in a stand-alone sense because successful design and delivery calls for partnerships and networks that involve many schools and many providers.
3   Establishing these partnerships and networks calls for high levels of trust and reciprocity, thus establishing the connection between social capital and spiritual capital, broadly defined in each instance. There are new skill sets for participants, the development of which should be given high priority for leaders in self-transforming schools.

13 The knowledge

There is almost universal agreement that the most important resource in securing success for all students in every setting is the knowledge and skill of teachers and others who support them. This refers to the intellectual capital (Caldwell and Harris, 2008) or the professional capital (A. Hargreaves and Fullan, 2012) of the school. Financial capital (Chapters 10 and 11) is important, but whether or not it makes a difference depends on how much money is provided and how it is deployed. Social and spiritual capital (Chapter 12) is important, but the support of the community must add value to what the school is endeavouring to achieve. The good news from these previous chapters is that outstanding models for allocating funds to schools have been developed and there is strong evidence that self-transforming schools know how to target their use, especially in helping to close the gap in achievement between low- and high-performing students. There are outstanding models of how funds and other support from the philanthropic, not-for-profit and corporate sectors can make a contribution. Learning how to utilise these models is part of 'the knowledge' for those who lead and support the self-transforming school.

The title of Chapter 13 ('The knowledge') is, of course, taken from the remarkable intellectual capital required of taxi drivers in London. They must learn 320 routes and the location of 25,000 streets and 20,000 landmarks before they are licensed. It may take up to three years for 'the knowledge' to be acquired. No analogy is intended, although the imagery can be transferred to the school setting to the extent that there may be 320 or more routes or pathways for students in a school if their needs, interests, aptitudes, ambitions and passions are to be addressed. The 'streets' and 'landmarks' are changing constantly for schools. Not only must initial teacher education be rigorous, extending to four years or more, but professional learning must be deep and continuous. This imagery is taken up again towards the end of the chapter.

The importance of initial teacher education

The purpose of Chapter 13 is to describe and illustrate selected approaches to building the intellectual capital of the self-transforming school. In some respects, Chapter 13 extends what was introduced in Chapter 9 ('The trans-formation of learning').

Much of the field is covered in comprehensive fashion by others. There is no need to make the point that initial teacher education, for example, is vitally important. It is a theme that runs through accounts of success in countries/ jurisdictions such as Finland (Chapter 4), and Hong Kong, Shanghai and Singapore (Chapter 5), where there are rigorous standards for selection to teacher education programmes and depth in design and delivery to the point that the community has confidence that high-quality teaching is assured in all schools regardless of the setting. Detailed accounts are provided elsewhere; for example, Pasi Sahlberg (2011) devoted an entire chapter in *Finnish Lessons* to what he called 'The Finnish Advantage: The teachers'. This is essential reading for those who wish to learn how Finland rigorously selects from the more than 20,000 seeking to enter the masters programme annually, of whom only about 2,000 are chosen.

A key indicator of intellectual capital is that 'staff allocated to or selected by the school are at the forefront of knowledge and skill in required disciplines and pedagogies' (Caldwell and Harris, 2008). Schools and their communities will have confidence that this indicator has been satisfied if the work described in the preceding paragraph has been done well. A system of education is, as a result, unlikely to have large disparities in achievement between low- and high-performing students, as the quality of teaching is uniformly high across all schools.

Chaining and unchaining

The focus in this chapter is on how the self-transforming school can build its intellectual capital in a manner that reduces its dependence on 'the system', in other words, how the school can 'take charge'. Particular attention is given to knowledge networks, and the chaining/unchaining metaphor in Chapter 3 is taken up. On the one hand, self-transforming schools should be 'unchained' from tight control by a system authority, exercising a relatively high degree of autonomy, with an open outlook in the way it draws ideas or practices from other settings. On the other hand, they join other schools with similar interests in sharing their knowledge, addressing issues of common concern and, where possible, sharing their resources. They participate in formal or informal 'chains' of schools.

Some of the best practices can be found in England, and brief descrip-tions were included in Chapter 4 of how schools are, in increasing num-bers, unchaining themselves from local authorities to become academies. It is appropriate to refer to England again for the way these academies are now operating in formal and informal chains. An example from England is included in the pages that follow (Bexhill High School), along with an exam-ple from Australia (Ballajura Primary School and the Haileybury Institute).

Figure 13.1 illustrates the possibilities for schools joining other schools in a chain in which there are common interests, that is there is knowledge to be

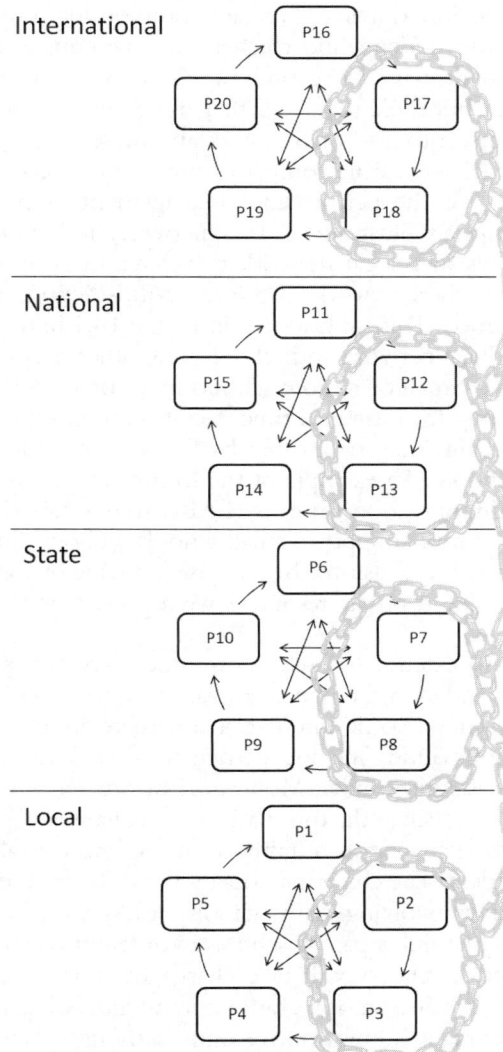

Figure 13.1 Chains of schools.

shared, there are issues of common concern to be addressed and there is the possibility that resources can be shared. Chains may be formal or informal, temporary or permanent. They may be created at the local or state (jurisdictional) levels or beyond, national or international.

Some jurisdictions organise schools into networks based on geographical location and, although there may be good networking of knowledge among participating schools, they are essentially administrative units. These typically consist of several secondary schools and the primary schools from which their students are mainly drawn. There are common interests, for example, the well-being of the students and teachers may be enhanced in transition arrangements from primary to secondary. These are good reasons for an administrative unit, but there may be little genuine networking. Some jurisdictions select a person to lead the network and these people are sometimes styled as 'network leaders'. Role conflict may be experienced if these people have responsibility for the performance management of principals. These kinds of relationships are illustrated as local networks in Figure 13.1.

However, schools in a local network may have more in common with some schools in another network in the same jurisdiction, and a chain of schools may be formed. This is illustrated in Figure 13.1 in the chains linking some schools in a local network and schools in another network in the same state or jurisdiction. Small or remote schools may come together in such an arrangement, meeting from time to time, face-to-face or online, and sharing resources. These chains may be created by the system itself, others on the initiative of the schools. An example of the former was cited in Chapter 11 in which Local Administration Bureaus (LABs) were established in Victoria to provide administrative support to small schools without diminishing their capacity to make the key decisions. In this case, an issue of common concern was being addressed and public resources were pooled or at least deployed more efficiently.

The chain may be extended to schools in other networks across a nation. Illustrations are provided in the two exemplars that are described later in the chapter. The chain may also be international if there are common interests. Examples of commonalities include particular models or philosophies of schooling, such as Reggio Emilia, Montessori or Steiner schools; particular models of curriculum, such as the International Baccalaureate; or foundational values or beliefs, such as schools of faith, including those established by particular religious orders. The chain may operate in different modes, including face-to-face or online, involving many schools, or less formal but nonetheless powerful activities that link a pair of schools in different countries.

In many instances, schools will take charge by 'unchaining' themselves from control by a jurisdiction, for example by withdrawing from local networks that are essentially administrative units, although they may continue their involvement if compelled or if they wish to maintain cordial professional relationships with colleagues in the same geographical area. A feature of the self-transforming school is that participation in a chain is, more likely than not, a voluntary association, with the school joining or withdrawing from a network to the extent that participation adds value to its operations.

Chains of academies in England

Some of the best examples of networking can be found in England, where academies, described in Chapter 4, are flourishing, especially at the secondary level. Andrew Adonis, who played an important role in establishing the academy programme, considered that 'academy chains are one of the most innovative aspects of the academy system, vital to its future'. Some of these chains are a function of the sponsoring organisation and he reported that, as of March 2012, 'nearly fifty organizations or individuals sponsor more than one academy' (Adonis, 2012: 204). In some instances, the chain emerged from the entrepreneurial leadership of a founding principal. Adonis cites an example:

> Still more ambitious is the Academies Enterprise Trust (AET), founded and led by David Triggs, the extraordinarily entrepreneurial head teacher of Greensward Academy in Hockley, Essex. AET now sponsors eighteen academies, both primary and secondary age, from nearby Clacton and Ashingdon in Essex to Ryde in Kent and Richmond in London.
>
> (ibid.: 199)

Co-author Brian Caldwell has followed the work of David Triggs over more than a decade and observed not only his entrepreneurship but also the comprehensive and coherent models of learning and teaching that have energised his efforts.

Characteristics of a successful network

David Hargreaves has done much to build the case for networks and networking, especially for innovation in learning, teaching, support, leadership and design, drawing extensively on practice in schools, notably in England. He concluded that networks in education tend to succeed when:

1 There is a clear and agreed outcome to the network's activity;
2 The benefits of networking – creating the network, operating it and maintaining it – exceed the costs, since lack of pay-off is disincentive to continuation;
3 The participants are committed to professional learning through collaboration, sharing and joint activity, with agreed ways of working;
4 The network contains high social capital and its two key components: trust between members and norms of reciprocity;
5 Leadership and management are distributed and supportive;
6 There is appropriate support in terms of time and/or resources, an appropriate model for professional development that connects innovation to normal professional practice;
7 There is a good balance in communication between face-to-face and electronic and virtual forms and e-networking is instituted after trustful, face-to-face networks have been established.

(D. Hargreaves, 2008: 33)

Item 6 in the list is noteworthy because of its recognition that networks will not be sustained unless time and funds are available. One of the most impressive networks in the first decade of this century was International Networking for Educational Transformation (iNet), established and supported by the London-based Specialist Schools and Academies Trust (SSAT). About 4,000 schools from more than 30 countries were involved. Although the network was supported by affiliation fees, the parent body (SSAT), dependent on government funding which was lost in the austerity measures following the global financial crisis of 2008, went into administration in early 2012 and momentum was lost.

Outside–inside networking

For each of the possibilities explored above, it is important to note that the intellectual capital of a self-transforming school is also built by sharing within the school what has been learnt through participation in wider networks. An illustration of how this can be done is drawn from practice at Brisbane Girls Grammar School (BGGS), a secular private school in Queensland, Australia.

In 2011, there were 1,165 girls enrolled in Years 8 to 12. Students are drawn from relatively advantaged communities but it is non-selective and does not offer scholarships. It describes itself on the My School website as 'internationally renowned for innovative educational practice and a consistent record of academic achievement'. It performs substantially above all other schools in NAPLAN tests and at the same level as or above 'like schools' on most tests since their inception in 2008.

Each year, senior staff of the school research and write a short report on a topic related to their area of responsibility. These reports are published in the school newsletter but brought together each year in *Insights*, a special publication which is distributed widely in the community of the school and beyond. Each report contains a small number of references to other publications. The authors are thus drawing from the wider world, often beyond education, and reporting in just a few pages what it means for the school.

In the 2011 edition, Emma Lowry, Acting Head of England House at BGGS, reflected on the tragedies arising from earthquakes in Christchurch, New Zealand, and, especially, the earthquake and tsunami in Japan. She concluded that 'what all these tragic circumstances had in common were the heroic and empathetic responses which, although varied in tone and expression in each culture, were evocations of the same human spirit of community and practical compassion to do for others what we would hope for ourselves' (Lowry, 2011: 49). Brendon Thomas, Co-Director of Technology Studies, noted from a short review of research that integrating games into teaching and learning 'is consistent with current educational theories and research, which emphasise the potential of digital games as pedagogical tools' (Thomas, 2011). The principal, Amanda Bell, wrote about the danger of applying too broadly the concept of creativity:

Education theorists and business gurus have remodelled creativity to apply in the most general sense to almost every circumstance, to the processes employed to undertake daily business. To use this interpretation of creativity is to reduce the rare and intricate natural talent of pure creativity to a tool that at its most base level will simply encourage us to look for other possibilities that may be better than the obvious.

(Bell, 2011: 109)

The BGGS approach to outside–inside networking of knowledge may not work in other settings. There are many ways to accomplish the same purpose.

Exemplar: Bexhill High in England

A school in England provides an example of a self-transforming school, descriptions of which would fit in with several of the chapters. It illustrates resolute action to 'unchain' the school from local authority control and become an academy (Chapter 3), innovation (Chapter 8) and the transformation of learning (Chapter 9). It is included in Chapter 13 because of the partnerships that have helped build the intellectual capital of the school. The school is Bexhill High in Bexhill-on-Sea in East Sussex. Co-author Brian Caldwell followed progress at the school over three years through regular briefings by its principal, Michael Conn.

Bexhill was faced with a stark choice a few years back when school performance fell below expectations, leading to an unsatisfactory inspection by OFSTED (Office for Standards in Education). One option was to close the school and re-open it with a different staff and possibly a different name. The other was to attempt a transformation, but profound changes needed to be made. The governing body chose the second option.

An important breakthrough was achieved in 2006 when the school was part of the East Sussex authority's bid for funds to rebuild the school. These were substantial: £34 million from the former Department for Children, Schools and Families and £4 million from the East Sussex authority. Significantly, Michael Conn and his team were able to devote £29 million to a design of their choice, with the remaining £5 million reserved for facilities for autistic students and for ICT. His first meeting with architects began, quite literally, with a blank sheet of paper. The only 'given' was that Bexhill would remain an 11–16 mixed comprehensive school serving a broad cross-section of socio-economic communities, including two of the most deprived wards in England, and offering a specialisation in technology. In addition, of course, there had to be dramatic improvement in student achievement. The school had good international links, especially in Europe through the Comenius Project (named after Jan Amos Comenius, regarded by many as the father of modern education in Europe). The school styles itself as an International Community Technology College.

Bexhill is organised into three schools: School of Culture and Communications (English, Modern Foreign Languages and Humanities); School of Discoveries (Mathematics, Science and Technology); and School of Well-being (PSHE and Citizenship, Careers, Physical Education and the Expressive Arts). The traditional timetable has been abandoned and there are no bells to delineate lessons. The day is divided into three sessions (3 h + 3 h + 2.5 h) with school commencing each day at 8.30 am and concluding at 5.00 pm, except on Fridays, when school finishes at 2.30 pm. Lunch break is for 30 minutes and is 'staggered', since there are more than 1,500 students at the school. Each teacher is free for one of these three sessions for preparation and personal professional development. Work–life balance for students and staff has been achieved by ensuring that all work is completed before 5.00 pm. Teachers do not take marking and preparation home; students do not do homework.

There is only one science laboratory. Most schools have several and that means large amounts of space are not being used for much of the day. The science laboratory accommodates 120 students organised by a large team of well-qualified technicians – each a trained scientist – under the supervision of science teachers. There is a camera and microphone above every student's work station so that an experiment may be filmed while the student dictates notes, with video and audio delivered immediately to each student's website.

Bexhill sought the assistance of Sir Dexter Hutt and his team. Hutt was Executive Headteacher at Ninestiles Community School in Birmingham and was knighted for his outstanding leadership and success as principal of Ninestiles, which is located in a particularly challenging setting. As described in several chapters, there are several innovations in school governance in England and these include the creation of federations or chains of schools and provision for outstanding leaders such as Hutt to provide support to schools that are underperforming. In Hutt's case, he led an enterprise known as 'Ninestiles Plus' that provided support for the Hastings Schools Federation, also in East Sussex, and these services were available to assist Bexhill (it is noteworthy that Hastings is located several hours by car or train from Birmingham). Hutt's team provided specialist 'best practice' teaching support in English and Mathematics. He has retired and the networked support of Ninestiles Plus has ceased.

Michael Conn secured the support of another eminent leader to help build the capacity of the leadership team. Dame Pat Collarbone was honoured for her work in the 1990s in leading the transformation of the Haggerston School for Girls in a disadvantaged community in the London Borough of Hackney. Since then, she has served as director of the London Leadership Centre and, among many other projects, led the far-reaching design of workforce reforms for those working in schools. She served as an international consultant in the development of the National Standard for School Principals for the Australian Institute of Teaching and School Leadership (AITSL), which was subsequently approved by every minister for education in the country.

The design of the new facilities was supported by the consultant Vincent McDonnell, Managing Director of Prospects, one of the largest private consulting companies in England. McDonnell had extensive experience in different education authorities and knowledge of developments elsewhere. Prospects is now the chief partner of Bexhill.

At the heart of the design for the school was the belief that students would be more successful if they were taught in larger groups accompanied by self-regulated project-based learning. Not only would this encourage students to take greater responsibility for their own journey of learning but it would promote a culture of team teaching and shared responsibility among staff for the success of students. Such was the commitment required to develop this new teaching and learning philosophy that, in May 2010, another visit from OFSTED led to Michael Conn devoting all of his working time to bedding down the innovations. Student achievement had fallen.

The local authority challenged the new learning design and the idea that young people should play such an active part in shaping their own learning journey. The governing body at Bexhill engaged Prospects to demonstrate the efficacy of the model, which was enhanced with the opening of the new facilities in late 2010. The level of interest was such that other schools started to visit and OFSTED conducted another inspection in early 2011 with a positive outcome. In addition, in early 2011, a team of investigative journalists from the BBC Insight Out programme visited, with the expert assistance of Sir Bruce Liddington, Children's Commissioner for England. There was positive media exposure as a result.

There were tensions along the way. Student achievement at the senior level continued to fall short of expectations and the local authority maintained its critical stance. The partnership with Prospects was strengthened through a commission to help with school improvement that included the development of new programmes tailored to the specific needs of the school and students.

In September 2011, Michael Conn secured the approval of the governing body for Bexhill to apply for academy status, as a 'converter school' with a partner, in this instance Prospects, which had formed similar partnerships with other schools across England that wished to become academies. Consultation with the local community led to a formal application, which was approved in October 2012. Another OFSTED inspection in March 2012 confirmed the merit of the somewhat radical approach to learning and teaching.

Michael Conn believes that a visitor to the school will find order, calmness and a quiet discipline of learning that sees its 1,600 students move around a building they control and manage. Learning is delivered to groups of up to 90 students working together in a learning zone, with each student aware of his/ her learning targets, measures of progress and expected outcomes. Teachers work in teams of three or four, supportive of each other and working within a themed subject, employing an investigative approach that is built around the needs and interests of students. Bexhill has created a learning environment that reduces distraction, encourages attention to learning and is now almost certain to achieve its best examinations results ever.

Bexhill is an example of how a self-managing school set out to become a self-transforming school, building its intellectual capital through networks and partnerships led by people such as Dexter Hutt and Vincent McDonnell, with the expert assistance of people such as Pat Collarbone. This was necessary if the radical changes in learning and teaching were to be made. However, Bexhill High is a special kind of exemplar. OFSTED found in February 2013 that the achievement of pupils and the quality of teaching, leadership and management were inadequate, and that the school required 'special measures' (OFSTED, 2013). It reported, in effect, that 'the knowledge' was not deep enough or sufficiently dispersed. Even with external expert support, it was clear that new strategies were needed if self-transformation was to be achieved.

Exemplar: Ballajura Primary and the Haileybury Institute in Australia

An impressive example of how schools can link together to learn from one another over great distances when there is common purpose is demonstrated in the achievements of Ballajura Primary School in Western Australia and its association with the Haileybury Institute in Victoria.

The back story is important because the leader of the Haileybury Institute, the national consultancy unit of the private school Haileybury College in south-east Melbourne, is John Fleming, whose previous appointment was as principal of Bellfield Primary School, in one of the most disadvantaged communities in Australia, in a north-east suburb of Melbourne. Under Fleming's leadership, students at Bellfield improved their performance from well below state-wide benchmarks to well above. A detailed account of how this was achieved was contained in *Raising the Stakes* (Caldwell and Spinks, 2008). Priority was given to explicit teaching and setting high expectations for students (Fleming and Kleinhenz, 2007). Bellfield became part of Charles La Trobe College in 2011, several years after Fleming's departure, in a merger of two primary schools and one secondary school.

In a remarkable professional coup, Fleming and several of his senior colleagues at Bellfield were headhunted by Haileybury to lift levels of achievement at the primary level, which were felt by the school's leaders to be below expectations. In general terms, Haileybury draws its students from more advantaged communities. Fleming became deputy principal at Haileybury and had an immediate impact through the introduction of approaches that proved so successful at Bellfield, to the point that Haileybury now has one of the most impressive profiles of student achievement in the country. As indicated on the My School website, which reports the performance of students in Years 3, 5, 7 and 9 in literacy and numeracy for every school in the country (National Assessment Program – Literacy and Numeracy), Haileybury outperforms all but one 'like school' at every level in literacy for each year level and leads all 'like schools' in numeracy. The Haileybury Institute was created as a vehicle to bring Fleming's expertise to schools across the country and he spends four weeks each term doing so. He supports approximately 100 schools, most of which are public schools.

Ballajura Primary School, a public school in an outer suburb of Perth, learned of Fleming's work at a conference and secured his services as a consultant. In fact, Ballajura was the first to receive this kind of support from the Haileybury Institute. Ballajura has about 580 students from a community where 30 different languages are spoken. Overall, the school serves a community with a moderate level of social disadvantage. The school offers specialist programmes in Indonesian, drama, physical education and music, as well as experiences for gifted and talented students. It has purpose-built music, drama and arts facilities, which is unusual for public primary schools in Australia. There has been a similar turnaround in the performance of students to the point that, in NAPLAN tests in 2012, Ballajura performed above 'like schools' in every area in literacy and numeracy in Years 3 and 5. The 'value added' from 2009 to 2011 was significant. According to the principal, David Wanstall (Ferrari, 2012), about 30 per cent of students failed to reach minimum standards at the start; only 3 per cent failed to do so at the end. The proportion of students in the top 20 per cent in Australia doubled over the three-year period.

In additional comments for this book, David Wanstall observed that 'our success has been achieved by setting a vision of what it is we want to achieve, applying whole school programs, having high expectations and retraining staff in the use of pedagogies that are effective for student learning'. He shares John Fleming's belief that 'just because you work hard and are committed to teaching does not mean you are effective'. He believes that what has been achieved at Ballajura is proof that 'significant gains can be made in student academic performance without large sums of money and resourcing being pumped into schools (although this would make it easier); it's about teacher practice!'.

In 2012, Ballajura became an Independent Public School (IPS) within the Western Australian system of public schools. Each IPS has a relatively high level of autonomy and a relatively low level of control by 'the system'. It clearly has an open outlook. Overall, it is an excellent example of how a school may be 'unchained', as illustrated in the model contained in Chapter 3. Ballajura maintains its commitment to the system of public education in Western Australia and to local networking. It was one of a cluster of three schools that entered the IPS scheme in 2012 as a 'coalition of schools'.

The networking of knowledge described above is exceptional and illustrates themes introduced earlier in the chapter. Each of the three schools (Bellfield, Haileybury and Ballajura) is a self-transforming school. The Haileybury Institute, a service provided by the private school, delivers support to about 100 mostly public schools across the country, each of which has a common purpose of lifting the performance of its students. The improvement at Ballajura over three years is noteworthy. These arrangements were made outside the traditional jurisdictional approach to setting up networks, most of which are limited to the local area. In these three instances, the schools took charge.

Mastering 'the knowledge'

The imagery of 'the knowledge' that must be mastered by those seeking a licence to drive London cabs was introduced at the start of the chapter. It is taken up again at this point. It was noted that applicants must memorise 320 routes, along with the location of 25,000 streets and 20,000 landmarks. It typically takes up to three years to master the knowledge. It is fair to ask why teachers and their leaders are not expected to master the evidence and implications that underpin the 138 factors that John Hattie drew from his study of 800 meta-analyses (Hattie, 2009). A capacity to navigate schools in dramatically different circumstances, in which change occurs often and in unexpected fashion, may be an educational counterpart to the thousands of streets and landmarks that must be negotiated in London. Hattie's more recent work, drawing implications for teachers, is equally authoritative and extends the list of 138 to 150 'influences on achievement' (Hattie, 2012). It is the imagery that is adopted here rather than a forced professional analogy. In any event, this is the depth of knowledge required in the teaching profession at this time and initial teacher education programmes and ongoing professional learning should be shaped accordingly.

In addition to the work of John Hattie, which should form the core of professional knowledge, there are other sources that self-transforming schools are drawing on. It is beyond the scope of this book to provide the detail; it is sufficient to note that such schools often select one or a small group of experts and shape policy and practice accordingly. Such experts include Viviane Robinson and Helen Timperley, who worked with John Hattie when he was at the University of Auckland; and David Hopkins, whose work in the Northern Metropolitan Region in Victoria, in association with the former Regional Director, Wayne Craig, was described in Chapter 10.

Reference was made in Chapter 1 to the work of David Hargreaves, who has written four publications for the National College for School Leadership on the development of a self-improving school system and how a capacity for school self-management was a prerequisite. In the fourth of these (D. Hargreaves, 2012), he demonstrated the connections between intellectual capital and other forms of capital in a way that is consistent with the alignment of the four forms of capital described in Chapter 3 (intellectual capital, social capital, spiritual capital and financial capital). He described the relationship between intellectual capital (abilities, skills, experience) and social capital (trust, reciprocity), and how organisational capacity is developed by drawing on both forms of capital. This requires organisational capital, which is created in large measure by leaders in the school. Taken together, these constitute what he described as 'collaborative capital'. He noted how schools with these capacities can work together to help create a self-improving school system:

This collaborative capital starts with a small group of schools in deep partnership, expands to the much larger group – an alliance, federation, trust, chain, local authority etc – and from there potentially to a whole region and nation.

(ibid.: 32)

Hargreaves believes that it will be school leaders who drive a system with a high level of collaborative capital and hence self-improvement. He noted the importance of a powerful narrative and one is presented in Chapter 15 ('Narratives in self-transformation').

The significance of what Hargreaves proposed, consistent with the position taken in this book, cannot be stressed too highly. The building block of the self-improving system is the self-transforming school. Although there are some strategies that should be employed in uniform fashion across a system of schools, reliance on a centrally driven approach alone, or even for most of the reform effort, will not transform the system. The most important strategy for those at the centre is to build a capacity for schools to become self-transforming. Underplaying such a strategy may account in large part for the disappointing outcomes reported at the start of Chapter 1 in countries such as Australia, England, New Zealand and the United States. This line of argument is developed further in Chapter 14 ('Governance ethos leadership policy').

Making the connections

Particular attention has been paid in Chapter 13 to the core of professional knowledge and how capacities can be built in schools across a system through networking. Part of the core includes capacities identified in previous chapters, including:

- Constructing a narrative for self-management, how it connects to learning, and the preconditions that enable these connections to be made (Chapters 1 and 2).
- Understanding trends and mega-trends in society and the economy, and how these shape developments in schools; strategically navigating so that the school is always well positioned to meet current expectations and future needs (Chapters 1, 2 and 8).
- Understanding change theory and choosing appropriate strategies for change and approaches to measurement; minimising dysfunctional approaches in each instance (Chapter 7).
- Being innovative; understanding the relationship between innovation, reform and change; searching out and sensibly adopting or adapting 'best practice' and 'next practice' (Chapter 8).
- Complementing Chapter 13, understanding and applying developments in the six leading edges of practice that transform learning; maintaining a focus on direct instruction; understanding what is fundamental change

and what is simply an adaptation of traditional approaches, driven by technology, including virtual learning and blended learning; anticipating the shift from national to global curriculum (Chapter 9).

• Building and drawing on financial capital (Chapters 10 and 11), social and spiritual capital (Chapter 12) and intellectual capital (Chapter 13); targeting each to meeting priorities for learning.

Important messages for policymakers and practitioners

1 The most important task for a school system is to build the capacity of its schools to be self-transforming.
2 The knowledge to be acquired for a school to be self-transforming may be effectively disseminated by networking within chains of schools, formal or informal, temporary or permanent, face-to-face or online. System-led dissemination may prove effective in some instances.
3 There is a substantial core of professional knowledge to be acquired and this should be embedded in programmes of initial teacher education and ongoing learning, updated as new evidence comes to hand.

14 Governance ethos leadership policy

The purpose of Chapter 14 is to draw together the major themes of the book in a short essay that describes the major features of schools and school systems where there is a degree of school self-management and an intention to push on to ensure that all schools are self-transforming. These features are organised loosely around governance, ethos, leadership and policy. The evidence is contained in preceding chapters, each of which addressed a particular theme. Each concluded with three short 'messages' for policymakers and practitioners. The intention in Chapter 14 is to achieve a degree of coherence among these themes rather than to revisit the evidence or compile a list of these messages.

The logic of self-management has settled in recent times with the primary intention agreed to be the improvement of outcomes for students. Earlier controversy about the practice was connected to inflated expectations or to purposes other than impact on learning, for example privatisation, community empowerment or blame-shifting. Each school contains a unique mix of student needs, interests, aptitudes, ambitions and passions and is situated in a unique community. A deep capacity for local decision making is necessary to ensure there is an optimal match of resources to strategies that will ensure the best possible outcomes for students, with resources defined broadly to include curriculum, pedagogy, professional expertise, community support, technology and money. There are commonalities among schools across a nation or school system, and common values and common approaches may call for common frameworks, but these do not detract from or override the uniqueness of each school. There is powerful evidence to show that connections to outcomes have been made, providing schools have the capacities to take up their authority and responsibility within a framework of accountability.

Creating a deep capacity for self-management may not be a high priority in some nations or jurisdictions where the driving imperative is to ensure that students and even staff attend school regularly, and that teachers have the knowledge and skill to deliver the basics. Even when these conditions are satisfied there may be a highly fragmented approach to learning and teaching within and among schools and there is little information on which to make judgements about the progress of students. It is understandable that governments as well as school and system authorities exert a high degree of control under these circumstances. Once a high level of alignment and coherence has been achieved then building the capacity of schools to make their own decisions should move up the order of priorities so that the school becomes self-managing within centrally determined frameworks, and ultimately becomes self-transforming.

A strong case can be made that there are too many levels of governance in some jurisdictions and that schools are excessively burdened with rules and regulations. This may be the case in countries such as Australia and the United States, each being a federation of states. Although constitutional powers to make laws in relation to education lie with the states, the federal governments in each instance exert control because they have power to make grants to the states with strict conditions being set for the ways in which they may be used. This seems straightforward; after all, it is argued, a federal government is best placed to serve the national interest. In practice, however, many of these arrangements may be power-coercive, with strict compliance a requirement if the grants are to be paid. Both countries have very large departments of education at the federal as well as the state level.

The contrast with Canada is striking. Canada has about 50 per cent more population than Australia and a similar land area, with 10 provinces and two territories compared with Australia's six states and two territories. Except in a few areas related to small numbers of students, the federal government in Canada has no power to make laws in relation to education and does not distribute funds for schools. A national perspective is readily achieved through a council of ministers.

The growth in the federal role in Australia and the United States is a relatively recent phenomenon. Previously, it was the states working directly with school districts in the United States, each of which administered a system of schools. In Australia, it was the states working directly with schools; the federal role was expanded half a century ago when there were inequities between and among systems of private and public schools, but the size of central bureaucracy continued to grow at all levels despite the development of outstanding practice in needs-based funding. There is evidence that the performance of students in both nations has flatlined or declined over the years of expanded federal involvement. In the light of experience in Canada, which out-performs both nations in the performance of its students, was the wrong approach to governance adopted or was what was right at the time sustained and expanded beyond what was necessary to the point that a federal role became dysfunctional? If the federal government has powers to raise revenue that is not available to the states, why not pay funds directly to the states within a framework determined by a council of ministers? There are options for the way such a change might be made. National agencies may still be established. The interests of private as well as public schools must be accommodated. The National Board of Education in Finland may provide a useful model.

Governance arrangements are much simpler in nations or jurisdictions that are high performers in international tests of student achievement and which seem more agile in responding to economic and social circumstances. The United Kingdom, specifically England, has moved in recent times to simplify governance, in this instance, maintaining a national framework and reducing sharply the role of the local education authority; meanwhile the capacities of schools to respond to the needs of their students has been strengthened.

An approach in all countries in the twenty-first century, once the basics as far as learning and resourcing have been addressed, should be to unrelentingly build the capacity of schools to be self-managing and then self-transforming, preferably maintaining at one level of government only a small but powerful regulatory regime that ensures that resources are allocated on a needs basis, which can step in when schools fail and be one among many sources of support.

A new framework for the governance of schools may take years to establish. Leaving aside the case for change in this respect, there is a compelling argument to 'unchain' schools that are already self-managing so that they have a high level of autonomy and low levels of central control and are open to ideas and practices from around the world. Not all schools will wish to shed the chains and not all will have the capacity to transform themselves even if they wish. Some governments are moving quickly to make this possible, notably in England, where the creation of academies has passed the tipping point. Schools were never shackled to any great extent in countries such as Finland, or the shackles were thrown off long ago in other jurisdictions, including top performers in East Asia and pioneers in self-management in Canada.

As in virtually every other field of endeavour, innovation should pervade a school and a system of schools. It seems that some systems actively discourage innovation on this scale, insisting that schools maintain their focus on the basics, securing good results in high-stakes tests. It is argued that 'the system' should identify the best innovations and take action to ensure that all schools adopt them. Strategies for dissemination that have often proved successful in the past are maintained in an effort to achieve a cascading effect. However, this is not the way things work in the twenty-first century, with advances in technology and outstanding formal and informal networking by schools ensuring that worthwhile innovations are adopted or adapted, often more effectively and much faster than if centrally driven. These schools do not wait around for direction from the top. An outstanding example is the adoption of the tablet computer, with some schools providing them to all students from the earliest years while the system was barely getting a field trial under way. Innovations that, at first sight, should be rolled out to all schools through a system-wide initiative, because it is efficient to do so, often fail because they do not meet the needs of schools. An example is failure on a grand scale in one state in Australia, with unacceptable budget blowouts and minimal take-up.

Innovation is just one of many functions that demand a change in ethos in schools and school systems. At the system level, the culture should be characterised by service to schools and every aspect of cultural change should be addressed in ensuring that this is the case, including how appointments are made, how performance is evaluated and how day-to-day interactions with those who work in schools are conducted. The self-transforming school is outward facing and this calls for an ethos that values the support of the wider community, which often means a change in how public education is understood. Although public schools may still be owned and operated by a public authority it is evident that support will be drawn from a range of public and private sources.

Philanthropic, not-for-profit and corporate contributions will be sought and new partnership arrangements will determine how cash and in-kind support will be deployed. That these contributions are invariably targeted to the support of high-needs students is just one aspect of how the notion of public education is being turned on its head. It is striking that in one state in Australia it is the not-for-profit sector that has come to the aid of schools that students are refusing to attend. In some developing countries, it is the private sector that is providing basic education where public education has failed or feared to tread.

Leadership of the highest order is required at all levels if self-managing schools are to become self-transforming. Leaders who seek to improve a system by working harder to make current strategies work more effectively may not be exercising leadership at all; at most, they may be managing more efficiently.

A transformation of learning has been under way for some time but, consistent with Peter Drucker's famously expressed view of transformation in every field of human endeavour, it may be occurring over decades rather than in sharp dislocations, and it is only towards the end of these years that there is widespread appreciation of what has transpired. Some changes in schooling are dislocating or 'disruptive', especially where technology is concerned, but leaders in the self-transforming school are taking charge rather than waiting around for cumbersome system-wide change processes to run their course.

A uniformly high quality of initial teacher education, as in Finland and in high-performing jurisdictions in Asia, is a prerequisite for self-transforming schools. Every teacher entering the profession must have deep knowledge, and a demonstrated capacity to apply that knowledge, about the factors that work together to secure high levels of achievement, for example the 150 factors identified by John Hattie. Professional learning must be deep and continuous, given advances in knowledge about learning.

Although system-wide strategies may still be helpful in some circumstances, it is face-to-face or online networking that is driving much of the effort in self-transforming schools. They join or leave networks to the extent that they add value in sharing knowledge, addressing issues of common concern or pooling resources. Some local networks are little more than administrative units in a traditionally organised school system and their value is likely to be minimal and short term. Increasingly, the self-transforming school is networking with schools elsewhere in the country and beyond. A global out-look may mean that aspects of the curriculum are global rather than national.

Policymaking is a critical function in the drive to create the self-transforming school. Regardless of the distribution of authority, responsibility and account-ability, policymakers at all levels should be concerned with the alignment of education, economy and society, and the same principles of formal and infor-mal networking apply. At the jurisdictional level, this may occur through large international organisations such as OECD or APEC (Asia–Pacific Economic Cooperation) or consortia such as the G8 or the G20, or, more informally and with a particular focus on education, such as the Global Education Leaders' Program (GELP), but the primary purpose should be acquiring knowledge of strategies that will help build the capacity of schools to be self-transforming, that is, lead to the success of all students in all settings, thus contributing to the social and economic well-being of the citizen and the nation.

These are the major themes that have emerged in successful efforts to build systems of self-managing schools over a quarter of a century and to energise efforts to go beyond so that they become self-transforming. What is almost certain to occur in the next quarter-century is addressed in Chapter 15.

15 Narratives in self-transformation

> Reports that say something hasn't happened are always interesting to me because as we know there are known knowns: these are the things we know we know. We also know there are known unknowns: that is to say we know there are some things [we know] we don't know. But there are also unknown unknowns – the ones we don't know we don't know. And if one looks throughout the history of our country and other free countries, it is the latter category that tends to be the difficult one.
>
> (Rumsfeld, 2011: xiii)

Donald Rumsfeld's statement was originally made during the Iraq War when he was Secretary of Defense for the United States in the administration of George W. Bush. It has rarely been cited outside this context, and certainly not in education. However, it is striking that the terminology has been adopted in several contexts, often without attribution, yet it applies perfectly to any attempt to write about the future of schools over the next 25 years, which is a purpose of this book.

The purpose of this short concluding chapter is to offer a possible, if not preferred, narrative for the future of the self-transforming school, extending for a further 25 years the narratives in Chapters 1 (self-managing schools) and 14 (self-transforming schools). There are 'known knowns', for example that further advances in technology will have a powerful effect on the future of schools. However, as made clear in several chapters, it is not possible to predict the particularities: what technologies will emerge at particular points in time and what their impact will be. In this respect, there are 'known unknowns', but schools should position themselves to take up the opportunities – to strategically navigate in the sense described in Chapter 8. There are 'unknown unknowns', that is there will be developments in some fields that we do not know about and we do not know what impact these will have on schools.

Scenarios for the future of schools

The best known attempt to describe possible and preferred scenarios for the future of schools was made in the OECD Schooling for Tomorrow project (OECD, 2001; Istance, 2003), which had a time horizon of 10 to 15 years from 2001. There were several spin-offs in different countries and, in particular, organisations. Templates to guide schools in the development of their own scenarios were prepared (Caldwell and Loader, 2010). Exploring those that derived from the OECD formulation is beyond the scope of this chapter other than to point out that elements of each scenario have come to pass, that some have continued far longer than necessary or is appropriate, and that others are likely to flourish.

Two scenarios saw the maintenance of the status quo. One was that bureaucratic systems would continue, with pressure to maintain uniformity, accompanied by resistance to radical change. Schools would continue as distinct entities. The second was known as 'the meltdown scenario', with teachers leaving the profession; crisis management and a fortress mentality would prevail.

There were two scenarios that envisaged *re-schooling*. One would see schools become social centres, with the school providing the core of a range of public and private services in support of students and the wider community. The other would see a strengthening of schools as learning organisations, with a focus on knowledge, specialisation, flatter structures and diversity.

There were two *de-schooling* scenarios, with one envisaging learning networks in a learning society, anticipating the powerful opportunities arising from advances in technology. The other would anticipate an extension of an educational market, with parents increasingly seeing schooling as a private good and exercising choice. A market for the delivery of a variety of services would flourish.

There was a general preference in seminars and workshops around the world for the re-schooling scenarios and concern about the meltdown and market possibilities. Participants in these events often felt that the most likely scenario was that the status quo would be maintained and that bureaucratic systems would continue. The reader will have little difficulty identifying examples of each of the six scenarios in the illustrations contained in this book and developments in jurisdictions around the world. It is almost certain that these scenarios, or variants thereof, will be evident over the next 25 years; that is, for two decades or more beyond the time frame of their initial formulation. Some are entirely appropriate in their contexts, consistent with the different stages in the journey to transformation, as illustrated in the report of McKinsey & Company (poor to fair, fair to good, good to great, great to excellent) (Mourshed *et al.*, 2010) as summarised in Chapters 1 and 3.

As made clear in Chapters 3 to 5, there are dangers in persisting with the bureaucratic model when self-managing schools have the capacity to be self-transforming. As Sahlberg (2011) has deftly pointed out, this has been the case in several nations that are falling behind on international indicators, notably Australia, England, New Zealand and the United States, compared with Canada, Finland, Hong Kong, Singapore and Shanghai. It as though the wagons have circled, tighter constraints have been placed on schools, innovation has been curtailed, outdated models of change have dominated and, in some instances, too many levels of government have wanted to take charge. In these circumstances, using the imagery introduced in Chapter 3, it is time to 'unchain' self-managing schools so that they become self-transforming.

Possible scenarios

Among the 'known knowns' is the probability that some of the OECD scenarios will emerge with the creation of the self-transforming school, notably those that involve networks and networking for the student and the profession, consistent with what has been described and illustrated in Chapters 9 ('The transformation of learning') and 13 ('The knowledge'). Although the particularities of change, especially as they concern technology, cannot be specified so far in advance, the schema presented in Chapter 9 based on the classification of Chen (2010) will assist in mapping what has occurred and what in general terms lies ahead. He referred to six 'edges' of innovation, with a continuum of possibilities in each instance: thinking (from either/or to both/and); curriculum (from traditional to twenty-first century); technology (from few empowered to many empowered); time/place (from place bound to any time, any place); co-teaching (from mainly teachers to partnerships of many); and youth (from students passive to students active). How these developments may be mapped and anticipated was illustrated in Figure 9.1.

Among the near certainties over the next 25 years is that large numbers of students now attending secondary schools will no longer attend a school in the traditional sense. Much of their learning will occur at any time and at any place, or in several places, depending on their needs, interests, aptitudes, ambitions and passions. For example, a young person may attend one centre to nurture their interests in the arts and another centre attached to a business where innovative and entrepreneurial skills are nurtured, with basic discipline-based learning occurring online and at home, or anywhere else. An international rather than national curriculum is likely to emerge under these conditions. There will be no difficulty assessing a student's knowledge and skills under these circumstances because online assessments, with the technology to assure identity, are already possible and are almost certain to be ubiquitous within 5 to 10 years. Such learning may still be publicly funded and the student needs-based approaches described in Chapters 10 and 11 will be honed to provide personalised learning entitlements. These have been advocated for years but developments along the lines set out above will require that they be implemented. Some students will have a 'home base', where some of their learning occurs and their entitlements are managed, and this will require leaders who can work with counterparts in other settings to ensure the delivery of services and the sharing of funds. Interestingly, this is already occurring in some jurisdictions for a minority of students who do not attend a school, refusing/declining to do so for one reason or another.

The possibilities that developments along these lines will occur in countries such as those described in Chapter 6 (Brazil, India and South Africa) should not be discounted. Nor should they be discounted in developing countries that do not feature in the list of possible powerhouses. It was noted in Chapter 6 that many of the initiatives and innovations are being taken by the private sector, and this is the case in Kenya, where most schools may be considered to be on the journey from poor to fair or, at best, fair to good. Private companies such as eLimu (Swahili for 'education') and Safaricom (a Kenyan mobile phone operator) are seeking to 'disrupt' current reliance on traditional textbooks and to provide online access in a context in which 'the flood of new pupils has overwhelmed state schools, which were already underfunded and poorly managed' (*The Economist*, 2012e: 62). The early adoption of tablet computers has led to improved outcomes for students.

Homeschooling should also be taken into account in assessing probabilities for the future. Joseph Murphy conducted a comprehensive study of the movement in the United States and noted that it had grown from 10,000–15,000 students in the 1970s to approximately 2 million students in 2010, exceeding the number of students in charter schools and in voucher programmes combined (1.5 million) (Murphy, 2012: 10–11). It is apparent that homeschooling has itself been transformed over four decades, now drawing on a much broader cross-section of students and their families. The 'essence' of this transformation may well describe the limited transformation that has occurred in mainstream schools. Murphy offered a 'theory of action' for homeschooling based on two dimensions: the instructional programme (1:1 teaching, efficient use of time, customisation) and the learning environment (safe/nourishing climate, personalisation) (ibid.: 155). Murphy noted a slowing of the movement in the 2000s, but it may well pick up speed again if parents perceive the loss of a 'safe/nourishing climate' in mainstream schools following the deaths of 20 children in the tragic shooting at the Sandy Hook Public School in Connecticut in December 2012.

Although it is beyond the scope of this book to provide the detail, account should be taken of the transformation of teaching and learning in higher education, which is driven to a large extent by the possibilities of technology. *The Economist* (2012f) described the astonishing growth of 'massive open online courses' (MOOCS). For example, Coursera was launched in April 2012 with a capital of $16 million. By December 2012, 2 million students had signed up for non-award subjects, including 180,000 students in a subject on 'how to reason and argue'. By that date, Coursera had 33 partners including the universities of Edinburgh, Melbourne and Toronto. In an extraordinary prediction, Sebastian Thrun, formerly at Stanford University before starting up MOOCS Udacity, suggested that in 50 years there may be only 10 universities in the world (ibid.: 96).

It is also highly probable that many schools will continue as discrete entities because the market will demand them. Included here will be private schools that have been established for decades (centuries, in some instances) and that will have long waiting lists far into the future. Although some parents will be happy for them to provide schooling in the traditional sense, it is striking that many are already at the forefront of developments mapped by Chen (2010), described above and analysed in Chapter 9. Some may become the 'home base' for students who may spend much if not most of their learning elsewhere. Some will provide services to public schools. The Haileybury Institute in Melbourne is a striking example, as described in Chapter 13.

A concise explanation of what is probable and what is preferred is contained in the following description – vision – offered by Houle and Cobb (2011) in *Shift Ed: A Call to Action for Transforming K–12 Education*. Such a vision accommodates each of the possible scenarios described above.

> A transformed school will not look like that brick building set apart from the society it is intended to serve. A transformed school will be an integrated part of the community and its students will be active participants and contributors to the community. In short, *a transformed school will look more like life*.
>
> (Houle and Cobb, 2011: 72)

Shaping the scenarios

Offering more detailed predictions is fraught with difficulty, if not danger. Ridley (2012) provided a convincing account of how many predictions over the last half-century about demographic, ecological, economic, scientific and social change were plain wrong. He cited Harford's contention in *Adapt* (Harford, 2011) that 'blind trial-and-error is responsible for most of the innovations that change the world, not intelligent design or planning', and argued that human 'ingenuity and inventiveness will prove all soothsayers wrong, pessimists especially' (Ridley, 2012: 264). The task of specifying the 'known unknowns' or preparing for the 'unknown unknowns' in education should be undertaken with a great deal of humility.

Addressing the five inter-related issues, the resolution of which will give shape to the 'contours of change', as described in Chapter 7, is a helpful starting point for those who seek to design the future. After that, the most important task is to build the capacity of every school to be self-transforming and the agenda set out in Chapter 13 is vital. The programmes for teachers and school leaders that are offered in many universities and in the centres of professional learning that have sprung up around the world are impressive, but in most instances they do not go far enough or deep enough.

Dame Pat Collarbone was cited in Chapter 13 for her ground-breaking work in workforce reform in England, as a consultant to schools such as Bexhill High, and in the development of the National Standard for School

Principals in Australia. She embraced the idea of the self-transforming school in the conclusion to *Creating Tomorrow* (Collarbone, 2009). She acknowledged the impressive progress in reshaping school leadership in England but warned:

> However, many organizations still have a tendency to revert to traditional industrial age thinking, particularly in periods of rapid change and disturbance or when faced with a crisis. They revert to a command-and-control style of leadership, uni-directional procedures for carrying out tasks, hierarchical structures and a tendency toward cultures of blame.
>
> (ibid.: 102)

This diagnosis matches that of the authors of *The Self-Transforming School*, marking the twenty-fifth anniversary of *The Self-Managing School* in Australia and the 1988 Education Reform Act in England. It is time to unchain the self-managing school in both countries and, progressively, in all schools around the world.

Acknowledgements

This is the fifth book in a series by the authors extending over 25 years, first with Falmer Press and now with Routledge. Bookending these were the leadership, encouragement and faith initially of Malcolm Clarkson (Falmer) and now of Anna Clarkson (Routledge). The editorial support of the Routledge team is acknowledged.

Fiona Longmuir, Consulting Researcher at Educational Transformations, provided invaluable research assistance in gathering information on developments in Hong Kong, Shanghai and Singapore reported in Chapter 5; Brazil, India and South Africa in Chapter 6; Finland in Chapter 8; innovation in Chapter 9; and the Local Learning Organizations project in the Southern Metropolitan Region of the Department of Education and Early Childhood Development (DEECD) in Victoria, reported in Chapter 12. Earlier work with Jessica Harris, Senior Consulting Researcher at Educational Transformations, now at the Queensland University of Technology, in the International Project to Frame the Transformation of Schools, is reported in Chapters 3, 12 and 13. Research for The Song Room conducted with Tanya Vaughan, also Senior Consulting Researcher at Educational Transformations and now at the Australian Institute for Teaching and School Leadership (AITSL), is reported in Chapter 12.

Leaders in schools shared information about transformation in their settings and confirmed the accounts reported in this book. These included Leung Kee-Cheong, Principal at the Fresh Fish Traders' School in Hong Kong, who hosted two visits over three years, as reported in Chapter 12, facilitated by Tsui Kwok-Tung, Associate Dean (Programmes/Quality Assurance), Faculty of Education and Human Development, Hong Kong Institute of Education. Information about developments at Ballajura Primary School in Western Australia reported in Chapter 13 was provided by Principal David Wanstall and John Fleming, who leads the Haileybury Institute at Haileybury College in Victoria that provided support at Ballajura. Michael Conn, Principal of Bexhill High in Bexhill-on-Sea in East Sussex, provided information for Chapter 13, updating the account he provided in 2010 for the Futures Focused Schools Project. Amanda Bell, former Principal of Brisbane Girls Grammar School, provided information on the networking of knowledge among school leaders reported in Chapter 13. Leaders at Mount Waverley Secondary College, Port Phillip Specialist School and Wooranna Park Primary School, all in Melbourne, shared information on developments in their schools at a workshop of International Networking for Educational Transformation (iNet) conducted in May 2012.

The partnership with David Loader in the Futures Focused Schools Project is also acknowledged, with several findings reported in Chapter 8, which also drew on reports of the Global Schools Innovation Network that publishes the twice-monthly online facility NOVA, edited by Steve Holden, Director of Communications at the Australian Council for Educational Research (ACER).

Leaders in several organisations shared information or provided opportunities for engagement. These included Michelle Anderson, Project Director, Tender Bridge, ACER, who also provided information about Leading Learning in Education and Philanthropy (LLEAP); Ben Jensen, Program Director, School Education, at the Grattan Institute (Melbourne); Anthony (Tony) Mackay, Executive Director of the Centre for Strategic Education (CSE) in Melbourne and a leader in the Global Education Leaders' Program (GELP); and Justine Munro, Executive Director, Education, Social Ventures Australia (SVA). The Australian Primary Principals' Association (APPA) and the New Zealand Principals' Federation (NZPF) provided an opportunity to field-test the model for 'unchaining' schools, reported in Chapter 3, in a workshop at their 2012 Trans-Tasman Conference on the theme of 'Our Primary Purpose: Leading Learning'.

Opportunities provided by the DEECD in Victoria are especially acknowledged. DEECD engaged each of the authors, separately or together, in several projects in recent years on topics related to the themes addressed in this book. Wayne Craig, former Regional Director, Northern Metropolitan Region, provided support and access to data related to themes in Chapter 10. Gus Napoli and Paul Dingle, Principals of John Fawkner College and Glenroy Secondary College respectively, shared their views on securing success for all students in high-needs schools. Nino Napoli, Director, School Resource Allocation Executive, provided information and advice on the resourcing of public schools in Victoria, as reported in Chapters 10 and 11.

Annabel Clowes, Manager of Communications at Educations Transformations prepared the manuscript for publication, a task that required considerable patience and a high level of skill, which she has in abundance, as does Marilyn Spinks, who prepared the index, the second time she has done so for our co-authored publications.

Special thanks are extended to Dame Pat Collarbone, Director of Creating Tomorrow, who generously agreed to write the Foreword. She models everything that we have advocated as her work over two decades includes head of a self-transforming school, leader of national workforce reform, outstanding impact at the London Leadership Centre, and a global consultant at Creating Tomorrow.

References

Adonis, A. (2012) *Education, Education, Education: Reforming England's Schools*, London: Biteback Publishing.

Anderson, M. (2011) 'Maximising the impact of philanthropy in education', *Teacher*, May: 56–59.

Anderson, M. and Curtin, E. (2012) *LLEAP Dialogue Series: Cases Companion Document*. A Tender Bridge project in association with the Ian Potter Foundation and the Origin Foundation. Melbourne: Australian Council for Educational Research.

Australian Government (2011) *Review of Funding for Schooling: Final Report*. Report of the Expert Panel, David Gonski (Chair). Canberra: Australian Government.

Bailey, A., Henry, T., McBride, L. and Puckett, J. (2011) *Unleashing the Potential of Technology in Education*, Boston: The Boston Consulting Group. Available at: www.bcg.com/documents/file82603.pdf (accessed 6 October 2011).

Barber, M. (2007) *Instruction to Deliver: Fighting to Transform Britain's Public Services*, London: Methuen.

Barber, M., Donnelly, K. and Rizvi, S. (2012) *Oceans of Innovation: The Atlantic, the Pacific and the Future of Education*, London: Institute for Public Policy Research.

Barber, M., Moffitt, A. and Kihn, P. (2011) *Deliverology 101: A Field Guide for Educational Leaders*, Thousand Oaks, CA: Corwin Press.

Barber, M. and Mourshed, M. (2007) *How the World's Best-Performing School Systems Come out on Top*, London: McKinsey & Company.

Barrera-Osorio, F., Fasich, T. and Patrinos, H.A. (2009) *Decentralized Decision-Making in Schools: The Theory and Evidence on School-Based Management*, Washington, DC: World Bank.

Battaglino, T.B., Haldeman, M. and Laurans, E. (2012) 'Education reform for the digital era', in Finn, C.E. and Fairchild, D.R.E. (eds.) *The Costs of Online Learning*, Washington, DC: Thomas B. Fordham Institute. Kindle Edition.

BBC (2012) 'Indian court orders toilets to be placed in all schools'. Available at: www.bbc.co.uk/news/world-asia-india-19811468 (accessed 31 October 2012).

Bell, A. (2011) 'Curating creativity to curating content: Are we being sculpted?', *Insights*, 6 October: 109–11.

Bergmann, J. and Sams, A. (2012) *Flip Your Classroom: Reach Every Student in Every Class Every Day*, Washington, DC: International Society for Technology in Education (ISTE).

Bitar, S. (2004) '3rd APEC Educational Ministerial Meeting – Sergio Bitar, Education Minister of Chile'. Speech by Sergio Bitar, opening the Education Ministerial Meeting at the third meeting of APEC, 29 April, Santiago, Chile. Available at:

www.apec.org/press/speeches/2004/0429_minsbitar_openemm.aspx (accessed 14 May 2013).

Bosma, N., Wennekers, S. and Amorós, J.E. (2012) *Global Enterprise Monitor 2011 Extended Report: Entrepreneurs and Entrepreneurial Employees across the Globe*, London: Global Entrepreneurship Research Association.

Braconier, H. (2012) *Reforming Education in England*. OECD Economics Department Working Papers, No 939. Paris: OECD. Available at: www.oecd-ilibrary.org/economics/reforming-education-in-england_5k9gsh772h9q-en (accessed 15 October 2012).

Business–School Connections Roundtable (2011) *Realising Potential: Businesses Helping Schools to Develop Australia's Future*. Canberra: Department of Education, Employment and Workplace Relations. Available at: www.deewr.gov.au/Schooling/Documents/RoundtableReport.pdf (accessed 23 May 2011).

Caldwell, B.J. (1977) 'Decentralised school budgeting in Alberta: An analysis of objectives, adoption, processes and perceived outcomes in selected school systems' (Unpublished doctoral dissertation, Department of Educational Administration, University of Alberta).

Caldwell, B.J. (2006) *Re-imagining Educational Leadership*, Melbourne: ACER Press.

Caldwell, B.J. and Harris, J. (2008) *Why Not the Best Schools?*, Melbourne: ACER Press.

Caldwell, B.J. and Hayward, D.K. (1998) *The Future of Schools: Lessons from the Reform of Public Education*, London: Falmer.

Caldwell, B.J. and Loader, D.N. (2010) *Our School Our Future*, Melbourne: Curriculum Services Australia (CSA), in association with the Australian Institute of Teaching and School Leadership (AITSL).

Caldwell, B.J. and Spinks, J.M. (1988) *The Self-Managing School*, London: Falmer.

Caldwell, B.J. and Spinks, J.M. (1992) *Leading the Self-Managing School*, London: Falmer.

Caldwell, B.J. and Spinks, J.M. (1998) *Beyond the Self-Managing School*, London: Falmer.

Caldwell, B.J. and Spinks, J.M. (2008) *Raising the Stakes: From Improvement to Transformation in the Reform of Schools*, London: Routledge.

Caldwell, B.J. and Vaughan, T. (2012) *Transforming Education through the Arts*, London: Routledge.

Chen, M. (2010) *Education Nation: Six Leading Edges of Innovation in our Schools*, San Francisco: Jossey-Bass.

Chin, R. and Benne, K.D. (1969) 'General strategies for effecting change in human systems', in Bennis, W.G., Benne, K.D. and Chin, R. (eds.) *The Planning of Change*, New York: Holt, Rinehart and Winston, pp. 32–59.

Christensen, C. and Horn, M. (2011) 'Disrupting how and where we learn: An interview with Clayton Christensen and Michael Horn', *Phi Delta Kappan*, 92 (4): 32–38.

Christensen, C., Johnson, C.W. and Horn, M.B. (2008) *Disrupting Class*, New York: McGraw-Hill.

Cisco (2008) *Equipping Every Learner for the 21st Century*. A Cisco Futures Report. San Jose, CA: Cisco Sytems.

Collarbone, P. (2009) *Creating Tomorrow: Planning, Developing and Sustaining Change in Education and Other Public Services*, London: Network Continuum.

Conservative Party (1987) *The Next Moves Forward*. General Election Manifesto. London: Conservative Party.

Cummings, P. (2012) 'World Wide Ed', *Good Weekend* (supplement to *The Age* and *Sydney Morning Herald*), 29 September: 20–25.

Dede, C. and Richards, J. (eds.) (2011) *Digital Teaching Platforms: Customizing Classroom Learning for Each Student*, New York: Teachers College Press.

Deloitte Access Economics (2011) *Assessing Existing Funding Models for Schooling in Australia*. Report prepared for the Review of Funding for Schooling. Canberra, ACT: DEEWR.

Deloitte Access Economics (2012) *The Socio-Economic Benefits of Investing in the Prevention of Early School Leaving*. Report commissioned by Hands On Learning (HOL). Kingston, ACT: Deloitte Access Economics.

Department of Basic Education (Republic of South Africa) (2012a) *Action Plan to 2014: Towards the Realisation of Schooling 2025*, Pretoria: Department of Basic Education. Available at: www.education.gov.za/Curriculum/ActionPlanto2014/tabid/418/Default.aspx (accessed 14 May 2013).

Department of Basic Education (Republic of South Africa) (2012b) 'Schooling 2025'. Available at: www.education.gov.za/Curriculum/Schooling2025/tabid/401/Default.aspx (accessed 14 May 2013).

Department of Education and Early Childhood Development (DEECD) (Victoria) (2010) *Teaching and Learning with Web 2.0 Technologies*, Melbourne: DEECD.

Department of Education and Training (DET) (Victoria) (2003) *The Blueprint for Government Schools*, Melbourne: Department of Education and Training.

Drucker, P.F. (1993) *Post-Capitalist Society*, New York: HarperBusiness.

Dyer, J., Gregersen, H. and Christensen, C.M. (2011) *The Innovator's DNA: Mastering the Five Skills of Disruptive Innovators*, Boston, MA: Harvard Business Review Press.

The Economist (2012a) 'Losing her stripes: Tiger mothers in Singapore', *The Economist*, 22 November: 31.

The Economist (2012b) 'The Pernambuco Model', *The Economist*, 27 October: 39.

The Economist (2012c) 'India, Special Report', *The Economist*, 29 September: 13.

The Economist (2012d) 'Cry, the beloved country', *The Economist*, 20 October: 11.

The Economist (2012e) 'Tablet teachers: Digital education in Kenya', *The Economist*, 8 December: 62.

The Economist (2012f) 'Learning new lessons', *The Economist*, 22 December: 95–96.

Edmonton Public School Board (2011) '2010–2011 Budget Highlights'. Available at: www.epsb.ca/budget/highlights.shtml (accessed 28 December 2012).

Education Review Office (ERO) (New Zealand) (2012) *Evaluation at a Glance: Priority Learners in New Zealand Schools*, Wellington: Education Review Office.

Ferrari, J. (2012) 'Improve the teachers, help the kids', *The Australian*, 12 December. Available at: www.theaustralian.com.au/national-affairs/education/improve-the-teachers-help-the-kids/story-fn59lz9-1226534899259 (accessed 19 April 2013).

Fleming, J. and Kleinhenz, E. (2007) *Towards a Moving School: Developing a Professional Learning and Performance Culture*, Melbourne: ACER Press.

Fullan, M. (2010) *All Systems Go: The Change Imperative for Whole System Reform*, Thousand Oaks, CA: Corwin Press (a joint publication with the Ontario Principals' Council).

Fullan, M. (2012) *Stratosphere: Integrating Technology, Pedagogy, and Change Knowledge*, Toronto: Pearson Canada (a joint publication with the Ontario Principals' Council).

Fullan, M., Hill, P. and Crévola, C. (2006) *Breakthrough*, Thousand Oaks, CA: Corwin Press.

GELP (Global Education Leaders' Program) (2012) *GENTE*, Rio de Janeiro. Available at: http://gelprio2012.rioeduca.net/rj_gente.html (accessed 14 May 2013).

Gladwell, M. (2001) *The Tipping Point*, London: Abacus.

Gunter, H. (ed.) (2011) *The State and Education Policy: The Academies Programme*, London: Continuum.

Hall, G.E. and Hord, S.M. (1987) *Change in Schools: Facilitating the Process*, Albany, NY: SUNY Press.

Hames, R.D. (2007) *The Five Literacies of Global Leadership*, London: John Wiley & Sons.

Hannon, V. (2007) *'Next Practice' in Education: A Disciplined Approach to Innovation*, London: Innovation Unit. Available at: www.innovationunit.org/sites/default/files/Next%20Practice%20in%20Education.pdf (accessed 28 December 2012).

Hannon, V. (with Hampson, M.) (2012) *The Evolving Role of Government: From Provider and Regulator to Broker and Facilitator*. Global Education Leaders' Program. London: Innovation Unit.

Harford, T. (2011) *Adapt: Why Success Always Starts with Failure*, London: Hachette Digital.

Hargreaves, A., Crocker, R., Davis, B., McEwen, L., Sahlberg, P., Shirley, D., Sumara, D. and Hughes, M. (2009) *The Learning Mosaic: A Multiple Perspectives Review of the Alberta Initiative for School Improvement (AISI): Summary Report*. Available at: http://education.alberta.ca/media/6412276/learning_mosaic_summary_report_2009.pdf (accessed 28 December 2012).

Hargreaves, A. and Fullan, M. (2012) *Professional Capital: Transforming Teaching in Every School*, London: Routledge.

Hargreaves, A. and Shirley, D. (2011) *The Fourth Way: The Inspiring Future for Educational Change*, Thousand Oaks, CA: Corwin Press.

Hargreaves, D.H. (2003) *Education Epidemic*, London: Demos.

Hargreaves, D.H. (2008) *Leading System Redesign 4*, London: Specialist Schools and Academies Trust.

Hargreaves, D.H. (2010) *Creating a Self-Improving School System*, Nottingham: National College for Schools and Children's Services.

Hargreaves, D.H. (2012) *A Self-Improving School System: Towards Maturity*, Nottingham: National College for School Leadership.

Harris, S. (2012) 'Failed, failed, failed: Blair said his priorities were education, education, education. But Labour billions did nothing to raise standards, says report', *Mail Online*, 11 September.

Hattie, J. (2009) *Visible Learning: A Synthesis of over 800 Meta-Analyses Relating to Achievement*. London: Routledge.

Hattie, J. (2012) *Visible Learning for Teachers: Maximizing Impact on Learning*, London: Routledge.

Higgins, D. (2011) *Lodestones: Leadership – From the Furnaces and Viking Raiding Ships*, Bendigo, Vic: Catholic Education Office Sandhurst.

Hillgate Group (1986) *Whose Schools? A Radical Manifesto*, London: Imediaprint.

Hinz, B. (2010) 'Australian federalism and school funding arrangements: An examination of competing models and recurrent critiques'. A paper presented at the Canadian Political Science Association Annual Conference, Montreal, 1–3 June.

Hogan, D. and Gopinathan, S. (2008) 'Knowledge management, sustainable innovation, and pre-service teacher education in Singapore', *Teachers and Teaching: Theory and Practice*, 14 (4): 369–384.

Hopkins, D. (2007) *Every School a Great School*, Maidenhead, Berkshire: Open University Press.

Hopkins, D. and Craig, W. (2011) 'Powerful learning: Taking education reform to scale in the Northern Metropolitan Region', in Hopkins, D., Craig, W. and Munro, J. (eds.) *Powerful Learning: A Strategy for Systemic Educational Improvement*, Melbourne: ACER Press, pp. 28–37.

Hopkins, D., Craig, W. and Munro, J. (eds.) (2011) *Powerful Learning: A Strategy for Systemic Educational Improvement*, Melbourne: ACER Press.

Horn, M. and Staker, H. (2012) 'How much does blended learning cost?', *The Journal*, 5 April. Available at: www.thejournal.com/articles/2012/04/05/how-much-does-blended-learning-cost.aspx (accessed 19 April 2013).

Houle, D. and Cobb, J. (2011) *Shift Ed: A Call to Action for Transforming K–12 Education*, Thousand Oaks, CA: Corwin Press.

IBO (International Baccalaureate) (2012) 'About the International Baccalaureate'. Available at: www.ibo.org/general/who.cfm (accessed 14 May 2013).

Information Society Programme (2006) *A Renewing, Human-centric and Competitive Finland: The National Knowledge Society Strategy 2007–2015*. Available at: www.epractice.eu/files/media/media1936.pdf (accessed 1 August 2011).

Interim Committee of the Australian Schools Commission (1973) *Schools in Australia: Report of the Interim Committee of the Australian Schools Commission*, Karmel, P. (Chair) Canberra: Australian Government Publishing Service.

Istance, D. (2003) 'The OECD scenarios', in Davies, B. and West-Burnham, J. (eds.) *Handbook of Leadership and Management*, London: Pearson Longman, pp. 644–652.

James, S. (ed.) (2012) *An Extraordinary School: Re-modelling Special Education*, Melbourne: ACER Press.

Jensen, B., Hunter, A., Sonnemann, J. and Burns, T. (2012) *Catching up: Learning from the Best School Systems in East Asia*, Melbourne: Grattan Institute.

Khan, S. (2012) *The One World Schoolhouse: Education Reimagined*, London: Hodder & Stoughton.

Knight, J. (2011) 'Education hubs: A fad, a brand, an innovation?', *Journal of Studies in International Education*, 15 (3): 221–40.

Koh, T.Y. (2012) 'Key ideas in behavioural economics – and what they mean for policy design', in Low, D. (ed.) *Behavioural Economics and Policy Design*, Singapore: World Scientific Publishing Co., pp. 17–34.

Leadbeater, C. (2011) *Rethinking Innovation in Education: Opening up the Debate* (No. 207 in the Seminar Series), Melbourne: Centre for Strategic Education.

Leadbeater, C. and Wong, A. (2010) *Learning from the Extremes*, San Jose, CA: Cisco Systems.

Lee, M., Seashore Louis, K. and Anderson, S. (2012) 'Local education authorities and student learning: The effects of policies and practices', *School Effectiveness and School Improvement*, 23 (2): 133–158.

Leong, L.C. (2012) 'Foreword', in Low, D. (ed.) *Behavioural Economics and Policy Design*, Singapore: World Scientific Publishing Co., pp. vii–xii.

Levin, B. (2011) 'Do we need more innovation?', in Zbar, V. and Mackay, T. (eds.) *Leading the Education Debate: Volume 3*, Melbourne: Centre for Strategic Education, pp. 166–177.

Levin, B. (2012) *System-Wide Improvement in Education* (Education Policy Series, No. 13), Paris: International Academy of Education.

Liberal Victoria (2010) *The Victorian Liberal Nationals Coalition Plan for Education*. The Victorian Liberal Nationals Coalition's Policy and Plans for the 2010 State Election. Melbourne: Liberal Victoria.

Lindberg, E. (2012) 'The power of role design: Balancing the principal's financial responsibility with the implications of stress', *Educational Assessment, Evaluation and Accountability*, 24: 151–171.

Lopez-Claros, A. (2006) *Executive Summary: 2005 Global Competitiveness Report*, World Economic Forum. Available at: https://members.weforum.org/pdf/Gcr/GCR_05_06_Executive_Summary.pdf (accessed 28 December 2012).

Loveless, T. (2011) *How Well Are American Students Learning? The 2010 Brown Center Report on American Education*, Brown Center on Education Policy at Brookings. Available at: www.brookings.edu (accessed 28 December 2012).

Low, D. (ed.) (2012) *Behavioural Economics and Policy Design*, Singapore: World Scientific Publishing Co.

Lowry, E. (2011) 'Crisis, determination, forbearance: Lessons from Japan', *Insights*, 19 May: 47–50.

Lykins, C.F. and Heyneman, S.P. (2008) *The Federal Role in Education: Lessons from Australia, Germany and Canada*, Washington, DC: Center on Education Policy.

Microsoft Corporation (2008) *Innovative Schools: Working Together. Shaping the Future of Education: Baseline Evaluation Report*. Available at: http://gtf.dicole.net/wiki/attachment/347/2259/318/ISP_Global_Baseline_Report.pdf (accessed 1 August 2011).

Miles, M., Thangaraj, A., Wang, D. and Ma, H. (2002) 'Classic theories, contemporary applications: A comparative study of the implementation of innovation in Canadian and Chinese public sector environments', *Innovation Journal*, 7: 1–23.

Ministry of Education (New Zealand) (2010) 'Assessment'. Ministry of Education discussion paper. Available at: www.minedu.govt.nz/theMinistry/PublicationsAndResources/AssessmentPositionPaper.aspx (accessed 19 April 2013).

Ministry of Education (People's Republic of China) (2010) 'National Outline for Medium and Long-Term Education Reform and Development 2010–2020'. Available at: www.gov.cn/jrzg/2010-07/29/content_1667143.htm (accessed 4 August 2011).

Ministry of Education (Singapore) (2011) 'Innovation and enterprise'. Available at: www3.moe.edu.sg/bluesky/ine.htm (accessed 8 August 2011).

Morgan, G. (1997) *Images of Organization* (second edition), London: Sage.

Mourshed, M., Chijioke, C. and Barber, M. (2010) *How the World's Most Improved School Systems Keep Getting Better*, London: McKinsey & Company.

Murphy, J. (2012) *Homeschooling in America: Capturing and Assessing the Movement*, Thousand Oaks, CA: Corwin Press.

Naisbitt, J. (1982) *Megatrends*, London: Future Press.

Naisbitt, J. and Aburdene, P. (1990) *Megatrends 2000*, London: Pan.

National Board of Education (Finland) (2011) *Knowledge and Education in 2020: Board of Education Strategy*. Available at: www.oph.fi/julkaisut/2011/osaaminen_ja_sivistys_2020 (accessed 2 August 2011).

National Library Singapore (2011) 'Singapore National Pledge'. Available at: http://infopedia.nl.sg/articles/SIP_84_2004-12-13.html (accessed 8 August 2011).

Northern Metropolitan Region (n.d.) *Curiosity and Powerful Learning: Northern Metropolitan Region School Improvement Strategy*, Melbourne: Department of Education and Early Childhood Development.

Nous Group (2011) *Schooling Challenges and Opportunities*. Report commissioned by the Review of Funding for Schooling Review (Australia). Available at: http://foi.deewr.gov.au/node/21550 (accessed 28 December 2012).

OECD (2001) *What Schools for the Future?*, Paris: OECD.

OECD (2008a) *Reviews of National Policies for Education: South Africa*, Paris: OECD.

OECD (2008b) *OECD Study on Digital Learning Resources as Systematic Innovation: Country Case Study Report on Finland*. Available at: www.oecd.org/dataoecd/25/21/41951860.pdf (accessed 1 August 2011).

OECD (2010) *PISA 2009 Results: Executive Summary*. Available at: www.oecd.org/dataoecd/34/60/46619703.pdf (accessed 3 August 2011).

OECD (2011) *Lessons from PISA for the United States, Strong Performers and Successful Reformers in Education*. Available at: www.oecd.org/dataoecd/34/45/46581016.pdf (accessed 3 August 2011).

OECD (2012) *Education at a Glance*, Paris: OECD.

OFSTED (2013) *Inspection Reports: Bexhill High School* (URN 138895). Available at: www.ofsted.gov.uk (accessed 24 May 2013).

Papert, S. (1993) *The Children's Machine: Rethinking School in the Age of the Computer*, New York: Basic Books.

Pope Pius XI (1931) 'Quadragesimo Anno: Encyclical on reconstruction of the social order'. Available at: www.vatican.va/holy_father/pius_xi/encyclicals/documents/hf_p-xi_enc_19310515_quadragesimo-anno_en.html (accessed 28 December 2012).

Putnam, R.D. (2000) *Bowling Alone: The Collapse and Revival of the American Community*, New York: Touchstone.

Quinn, R.E. and Sonenshein, S. (2008) 'Four general strategies for changing human systems', in Cummings, T. (ed.) *Handbook of Organizational Development*, London: Sage, pp. 69–78.

Ridley, M. (2012) 'Of predictions and progress: More for less', in Franklin, D. and Andrews, J. (eds.) *Megachange: The World in 2050*, Hoboken, NJ: John Wiley & Sons, pp. 264–275.

Rogers, E. (1962) *Diffusion of Innovations*, Glencoe, IL: Free Press.

Rumsfeld, D. (2011) *Known and Unknown*, New York: Sentinel.

Sahlberg, P. (2011) *Finnish Lessons: What Can the World Learn from Educational Change in Finland?*, New York: Teachers College Press.

Schleicher, A. (2011) 'Is the sky the limit to education improvement?', *Phi Delta Kappan*, 93 (2): 58–63.

Schütz, G., West, M.R. and Wößmann, L. (2007) *School Accountability, Autonomy, Choice, and the Equity of Student Achievement: International Evidence from PISA 2003* (Education Working Paper No. 14), Directorate of Education, OECD. Available at: www.oecd.org/edu/39839422.pdf (accessed 27 November 2009).

Seddon, J. (2010a) *Systems Thinking in the Public Sector*, Axminster, UK: Triarchy Press.

Seddon, J. (2010b) *The Economics of Localism*. Available at: www.systemsthinking.co.uk/6.asp (accessed 28 December 2012).

Sedlacek, T. (2011) *Economics of Good and Evil: The Quest for Economic Meaning from Gilgamesh to Wall Street*, New York: Oxford University Press.

Sexton, S. (1987) *Our Schools: A Radical Policy*, London: Institute of Economic Affairs.

Singapore Economic Development Board (2011) 'Singapore: A global schoolhouse'. Available at: www.sedb.com.cn/content/edb/sg/en_uk/index/industry_sectors/education/global_schoolhouse.print.html (accessed 28 December 2012).

Sloan, J. (2012) 'Sludge-producing OECD has outlived its welcome', *The Australian*, 6 October. Available at: www.theaustralian.com.au/opinion/

sludge-producing-oecd-has-outlived-its-welcome/story-e6frg6zo-1226489031440 (accessed 2 January 2013).

Social Ventures Australia (SVA) (2013) 'Making a difference in education'. Available at: www.socialventures.com.au/education/making-a-difference-in-education/ (accessed 19 April 2013).

Spinks, J.M. (2006) *Resourcing Schools for the 21st Century – 2: Models*, London: Specialist Schools and Academies Trust.

Subramaniam, R. and Lee, J.C.K. (2011) 'Educational Reforms and School Improvement in Singapore', in Lee, J.C.K. and Caldwell, B.J. (eds.) *Changing Schools in an Era of Globalization*, London: Routledge, pp. 85–104.

TechSmith Corporation (2012) 'What is the flipped classroom?'. Available at: www.techsmith.com/flipped-classroom.html (accessed 12 April 2013).

Tekes (2007) 'InnoSchools: The innovative school concept for the future'. Available at: http://innoschool.tkk.fi/framet/brochure_new.pdf (accessed 1 August 2011).

Thomas, B. (2011) 'Games-based learning: Creative steps to a digital future', *Insights*, 23 June: 67–70.

Thomson, S., Hillman, K., Wernert, N., Schmid, M., Buckley, S. and Munene, A. (2012) *Highlights from TIMSS & PIRLS 2011 from Australia's Perspective*, Melbourne: Australian Council for Educational Research (ACER).

Tooley, J. (2009) *The Beautiful Tree*, Washington, DC: Cato Institute.

Topsfield, J. (2012) 'Australia's disaster in education', *The Age*, 11 December: 1.

Ubiquitous Information Society Advisory Board (2008) 'Ubiquitous information society: Action programme 2008–2011'. Available at: www.Lincompany.kz/pdf/Esite_englanniksi_fin.pdf (accessed 19 April 2013).

UNESCO (2012) 'Education for all in Brazil'. Available at: www.unesco.org/new/en/brasilia/education/educational-governance/education--for-all/ (accessed 30 October 2012).

Vaughan, T., Harris, J. and Caldwell, B.J. (2011) *Bridging the Gap in School Achievement through the Arts: Summary Report*, Melbourne: The Song Room.

Victorian Auditor-General (2012) *Learning Technologies in Government Schools*. Report to the Parliament of Victoria.

Wardlaw, C. and Dawkins, P. (2010) 'Victorian education system: From improvement to transformation'. A paper presented at the Global Education Leaders' Program (GELP), Beijing, November 2010 (PowerPoint) (copy provided to the authors).

Wößmann, L., Lüdemann, E., Schütz, G. and West, M.R. (2007) *School Accountability, Autonomy, Choice, and the Level of Student Achievement: International Evidence from PISA 2003* (Education Working Paper No. 14), Directorate of Education, OECD. Available at: www.elternlobby.ch/deutsch/argumente/pdf/fbw13woessmann.pdf (accessed 27 November 2009).

Zhao, Y. (2009) *Catching Up or Leading the Way: American Education in the Age of Globalization*, Alexandria, VA: Association for Supervision and Curriculum Development (ASCD).

Zhao, Y. (2012) *World Class Learners: Educating Creative and Entrepreneurial Learners*, Thousand Oaks, CA: Corwin Press.

Index

Note: page numbers in **bold** indicate the principal or key pages for the entry.